Online
INVESTING

The Wall Street Journal Interactive Edition's Guide to

Online
INVESTING

Become a Successful Internet Investor

Dave Pettit
and
Rich Jaroslovsky

and the reporters and editors of
The Wall Street Journal Interactive Edition
Jason Anders, Lisa Bransten, Rebecca Buckman,
Terri Cullen, Aaron Elstein, Andrew Fraser,
Carrie Lee, Brian Tracey, and Nick Wingfield

CROWN
BUSINESS

With love to Mindy, David, and Becca—the partners in the firm. And Trish, Ryan, Alex, Hannah, Emma, Jerry, Gerald, Rashaun, Edith Joyce Fraser, Denise, and Amanda.

Copyright © 2000 by Dow Jones & Co., Inc.

All rights reserved. No part of this book may be reproduced or transmitted in any form or by any means, electronic or mechanical, including photocopying, recording, or by any information storage and retrieval system, without permission in writing from the publisher.

Published by Crown Publishers, New York, New York. Member of the Crown Publishing Group.

Random House, Inc., New York, Toronto, London, Sydney, Auckland
www.randomhouse.com

Crown Business is a trademark of Random House, Inc.

Owing to limitations of space, permission acknowledgments can be found on page 323.

Design by Joseph Rutt

Library of Congress Cataloging-in-Publication Data

Pettit, Dave.
    Online investing : the Wall Street journal interactive edition's complete guide to becoming a successful Internet investor / Dave Pettit and Rich Jaroslovsky and the reporters and editors of the Wall Street journal interactive edition.
        p.   cm.
    Includes index.
    1. Investments—Computer network resources.   2. Internet (Computer network)
    3. Electronic trading of securities.   I. Jaroslovsky, Rich.   II. Title.
HG4515.95.P38 2000
332.64'0285'4678—dc21   99-053668
ISBN: 0-8129-3250-1

10 9 8 7 6 5 4 3 2

FIRST EDITION

CONTENTS

For updates to *Online Investing*, see *The Wall Street Journal Interactive Edition* at **investing.wsj.com.**

Online
INVESTING

An Introduction to Online Investing

G ary Kline has had a beating heart at his fingertips. A skilled cardiac surgeon on the faculty of the Albert Einstein College of Medicine, he obviously isn't a guy afraid of responsibility. But for years, when it came to making investments, he left the decisions up to someone else. Most of his ideas came from his Salomon Smith Barney broker.

Then came the Internet.

Today, he gets most of his stock picks on the Net and places trades through an online trading firm. "I've kind of cut myself off from brokers," he said. "I just don't view them as having the same credibility." Dr. Kline is a frequent visitor to online stock-discussion sites, where he swaps information with other investors. He believes individuals who do enough research can be every bit as savvy about the market and stocks as any broker—and going online yourself is a lot cheaper and easier. So much is just a mouse click away.

Gone are the days when investors had to call their broker at every turn for stock quotes, for investment tips, for business news. Gone, too, are the $100, $200, or $300 commissions they once paid for the simplest of stock trades. Those are sky-high by the standards of today, when you would be hard-pressed to find an online broker charging more than $30 for the same trade. Shop around, and you'll pay less than $10.

When it comes to personal investing, the Internet has changed all
the rules. Sure, other businesses have been altered by the Net—book-
stores, drugstores, even telephone and cable television companies. But
no other field has been transformed, so totally and so rapidly, as has
personal investing. Trading securities is all about obtaining information and executing transactions. The Internet offers quicker, cheaper,
and more efficient ways to do both.

It is quicker and cheaper than traditional trading because online
trading allows you to get rid of the middleman—your traditional full-
service broker. It is more efficient for several reasons. Few would dispute the revolutionary nature of the Internet as a means of
communication. And tapping an order into your computer often offers
a clearer shot into the stock market than reading it into the phone.

All this has been quite a blow to your broker. After all, for years he
has been the nexus for trading and information. That arrangement
provided for him quite well. If he had you on the phone, maybe he
could sell you on a trade. And if you had enough money, he'd try to
get you on the phone all the time. Under this traditional, commission-
based sales structure, every trade was more money in the bank—for
him.

Now, you log on to the Net. You can check out price quotes on any
one of hundreds (maybe thousands) of Web sites. You can comb for investing ideas on financial news and information sites—or on online
message boards, where investors swap ideas among themselves. You
can dig into company information and Wall Street research, or pick
and choose mutual funds with screening tools that used to sit only on
your broker's desk. And, of course, you can hop on to any one of
scores of online brokerage sites to place a trade.

All of this emerged just as two other powerful forces were being felt
on Wall Street. Since the mid-1980s, individual investors have become
more and more interested in managing their own finances—partly out
of necessity as old-time pension plans have been replaced by so-called
self-directed plans, such as 401(k)s. Meanwhile, the stock market was
enjoying an unprecedented bull market: During the 1990s, stocks rose
higher (and more consistently) than they ever had—in history. In what

seemed to be a can't-lose environment, it was easy to become a do-it-yourselfer.

Of course, it isn't really a can't-lose environment. You can lose—and many do—often with the help of the Internet. The same attributes that make the Net a quick and efficient way to invest also make it an easy conduit for quick losses. Even as it puts more power in your hands, it has breathed new life into the same investing scams that have been around for years by making it easy to reach many thousands of people more quickly than ever before. Now, instead of using the phone to hype stocks, scamsters can use phony investing Web sites or message boards, cloaking their identity.

The efficiency of online-trading sites has given birth to a new generation of stock speculators, who quickly dart into and out of stocks, not investing so much as gambling. Some people quit their jobs for what they believe will be an easy, work-at-home life of day trading. But a study by state regulators shows that most people lose money day trading. If trading stocks for a profit every day were as easy as many people seem to think, brokers wouldn't waste their time pitching stocks over the phone—they would have all retired rich by now.

Words to the wise: The basic rules of the markets and of investing haven't changed. The lucky soul who takes a flier in the market and retires with a fortune remains the rare exception. Selecting investments carefully and holding them for the long term is still the best way to make a buck in the markets. The Internet has simply given you new tools—in many ways better tools—to select, buy, and sell those investments.

That isn't to say, as one popular electronic trading firm puts it, that you should necessarily "boot your broker." There is no reason to keep paying hundreds of dollars for each stock trade, and you don't need your hand held for every decision, and at every step, on the way to planning your financial future. But you probably will need some professional guidance from time to time. Web-site calculators and software tools that help you pick stocks or create a retirement savings plan can't always take the place of human interaction and professional help. Sometimes a second opinion can help, especially when markets are moving quickly and you are tempted to make hasty—and possibly panicky—decisions.

When choosing an investment or setting up an investing plan, think of the Net as both a starting place and an ending place. You can troll for investment ideas on message boards, cull insights from data and research housed on Web sites, and answer simple questions using online calculators, worksheets, and the like. And once you have developed a plan and are ready to buy, the Net is clearly the best place to make your actual trades and monitor the performance of your investments. Scores of sites feature online portfolio-tracking tools to help you do this. But in the middle of this process—between the spark of an idea and the transaction that brings it to fruition—questions and concerns may come up. That's when it's time to get some human advice.

How much help you want and need depends on you and your level of comfort with personal finances. And that may change over the course of your life. Some young people who are just starting to invest may do just fine for years, picking some mutual funds and stocks and making regular investments. But as their portfolios grow in size, as they need to begin thinking about things like a will to keep things in order for their children, and as they approach retirement years, they may find it is time to seek out some help.

Financial issues seem to become trickier with age. Tax planning, for instance, can be complex. From understanding capital gains to figuring out how to save for your children's education without wasting too many precious investment gains on payments to the government, you'll find that you need to consider different—and sometimes more confusing—types of investments as you get older. A portfolio of stocks and funds that made perfect sense at age 30 probably should be partly diversified into bonds at age 60. Knowing the ins and outs of bond investing can be a challenge.

If you aren't paying your broker through a commission charged at the time you make a trade, just how do you hook up with someone who can give you advice? As it turns out, brokers today rarely call themselves brokers, using instead a term such as financial adviser, financial planner, or financial consultant. Many of them offer their services in exchange for an annual fee, which is set as a percentage of the assets you have in accounts at the firm. Some firms will allow you to make cheap trades and track your investments online, yet call upon an adviser when you need a hand. You can also use an independent financial planner: someone who doesn't work directly for a brokerage firm, but rather dispenses advice in exchange for a flat or hourly fee. These advisers may offer you less biased information than a broker, who may have an interest in steering you to certain investments.

Stocks were the first investment vehicle to move online. Some types of online trading—involving special software and a dial-up modem connection into a brokerage firm's computer—were launched as early as 1985, years before the Web even existed. (The first trade over the Internet was executed in 1994 by K. Aufhauser & Co., which is now part of Ameritrade.) By now, every aspect of personal finance is available on the Internet. Online banking services, also first offered on a dial-up basis, are exploding on the Web, as is the opportunity to shop for a mortgage, insurance, and credit cards. In each case, online firms can promise speed, efficiency, and often lower prices.

A BRIEF HISTORY OF THE NET

The Internet as most people know it—with its colorful Web pages and point-and-click navigation—has only been around since the mid-1990s. But its roots go back more than 30 years, to a secret military project.

The Internet's history can be traced to the Cold War paranoia that gripped American society in the 1960s. Military researchers spent considerable effort thinking about doomsday, and tried to find a way that forces around the country could communicate with one another following a nuclear attack. The networks of the day were point-to-point—destroy one piece, and the whole

(continues)

system would fail. Researchers believed that if they could find a way to let data flow across several different networks crisscrossing the country, then, in the event of an attack, the data could just navigate a different path from point A to point B.

In the early 1960s, the Department of Defense's Advanced Research Project Agency (ARPA), formed as a response to the Soviet launch of Sputnik 1 in 1957, began pushing plans for a nationwide network to be known as Arpanet. At the end of the decade, after years of planning, academics created the first network, which linked four universities.

Instead of using the network to access remote computers and experiments, as the founders intended, users quickly got hooked on the Arpanet's electronic-mail feature. The Net's evolution from an academic tool to a social network reached a milestone in 1979, when three college students set up the first Usenet newsgroups—precursors to today's message boards—and users from around the world logged on to voice opinions on topics from politics to entertainment.

The Internet got its biggest boost in the 1980s. Researchers developed a common protocol—or computer language—for the network, known as TCP/IP. This transformed the Arpanet from a string of connected networks into one seamless web of computers, all speaking the same language. The Internet was born.

And just in time. The 1980s brought the personal computer boom. Falling prices and increasingly user-friendly designs made the boxes popular to home users, and proprietary online systems like Prodigy, and later America Online, established themselves as online gathering places.

In 1991, Marc Andreessen and a group of student programmers at the National Center for Supercomputing Applications, located on the campus of the University of Illinois at Champaign-Urbana, began work on Mosaic, the first graphics-based Web browser. Its release in 1993 spurred an explosion in Internet traffic. Suddenly, lifeless pages of data came alive with pictures (and, soon, sounds and video). Just a year later, Mr. Andreessen and Jim Clark formed Netscape Communications Corp., and Mosaic evolved into Netscape Navigator.

Part One

ONE

Trading Stocks Online

I t started out as a curiosity, quickly became a fad—and now it's a revolution. The simple act of tapping a stock trade into a personal computer has transformed a multi-billion-dollar industry. The biggest names on Wall Street have had to tear up their business plans. "My broker says" has been replaced by "I read on the Net." Some of this interest will be fleeting. The public's fixation with stocks and trading clearly could never have come about without the historic bull market that swept stocks higher through much of the 1990s. It is a lot more fun to talk about stocks—and easier to make money trading them—when prices seem to do nothing but rise. A long bear market for stocks (or even a period of stagnation where prices barely move) quickly takes the glamour out of stock trading.

Indeed, for some time, many on Wall Street bet that a bear market would quickly snuff out online investing. (In fact, the Internet itself was considered a fad at first. Many predicted that interest in the Net would quickly fade out—a 1990s version of America's brief 1970s infatuation with citizens band radios). But that talk petered out as Internet-accessible brokerage firms posted year after year of growth figures.

Charles Schwab & Co. (**www.schwab.com**) was the first established brokerage firm to embrace the Net, and it quickly saw thousands of its clients give up its toll-free phone lines and place their orders online. By

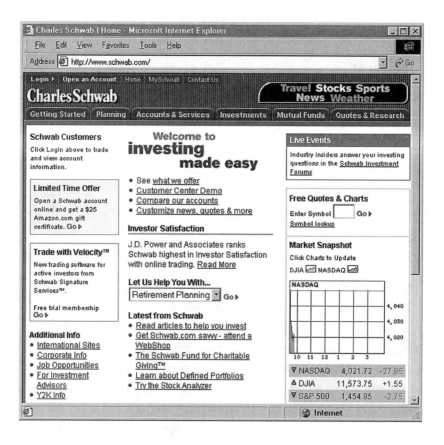

the end of 1998, more than half of its stock trades came in over the Net, and across the industry, roughly one in six stock trades originated from orders that were placed online. There were 7.1 million online brokerage accounts, up from just 1.5 million two years earlier, according to Gomez Advisors, an Internet consulting firm in Lincoln, Massachusetts. The number of accounts is expected to hit a whopping 18 million by 2001.

As if any more evidence were needed that Wall Street couldn't afford to remain aloof from online investing, Schwab's total stock market value edged above that of Merrill Lynch & Co. (**www.ml.com**) in late 1998. If there is one measuring stick that always has Wall Street's attention without fail, it is the stock market. Schwab, a discount-brokerage firm barely 25 years old, was king of the hill. The two companies continue to swap the leadership position in terms of market value.

And Schwab wasn't the only upstart to ride the Internet wave. Consider Ameritrade: J. Joe Ricketts, its chairman, borrowed $10,500 to start the brokerage firm (**www.ameritrade.com**) that is now Ameritrade in 1975. At one point in 1999, the company's market value topped $8.6 billion, while Mr. Ricketts's and his wife's combined stake in the Omaha, Nebraska, company soared to more than $4.7 billion. E*Trade Group (**www.etrade.com**), founded in 1991 and launched on the Web in 1996, saw its market value hit $16.8 billion at its high.

All of these market values will continue to zigzag with the stock market, but few people now expect online stock trading to go away. The phenomenon has clearly touched a nerve with the investing public and tapped into investors' desires to use technology as a means to accomplish things cheaper and faster. "Take my word, it's really easy," said Charles Schwab, founder of the company that bears his name. "Even I can do it, and I'm all thumbs." Mr. Schwab called online trading "the ultimate empowerment of the individual." As Home Depot discovered, we really are a nation of do-it-yourselfers—whether it's hanging wallpaper or buying a stock.

FIRST AND FOREMOST: IT'S CHEAP

There are many reasons to trade online, but the most obvious one— and the one that first caught the attention of investors—remains its biggest selling point: Online brokers are just so dirt cheap.

E*Trade, one of the first cyberbrokers and the one that first really captured Wall Street's attention, stunned the industry in 1996 when it went on the Internet with a $14.95 stock commission—and launched its in-your-face "Boot Your Broker" advertising campaign. Like the discount brokerage firms (which offer trading but little or no advice) that sprang up in the mid-1970s after the Securities and Exchange Commission put an end to fixed stock commissions, online brokers had found a cheaper way, through new technological efficiencies, to offer an old service.

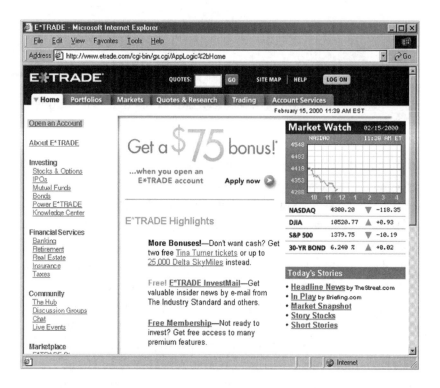

Because of the way brokerage firms charge for stock trades, it's difficult to compare prices precisely. Internet brokers usually charge flat rates, often for transactions up to 1,000 shares, with additional fees for larger or more complicated orders. Traditional brokers, by contrast, levy fees based on how much stock an investor wants to buy or sell, and how much the stock is trading for at the time. But, even factoring in the discounts many big brokerage firms reserve for their best customers, online brokers charge commissions anywhere from half to one tenth, or even one twentieth, the cost of their full-service counterparts.

That's changing—but not because online brokers are becoming more expensive. Instead, traditional firms are reworking their pricing structures to become more competitive. Even mighty Merrill Lynch, long the most popular brokerage firm for individual investors, and one that for years dismissed the online trading phenomenon, now offers two kinds of Web accounts designed to stem the flow of business out of the firm. One type of account offers trades for $29.95, but no advice from a broker. The other promises unlimited trades, either over the Internet, by phone, or with a broker, for an annual fee based on a customer's assets. Right now, Schwab is charging many of its customers a relatively steep $29.95, but that's still far less than the $300 a customer in a traditional Merrill account (it's still offered) would have paid at one point last year to buy, say, 300 shares of Internet portal site Yahoo!. The same trade would have cost $19.95 at E*Trade (because trades for Nasdaq stocks cost more than those for issues listed on the New York Stock Exchange), and $9.99 at high-tech Datek Online. The fee at George Brown & Company, a niche firm based in Boston and now owned by Chase Manhattan Bank? A mere $5.

Traditional brokers, of course, also offer sophisticated advice and financial planning along with their stock trades. That's the card full-service firms, such as Merrill and Salomon Smith Barney, hope to play as they try to woo cyber-savvy customers with their new Internet-based accounts. These firms are betting that investors still want—and need—the help of a broker. Schwab, which controls the biggest share of the online stock-trading business, seems to agree, at least up to a point. In another example of how the Net has turned things upside down, Schwab—which made its name offering stripped-down service and low prices—now markets itself, in part, by calling attention to the service and advice it offers customers, contrasting them with the bare-bones firms that offer still cheaper trades. Those even less expensive firms offer no apologies for their lack of bells and whistles. That, they say, is what their customers want. "Our customers are financially literate," explained Jeffrey Citron, the former chief executive of Iselin, New Jersey–based Datek. "They know exactly what they want to buy."

Not everyone is that sophisticated. But even less savvy investors probably realize that most professionals, with all their stock-picking prowess, usually can't beat the returns of major stock market indexes. So why pay more for their services?

"If you're paying 1.5% each way on a trade, or if you're paying 1.5% or 2% a year (to have your money managed) and you're not even doing as well as the averages, how do you ever make up the cost of this intermediary who's actually sucking value away from you?" said Samuel Hayes, a professor of investment banking at Harvard University. But that's not to say that people who opt to do it themselves necessarily do the right thing on their own. Many investors jump "from the frying pan into the fire" trying to pick a handful of winning stocks once they are out on their own, rather than buying and holding a selection of mutual funds (mostly index funds) as the bulk of their portfolio.

Ever-falling commissions marked the online brokerage industry's first few years. The $14.95 commission at E*Trade was followed by the $8 trade at Ameritrade in late 1997, promoted by a huge advertising campaign. Soon after, Quick & Reilly, now a unit of Fleet Boston Financial Corporation, launched a deep-discount broker called Suretrade (**www.suretrade.com**), which boasted a base commission of just $7.95 a trade. Many other sites emerged offering commissions of $10 to $12 a trade, including Datek Online (**www.datek.com**) and TD Waterhouse Securities (**www.waterhouse.com**), which are now two of the biggest online firms.

To some extent, online commissions stabilized after that push below $10, though many firms offered even deeper discounts to active traders or very wealthy customers. In 1999, American Express Company went so far as to offer some free online trades to customers who brought $25,000 or more to the firm and early in 2000, Schwab cut the commissions it charges its most active clients to as low as $14.95. Now, the battle largely has shifted to competition over who will offer the best services—such as Wall Street research and the ability to buy into lucrative initial public offerings of stock. According to investment firm Credit Suisse First Boston, the average online stock commission remained flat, at between $15 and $16, during 1998 and 1999.

GOOD-BYE, CHURN AND BURN

Stockbrokers have never had rock-solid reputations as trusted professionals. A 1997 Gallup public opinion poll found that in terms of honesty and ethical standards, stockbrokers ranked higher than lawyers and car salesman—but lower than journalists and building contractors.

Online brokers know that, and they're milking it for all it's worth.

Most stockbrokers are honorable, well-trained people. But for years, investors have lodged very legitimate complaints about traditional brokers who were more concerned with pushing a stock underwritten by their firm—in other words, a stock the firm needed to unload—than finding solid, suitable investments for their customers. At many brokerage houses, brokers get paid more for selling in-house products, such as mutual funds managed by the firm's portfolio managers, than outside products, regardless of the funds' performances. Even today, securities arbitrators, who handle all disputes between brokers and their clients, routinely face cases in which investors allege that brokers simply "churned" their accounts, recommending transactions mainly to generate commissions for themselves and without regard to the portfolio's rate of return.

"I have no doubt that some of the people who have gone online are the people who have had the horror stories," said Harvard's Professor Hayes. Indeed, it's hard to forget disasters such as brokerage firms' aggressive sales, in the 1980s, of limited partnership investments in everything from oil exploration to real estate. Many investors eventually filed claims charging they were never informed of the hefty risk of such investments. Prudential Securities, for one, paid $330 million in 1993 to settle SEC civil claims of widespread fraud in selling limited partnership interests. Its parent, Prudential Insurance Co. of America, has paid nearly $2 billion in legal fees and restitution.

That fundamental conflict—between generating income for the brokerage house and creating a safe, suitable portfolio for the investor—is something online brokers have exploited and parlayed into a resonant marketing message, and one that has undoubtedly helped their business. A famous television advertisement from E*Trade plays off the public's distrust of brokers and envy of their big paychecks by opening with an enticing shot of a brick mansion. An attractive, well-dressed couple strolls up the front walk. When the two reach the front door and turn around, an announcer intones, "Your investments paid for this dream house." The man and woman turn around, smirking. Then the kicker: "Too bad it belongs to your broker."

Many cyberbrokers, most notably Charles Schwab, tout their services as "unbiased," saying they have no interest in peddling any particular product. Schwab doesn't underwrite any stock deals, and its employees don't get paid based on the commissions generated by each customer. Though firms like Schwab and E*Trade make more money as the number of trades they execute grows, most of their employees receive flat salaries and bonuses, compared to the commission-based pay structure at most traditional brokerage firms. There are no "cold calls" from online brokers interrupting dinner or aggressively selling tiny stocks you've never heard of. Instead, the new Internet brokers have positioned themselves as mere trading and investment-information vehicles.

But even though online brokerage firms don't employ any unscrupulous individuals who aim to churn your account in search of commission fees, that doesn't mean plenty of online trading accounts aren't churned. Typically, though, the guilty party in these cases is the online investor himself. With the ease and low cost of making trades from the comfort of their office or home, many investors trade far too frequently and thereby rack up commission costs, instead of buying and holding stocks and funds.

THE CULTURE OF INVESTING

Even before online brokers burst onto the financial scene in 1996, Americans' love affair with the stock market had already blossomed. The reason was simple: For nearly 20 years, companies had been gradually shifting more responsibility for retirement saving and planning into the hands of their employees, instead of managing big pension funds themselves.

The rise of the tax-deferred 401(k) account, coupled with growing concerns about the adequacy of Social Security, meant many Americans had no choice but to focus on saving and to bone up on investment strategies. How could they amass enough money to retire if they couldn't figure out which mutual funds to buy and how long to hold them? That meant understanding expense ratios (a measurement of annual fees charged by funds), interpreting 10-year performance charts and wading through thick fund prospectuses. Many have done it: By 1999, about 44% of Americans owned mutual funds, up dramatically from about 6% in 1980, according to the Investment Company Institute.

The robust bull market of the 1990s intensified this investing fervor and made Americans more confident about investing in mutual funds as well as in individual stocks, whether through retirement plans or brokerage accounts. In 1999, the Dow Jones Industrial Average crossed the 10,000-point barrier, a milestone emblematic of the country's economic strength and Americans' seemingly unshakable faith in the stock market. The industrial average had tripled in just seven years.

In some ways, the charging market and the rise of online investing have fed off each other: The market's rise has created a new class of eager first-time investors who are confident enough to invest on their own, without a traditional broker. At the same time, the new, cheap channel of electronic investing has changed the rules of the stock-trading game. It's given average individuals—not just professional investors—the power to move stocks. Many experts name active online investors as a significant force behind the otherwise inexplicable gains posted at times by many Internet-related stocks, which many Web investors seem to favor over traditional industrial companies. Chatter on Internet message boards such as those run by Yahoo! Finance (**finance.yahoo.com**) and Silicon Investor (**www.siliconinvestor.com**) helps fuel the trading, with investors prodding their online friends to get in on the next can't-miss investment.

It's not just hard-core day traders—those investors glued to their computer screens throughout the day, making scores of rapid-fire trades—who have helped create what many call a new culture of investing. Everyone, from grandmothers to midlevel executives to tradesmen, now participates in the stock market. CNBC has become as accepted as other cable networks like ESPN and MTV. College students buy and sell stocks to pay for tuition.

In Nanuet, New York, three auto mechanics at the All Transmissions repair shop dart in and out of Internet stock chat rooms between fixing cars. One of the mechanics, Steve Murphy, said that after arriving at work at about 7:20 A.M., "The first thing I do is get on the computer and see what they're talking about in the chat rooms." Coworker Henry "Hank" Kraszewski is "in at seven-thirty right behind me," Mr. Murphy added. "The first thing he asks me is, 'Are you online yet?' "

THE INTERNET AS A COMMUNICATIONS MEDIUM

The communications power of the Internet is evident in the way it has transformed business, academia, and the way people interact with one another—all in just a few years' time. People now buy books, plan vacations, and talk to their friends online. They research medical issues, get news, and even watch live video programs via the Web. The Internet could soon become as ubiquitous as the telephone or the television set. By early 2000, more than 65 million Americans were accessing the Web from home or work, according to Media Metrix, a group that tracks Internet use.

Online stock trading wouldn't have exploded without the accompanying growth of the Internet at large. Indeed, people could trade using dial-up software for years, but the online-trading boom didn't ignite until the Web emerged. The Web is cheap and easy to use, and as a result, it has quickly become the clearinghouse for enormous amounts of information. That information has unlocked the secrets of Wall Street for many investors.

Web sites such as Yahoo! Finance, America Online (**www.aol.com**), MoneyCentral (**www.moneycentral.com**), and Quicken.com (**www. quicken.com**) are just a few of the central places on the Internet where investors now gather to get up to speed on the stock market. On some of these sites and countless others, visitors can get up-to-date stock quotes in seconds. They can pick a stock and almost instantly create a chart showing its price history. They can read about stock sales by company insiders, peruse the company's latest quarterly report, and get the latest market-moving news.

And if they have questions about a stock or an investing strategy, online aficionados don't need to call a broker. They can simply post a message on any of the scores of finance-oriented message boards or chat rooms on the Internet. Almost any publicly traded company has its own "board" somewhere. Many investors religiously follow the picks and musings of some of the new cyber-investing gurus, who have their own discussion groups, and dispense tips and observations to their followers.

Tim Luke Stefanich, a bodyguard turned day trader from Los Angeles, moderated several stock message boards on Silicon Investor before becoming so popular that he tried to form his own stock Web site—and charge people to use it. That venture didn't work out, he said, but Mr. Stefanich is back on Silicon Investor tending to his flock.

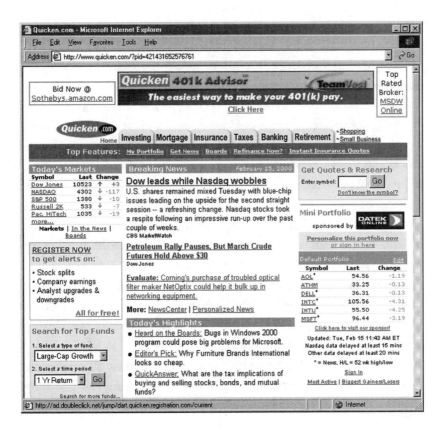

"I probably have 2,000 to 6,000 people who follow it daily," he said of his main discussion group. The thread claims it is a "clean site free of any fights, scams, and pumps and dumps."

BEFORE YOU JUMP IN

It's easy to understand why online trading has become so popular. But there are plenty of drawbacks to consider before taking the plunge. You may find that you only want to tiptoe into online investing, or maybe you don't want to do it at all. Not everyone is suited to picking their own investments. Those who are will find that there are plenty of pitfalls to Web trading that you don't hear or read about in all those slick online brokerage TV commercials and magazine ads. Here are some of the biggest negatives to trading over the Internet:

No Formal Advice

Internet trading right now is primarily for do-it-yourselfers. But what if you don't want to do it yourself? The stock market can be a frightening, unpredictable animal, particularly for people who have never invested before. These days, even sage old Wall Street hands are struggling to understand new market dynamics, which include wildly volatile Internet stocks and shaky foreign markets that, increasingly, dictate market movements on Wall Street. And although the Web has for the first time made all sorts of investing information available to nonprofessionals, that information is so expansive it can easily overwhelm novices.

That's why many investors continue to turn to professional stockbrokers, or even independent financial advisers, for help. These pros can help you draft a financial plan and suggest ongoing changes to your portfolio. They can also anticipate major changes in your financial life, such as getting married, sending a child to college, planning for retirement—or even buying a vacation house you've always wanted. A seasoned professional can also help you stay calm during a market dip, when CNBC and Internet message boards are issuing alarmist statements and predicting permanent doom and gloom.

Of course, many of the tools that professional advisers use to help guide their clients are increasingly available online—for free and without the middleman. Some big online brokers and other Web sites offer stock and mutual fund "screeners" to help you pick investments compatible with your risk tolerance. Others can tell you exactly how much money to put away each month to save for a particular goal, such as sending four children to Ivy League schools. There are also sophisticated "alerts" that send you an instant message when one of your stocks has hit a predetermined target, allowing you to sell the stock or buy more right away. Even Merrill Lynch is using automated advice for customers in its massive 401(k) business. The firm in 1999 announced a pact with Financial Engines (**www.financialengines.com**), a Web site dreamed up by Nobel laureate and finance professor William F. Sharpe that selects specific mutual funds for customers and tells them exactly how likely they are to meet their retirement goals with a particular portfolio.

But for some people, there is no substitute for that human touch. No matter how nifty an online tool looks, nothing can beat the experience and nuance that a seasoned and caring human can offer. (For more on online investing resources, see "Tools of the Trade," Chapter 6.)

Technical Meltdowns

Let's say you're ready to take the plunge. Maybe you already have a financial plan drawn up by an adviser or a Web-based service. You're knowledgeable, empowered, and ready to trade online.

What if you can't?

As more and more customers have swarmed online, many big Internet brokers have been slammed with technical problems that have locked customers out of their Web sites and left them unable to trade—and in some cases, even unable to view their account information. In late 1999, the New York attorney general's office released a critical report that said many big online brokers, at least in the early part of 1998, simply couldn't handle the hordes of new customers they attracted with their ubiquitous advertising. Demand for brokers' Web sites often exceeded computer capacity, the report said, and customers at one firm had to wait 90 hours—nearly four days—to get e-mails answered from customer-service representatives. Many of the glitches stemmed from overwhelmed computer systems that were designed for much lower levels of activity. In late 1998 and early 1999, Charles Schwab actually tricked its computer systems into operating on two mainframe computers, instead of one, until it could devise a more permanent fix to handle its exploding trading volume. In other cases, bottlenecks have developed in specific software systems, such as the faulty software that intermittently disrupted business at Ameritrade in 1998.

Still other meltdowns arose from sources outside the firms. Though placing a trade online may seem like a simple process for the investor, it actually involves a series of transactions and communications involving several parties, any one (or several) of which can get backed up when trading activity is brisk. One example: Since most online brokers don't have their own trading desks and must send orders to other trading firms to be executed on the Nasdaq Stock Market or New York Stock Exchange, slow response times there can cause backups and sometimes create confusion as to whether orders have actually been executed. Backups are especially common for investors trading hot Internet stocks, since trading firms sometimes have a hard time finding customers to take the other side of trades. During a particular bullish spell, firms might have a thousand orders to buy shares of Amazon.com, and not enough people aiming to sell.

In times of heavy trading, it's not unusual for an investor to place a trade, not get the usual quick confirmation, and then place *another* order for the same stock—believing the first one wasn't executed. When the systems catch up, the investor may find that he or she made several purchases. Other customers repeatedly place and cancel orders, further jamming up communications lines. Those who can't figure out if they've actually bought or sold stock often call the firm's toll-free telephone line, where waits of 30 to 90 minutes have been reported at some firms.

The phone lines jam up because so many customers are calling with the same question: Was my order executed? In October 1997, after a one-day market plunge and subsequent rebound triggered staggering volumes on the nation's stock exchanges, Schwab actually instituted a new program for exactly such conditions, under which customers could drive to a branch office and get $500 worth of free commissions. Schwab still puts the offer into effect when its Web site and phone lines are jammed.

Nightmares with technical problems were also common in the first month or two of 1998, when online trading volumes spiked and caused temporary meltdowns at firms like Schwab, E*Trade, and TD Waterhouse Securities, which is part of Toronto-Dominion Bank. For the most part, these firms have worked furiously to increase their capacity and to install new software to handle future trading volumes. Some have also embarked on serious hiring sprees: Ameritrade opened a brand-new customer service center in Texas that will employ up to 1,200 people, while Schwab ran a huge newspaper ad advertising 1,000 job openings. Still, online investors should know that computers do break—and they won't always have access to their money when they want it.

Despite the periodic trouble with jammed phone lines, online-brokerage officials still point to their toll-free lines as the best route to take when Internet trading is out. Gomez Advisors, the Internet consulting firm, advises online investors to have more than one online-trading account to protect themselves from technical meltdowns.

Still, officials note that the expectations of online investors are often much higher than those of full-service customers. Internet investors are accustomed to instantaneous trade execution and howl when they don't get it.

Hidden Costs

Stock trades for $9.99. Even $7.95. It sounds almost too good to be true.

Sometimes it is.

Increasingly, sophisticated online investors are waking up to the fact that trading over the Internet can be more expensive than advertised. Take base commissions, for example. E*Trade constantly touts its base rate of $14.95, but reveals only in the fine print of its ads and brochures that placing a trade for a Nasdaq stock—which represents the bulk of its business—costs $19.95. So do limit orders, or orders to buy or sell a stock at a certain price, instead of at the prevailing market price. Similarly, Ameritrade trumpets its rock-bottom commission of $8, but analysts note that its average commission is closer to $15. The reason for the discrepancy? Many customers place trades for limit orders, which cost $13, and also buy and sell complicated stock options, where the minimum charge is $29.

Deep in the mechanics of online trading lies another hidden cost for investors. Some cybertraders are unaware that most Internet trading houses don't have a presence on the floor of the New York Stock Exchange, or run their own Nasdaq trading desk. Instead, these firms route their orders to outside trading firms to be executed, and are often paid for sending business to certain firms in a practice known as payment for order flow. That is good for the online brokerage firm's bottom line, but some question whether the firm's clients are as lucky. The practice has raised questions as to whether Nasdaq market makers, professional traders charged by Nasdaq to maintain orderly trading, always have the best interests of customers at heart. If online brokers sell orders, they might not be motivated to find the market maker offering the best possible price, some fear.

Consider this example: You're watching your computer screen and see that the lowest "offer" price for a stock you want to buy is $20. You enter your order to buy 100 shares, expecting to buy the stock at $20. But if the stock is moving fast, and if the dealer takes its time in selling you the stock—perhaps because the dealer doesn't have any of its own to sell and can't find any, except at a higher price—your order might be filled at $21. That means you paid $100 more than if the order had been handled differently, and it makes your cheap $10 commission seem somewhat meaningless.

Scenarios such as this have prompted stock regulators to remind customers they're often better off placing limit orders. If in our example you had placed a limit order to buy 100 shares at $20, the order wouldn't have been filled unless the dealer could make a trade for that exact amount.

Online brokerage firms and Nasdaq dealers generally deny that payments for orders influence execution decisions. Still, the issue has helped fuel the popularity of online trading firms that can match orders automatically, without the help of a market maker. Datek, for one, also owns a company called Island ECN, which runs a high-tech, off-exchange trading network that only matches customer buy and sell limit orders. That means there is no dealer who profits off those trades, though Island does charge broker participants a small, per-share fee to participate in the network. In addition, unlike a market maker, Island doesn't step in to buy stock from a seller if another buyer isn't present. So an investor won't always have his order filled at the price he wants. (Market makers, on the other hand, are required by Nasdaq to buy or sell stock for a customer if no other buyers or sellers are available to trade.)

Online Scams

Investing scams have been around as long as, well, investing itself. But the Internet makes them easier to pull off.

Investing over the Internet—and gleaning financial data from Web sites and chat rooms—means you could fall prey to a cyber-rip-off. Sleaziness abounds online, including old-fashioned pyramid schemes and "pump-and-dump" setups updated for the online world. The anonymity and breadth of the Internet has created new headaches for investors and the securities regulators trying to keep cyberspace clean.

One of them is spam, or junk e-mail that can be disseminated to thousands of people at almost no cost. A spam might contain an invitation to buy a bogus security or invest in some other ill-advised venture. Fraudsters have always peddled illegitimate investments, but they

A FEW WORDS ABOUT SPREADS

Amid the excitement about the low commissions that are available from online brokerage firms, it is important to remember that there is another significant cost to trading stocks: When buying and selling a stock position, you are effectively being charged an amount equal to the difference between the price at which a market maker is willing to sell you the shares and the price he or she is willing to buy shares. Known as the spread, this is the difference between the bid and ask price of a stock.

Spreads are relatively slim on the biggest, most heavily traded stocks, but they are considerably wider on small stocks. Spreads have been a big issue on the Nasdaq Stock Market, though they have narrowed there following several securities rules changes that were instituted by regulators in 1997.

Still, the costs can be significant. Consider an investment involving $10,000 worth of stock. You may pay just $20 in commissions buying the shares and later selling them—hopefully, for a profit. But the difference between the bid and ask prices at the time of your transactions may be equal to 1% of the share price for a blue-chip stock—and perhaps 4% of the share price on a small stock. That means you would have paid $400 on the trades in a blue chip, and $500 on the trades in a small cap.

One way to reduce the amount lost to spreads is to execute your trades using limit orders placed directly into an electronic communications network. In some cases, that would allow you to eliminate the middleman—the broker—who is collecting the profits on spreads, but making trades this way isn't always pos-

sible. Though changes are afoot, ECNs so far only have
meaningful trading activity in Nasdaq stocks, not in
New York Stock Exchange issues. (Many trades on the
Big Board floor are also executed without losses to a
spread, when a buyer and seller are matched up in what
is known as an agency trade. More on how the exchange
works later.) And even when trading Nasdaq stocks on
an ECN, you may not be able to find a buyer or seller
at the price you want, when you want it.

can reach many more victims through the Internet than they could just a few years ago, when the telephone was their primary tool.

The Web has also created a new market for bogus investment newsletters. Now, instead of going through the costly procedure of printing them up and mailing them to unsuspecting investors, securities cheats can simply put up a Web site and list their latest picks. Often the authors of these newsletters have been paid by the companies they're touting to recommend them—meaning the "expert" authors have very biased opinions. SEC rules require that newsletters disclose the exact amount and nature of any payments authors receive for recommending securities, but fraudsters often omit or hide those disclaimers. Don't be taken in by a polished appearance or lots of whizzy features, either; the nature of the Web makes it just as easy for scam artists as for legitimate outfits to have an impressive-looking site.

There is also the cyber-smear, a new Web-based scheme to discredit certain companies or stocks. Usually, someone with an interest in hurting a company or stock—often a short seller, an investor who is betting that a stock will decline in value—will load up Internet message boards or chat rooms with negative information about a company. The writer might insinuate that the company has committed accounting fraud, or that its CEO has lied on his résumé. Whether true or not, such allegations, given legitimacy because they're published for all to see on the Web, can send stocks plummeting.

For more on online investing scams and how to avoid them, see "Scams and Deceptions," Chapter 8. And for a discussion on what to do if you have been the victim of a fraud, see "Recourse," Chapter 9.

Addiction

It may not be as addictive as smoking cigarettes or shooting craps, but trading stocks online has turned some investors into bona fide Web junkies. Lured by the casino-like excitement of the stock market and the flashy, fast-moving action on their computer screens, some Internet investors acknowledge they're hooked—and their inability to stop trading has cost them plenty of money.

The addictive aspect of online trading is so big that there's a message board on Silicon Investor dedicated to discussing it: "Are you mortgaging your house to fund your brokerage? Are you tapping into credit cards to cover your margin calls? Is your family suffering because you are neglecting their needs? Let's talk."

One 29-year-old California man, under the name "Mktbuzz," posted his tale of woe. He described how he borrowed nearly $40,000 from his credit cards and quit his job at a bank to trade stocks full-time—only to lose virtually all of his money when a few trades went bad. After moving back home with his parents—and squeezing his king-size bed into his boyhood room—he eventually got back on his feet and took another job with a software company. (He also moved into a new apartment by himself.) But as of 1999, he was still trading, he admitted, hoping he'd score big and be able to pay down the debt he racked up from his last trading debacle. "It's like playing Missile Command with your brokerage account," he said.

Gambling and addictions specialists report they're now seeing people who are hooked on online trading. David Osinga, a therapist at the tony Sierra Tucson center in Arizona, said he's treated patients who "spend inordinate amounts of time in front of the computer screen, monitoring their stocks and every minutiae of every turn in the stock market." New Jersey's Council on Compulsive Gambling held a seminar that addressed compulsive Internet trading at a statewide conference. It's easy to see how people with addictive personalities can get hooked on the market, according to Kimberly S. Young, a clinical psychologist who wrote a book about Internet addiction called *Caught in the Net*. Telltale signs of a problem include spending twelve to fourteen hours a day at the computer, hiding or lying about trading losses, or neglecting jobs and loved ones.

Most online investors aren't at risk of developing a gambling addiction. But handling part or all of your financial portfolio on the Internet is a big step, and one that shouldn't be taken lightly. You need to make sure you have the time, the savvy, and the desire to learn about the markets and keep up with all the latest news that could affect your financial well-being. You must also be able to recognize at what point in your financial life the Net isn't enough, and when you need professional advice.

If you're ready for it, though, you'll find the Net to be the most powerful tool ever put into individuals' hands for managing their money. And as the country's biggest financial companies take steps to embrace it, its power will only continue to grow.

LEARNING THE ROPES

According to a 1999 survey by the Securities Industry Association and the Investment Company Institute, almost half of U.S. households own stocks, either directly, in the form of actual company shares, or indirectly, through a mutual fund or employer-sponsored investment plan. That figure has climbed by 48% since 1989.

Why the growth? It's easy: almost irresistible investment returns, thanks to the stock market's biggest rally in history during the 1990s. As the decade began, the Dow Jones Industrial Average stood at 2750 and the Nasdaq Composite Index at just 455. By 1999, the industrials had topped 11000 and the Nasdaq composite exploded above 4000 as the decade came to a close. But even if the 1990s hadn't been a such a boom time, investment advisers say individuals would still have good reason to park a big part of their portfolios in stocks. Since 1926, stocks have gained, on average, 11.4% a year, and have suffered annual losses just 20 times, according to Ibbotson Associates, a Chicago re-search firm. By contrast, long-term government bonds have returned 5.1% and cash holdings, i.e., Treasury bills, just 3.8%. (This calculation was made using the 30-day bill.)

Of course, stocks aren't for everyone. Some people simply can't stomach the risk of holding stocks. After all, although the market tends to rise over time, there are a considerable number of nasty bumps along the way. Ibbotson's statistics show that the stock market has plunged more than 20% on 11 separate occasions since the 1920s. In one case, the market dropped 43% from peak to trough—during 1973 and 1974. Risks like that mean that investors need to consider their goals before plunking their money down for stocks. If retirement is just a few years away, or you are saving money for a down payment on your first house, you probably should cut back on your stock holdings. You could come up short on cash if a bear market strikes at just the wrong time.

But for people with a long time horizon—people in their 20s, 30s or 40s who are saving for a retirement that is still many years away—stocks are the best place to be, financial advisers say. Their recommen-dations vary (and, again, much of this has to do with your personal tolerance for risk), but professionals often advise investors to put be-tween 70% and 90% of their money into stocks over the long term—and to be prepared to ride out the bumps that will surely come.

Many people invest in stocks without ever directly owning a single share. Instead of picking investments among the thousands of stocks that trade on the major U.S. markets, and even overseas, they purchase shares of mutual funds or invest money through employer retirement plans, such as a 401(k) or profit-sharing plan. This can be a good in-vestment policy for many people, because most funds give you diversi-fication.

One of the biggest risks you can face in the stock market is picking a loser. Even in a boom time for the market, individual stocks (or stocks in specific industries) regularly go into a funk, and companies sometimes go broke. If you put too much money into a stock that goes bad, your portfolio could be in tatters even if the stock market rallies.

Consider precious metal and pollution-control stocks. They lost 48% and 42%, respectively, as measured by the Dow Jones U.S. Industry Groups, between 1995 and 2000, despite the roaring gains elsewhere in the market. Separately, plenty of hot Internet stocks crashed after making their debuts in the market with exciting initial public offerings.

BASIC RETIREMENT PLANS

Profit-sharing. This is one of several popular types of defined contribution plans, in which employers make a specific annual contribution toward workers' retirements, but don't guarantee a specific level of benefits. The employer agrees to pay a percentage of its profits to employees, in amounts based on a specific formula. Employees typically can choose to direct the money into several investment options, and investment returns grow tax-free until retirement.

401(k) plans. This is another type of defined contribution plan, named after a section of the tax code. You contribute a percentage of your pretax salary into the plan, and your employer may make an additional contribution to your account, based on the size of your contribution. You choose from several investment options, and the money grows tax-free until retirement. There are also 403(b) plans, which are similar to 401(k)s, but are available to employees of nonprofit organizations.

Traditional pension plans. These defined benefit plans promise a specific level of benefits that will be paid during your retirement years, but you have no say in how the funds are invested. These plans typically are more expensive for corporations and have been falling out of favor.

Even if your stock picks aren't losers—dogs, in the parlance of Wall Street—you still may have trouble matching the performance of the overall stock market. Even professional investment managers struggle to keep pace with major stock market averages. In 1999, for instance, about 40% of U.S. mutual funds outperformed the Standard & Poor's 500-stock index (the market yardstick by which investment managers' performances are most often measured), according to Lipper Inc., a Summit, New Jersey, research firm. Over the prior five years, no more than 25% of general U.S. stock funds outperformed the S&P on any given year. That is why financial advisers often recommend keeping much of your stock holdings in a mutual fund that is designed to track the performance of the overall stock market. These index funds buy shares of many stocks that are contained in a major index, such as the S&P 500, aiming to match the index's performance. (For more information on mutual fund investing, including online tools you can use to select funds and Web sites you can use to make purchases, see "Mutual Funds," Chapter 4.)

But for all the alternatives to investing in individual companies, Americans remain rabid stock pickers. The Securities Industry Association/Investment Company Institute survey showed that 26 million American households directly own stocks. Some people buy shares in a range of companies—across several industries—in an attempt to create a diversified portfolio, which they can fine-tune more precisely than they ever could through mutual fund investments alone. Other people supplement their fund holdings with a handful of individual stock picks that they believe—or their brokers have suggested—will outperform the overall market. Still others chuck diversification altogether and simply take a flier on a handful of stocks they hope will make them rich.

When you invest in a stock, you are taking an ownership stake in the company that issued the shares. That stake is often tiny (International Business Machines Corp., for instance, has a total of 1.8 billion shares outstanding), but it does give you an interest in the company's earnings power. It sometimes entitles you to a dividend payment, and depending on the terms of the specific stock, it usually gives you the right to vote on certain matters related to the way the company is run.

BUYING ON MARGIN

Some investors take out a loan with their broker in order to buy stocks. That way, they don't have to put up the entire cost of the stock in order reap the benefits from any gains in its share price. Doing so is called buying on margin and requires you to set up a margin account with your broker. There are strict rules, though, limiting the amount of money that you can borrow (or, as they say on Wall Street, how much you can leverage your position) to buy stock. Broad limits are set by regulators, but firms may have even tighter controls of their own—sometimes called house limits—and they can change those limits.

There are two ways to look at the limits on margin. In any single transaction, Federal Reserve rules let you borrow no more than 50% of the purchase price. There is also a separate margin maintenance requirement that is set by the major markets and by brokerage firms. You must have equity in your margin account (the value of the stock purchased on margin, minus the amount you owe the broker, plus any cash and other assets kept in the account) that equals at least 25% of the current market value of the stocks you purchased on margin. (Requirements are somewhat different for short-sale and day-trading positions.) If the value of the stocks in that account fall, pushing the reserve below 25%, your brokerage firm will ask you to deposit cash or securities in the account. This is called a margin call. If you can't, or won't, supply additional cash or securities, the firm can sell stocks you own—without your permission—to raise the money needed to meet the maintenance requirement.

(continues)

Margin requirements are sometimes changed by brokerage firms during unusual market conditions. If
stocks enter a period of sustained losses or wild
volatility, margin requirements may be raised to protect firms from potential losses on margin loans they
made. Requirements may be increased for specific
stocks that are particularly volatile—and sometimes
margin purchases are prohibited entirely on individual stocks. Requirements on Internet stocks, for instance, were tightened by many firms in 1999. The
Federal Reserve sometimes adjusts its margin requirements in response to market conditions, too, but it
hasn't done so since 1974.

Most people don't buy shares in order to have a voice at a particular company (although some do—there are several socially responsible
investment funds that take positions in companies to try to influence
they way they are run), or even to collect dividends. The majority of
people buy stocks in hopes they will rise, seeking capital appreciation.
More to the point: They want to buy low and sell high.

Your gains, though, aren't simply the amount by which a stock has
risen or fallen. Investors should pay most attention to their total return
on an investment, and there are pluses and minuses to that. On the
plus side, you can add any dividend payments you have received to the
gains that have occurred in your stock's share price (or use the dividend payments to offset part or all of any losses). On the negative side,
you must deduct the costs of brokerage commissions from any gains
you have realized.

Investing for Dividends

Some investors are more interested in the dividends that companies
pay out than in the appreciation of stock prices, but that form of in-

vesting has become less prevalent during the past ten years. The long bull market made capital appreciation much easier to attain. Investors have been able to earn much, much more on the gains in stock prices than in the cash from dividends. The dividend yield on stocks—that is, the total amount of dividends paid out each year divided by the stock's share price—hit a record low of little more than 1% in 1999, as measured by the yield on the stocks in the S&P 500. That was paltry compared with the 19.5% advance that the index posted for the year. Just a few years ago, a dividend yield below 3% was considered a sure sign that the market was "overvalued" and due for a setback.

Many of the hottest stocks of the past decade, most notably those of companies in the technology industry, paid no dividends at all. Traditionally, it hasn't been unusual for young companies to opt against paying dividends because, the argument goes, they need to conserve their cash—keep it in-house to reinvest in the business rather than pay it out to shareholders. But many of the biggest, most powerful companies in the technology sector have decided against paying dividends, even though they could easily afford to do so. Microsoft pays no dividend, and Intel, a mere 12 cents a year.

Hefty dividends are still available in certain areas of the market, most notably utilities and real estate investment trusts. Some of these still have yields between 5% and 7%, said Arnold Kaufman, editor of *The Outlook,* an investment newsletter published by Standard & Poor's. Utilities tend to pay high dividends because they have big assets already in place, in power-generating plants, for instance, and don't need to hold on to earnings for further investment in their businesses. Real estate investment trusts, meanwhile, are required by law to pay out 90% of their earnings in dividends.

Investing for the sake of earning big dividends will be back in vogue when the stock market falls into a bear market, or even just when it enters a period when stock prices remain little changed. At that point, with gains for capital appreciation hard to come by, investors will demand bigger dividends as a reward for holding stocks. But many experts, like Mr. Kaufman, believe the world where 3% or higher dividend yields were common may be gone for good.

Short Selling

Most people who invest in the stock market are doing so in the hope that prices will rise. But it doesn't take a bull market to make a buck in stocks. You can profit from falling prices by selling stocks short—that is, selling shares that you don't own. (In the language of Wall Street, if you don't own something, you are short; if you do own it, you are long.)

That may sound confusing, but it works this way: You simply borrow shares from a broker, much the same as you borrow cash from a banker, and then sell those borrowed shares in the market. If the shares fall in price, you'll profit by buying them at the new lower price, and then using them to repay the loan. (That act of buying stock to get rid of a short position is known as covering a short.) Your profit is the difference between the amount of money you received when selling the borrowed stock, and the amount of money you paid to buy the shares to pay off the loan.

Short selling is risky because a short seller's losses, in theory, are limitless. When you buy a stock, the worst that can happen to you is that the company will go broke, your shares will be worthless, and you will have lost your investment. But a short seller's losses don't have a floor. If a short seller bets wrong—and the stock rises instead of falls—the losses could grow and grow. If you short a $10 stock that subsequently rises to $20, you are out $10. If it goes to $50, you are out $40. If it goes to $100, you lose $90. Worst case: The stock you short could be the next Microsoft.

Of course, reasonable short sellers would bail out and cover their positions long before they lost a bundle of money. It pays to set limits when you take on a short position. You can give your broker standing orders to cover a position if the stock climbs to a specific price—called a stop-loss order—to make sure that your losses don't get away from you.

Exchanges and Markets

Stock investors in the United States enjoy some of the fairest, most open markets in the world. Companies whose shares are publicly traded in a major stock market are required to file detailed information on their business and financial condition with the Securities and Exchange Commission at least quarterly, and those documents are almost immediately available to the public. The markets themselves are closely monitored by regulators to ensure that investors' orders are filled at the best available price, that brokers live up to the stock prices that they quote to one another, and that trades are completed as promised—that the money and the stock are actually delivered. The markets themselves have strict rules of conduct for their traders and member firms.

Of course, regulators can't catch everything, and people will always try to beat the system and break the rules until they are caught. Hundreds of individuals and scores of firms are disciplined each year by the SEC, the New York Stock Exchange, and the National Association of Securities Dealers, a group that regulates brokers and runs the Nasdaq Stock Market. Many times, though, critics complain, the punishments that are handed down aren't nearly severe enough to hurt the rule breakers. In some cases, the guilty party merely accepts a censure, and promises not to violate the rules again. In other cases, unscrupulous brokers quietly leave the business and never pay the fines that are levied. But for all their warts, the American markets are still the envy of the world in terms of investor protection.

Just as has been true for some 200 years, most of the biggest and most important companies—in terms of the total market value of their stocks—are traded on the New York Stock Exchange, often called the Big Board. That may seem surprising, considering the attention that the Nasdaq Stock Market received during the 1990s bull market. Nasdaq exploded in terms of trading volume and the number of stocks traded during the past decade, and it captivated investors with the towering gains that were posted by its dominant technology sector. Indeed, share volume on the Nasdaq market ran about even with the New York Stock Exchange late in the 1990s, with both setting single-day volume records just above 1 billion shares traded. But the total value of U.S. stocks listed on the NYSE, at $10.8 trillion, remained far above Nasdaq, at $4.9 trillion.

The American Stock Exchange, which merged with Nasdaq in 1998, remains a distant third player in the U.S. markets. Its daily trading volume is often well below 50 million shares and the total market value of stocks traded on the exchange is just $100 billion. The Amex, once the proving ground for small companies, was crushed by Nasdaq during the 1980s and 1990s.

Trading on a stock exchange is vastly different from trading on the Nasdaq Stock Market. Exchange trading takes place on what is called an auction market—orders are consolidated on the exchange floor before a single trader, called a specialist, who helps match up the buyers and sellers. Because brokers at the exchange are acting as agents for customers—helping buyers to find sellers—the exchange is known as an agency market. Brokers earn money on commissions from the trades they arrange. Nasdaq trading, on the other hand, takes place in a dealer market, where many traders—called market makers—post competing prices to buy and sell shares. Orders are executed at the best available price using a computer system, rather than face-to-face contact, to communicate and execute trades. Dealers earn money from the difference, or spread, between the price at which they buy shares of a stock and the price at which they are willing to sell those shares.

Despite these fundamental differences in the way the two types of markets operate, the differences are narrowing. For instance, exchange specialists at times will act like dealers, trading directly with customers. (Specialists are required to do so if other buyers or sellers aren't available to fill a customer's order, part of the specialists' obligation to maintain an orderly market in each stock they trade.) Also, some orders for Big Board stocks are routed to dealers on the Nasdaq market. Meanwhile, trades in Nasdaq stocks—most notably limit orders—are increasingly being sent into electronic communications networks. ECNs match up buyers and sellers without intervention from a dealer. Nasdaq officials say they are moving toward creating a "central limit-order book" for that market that would do roughly the same thing. Although the New York Stock Exchange evokes images of its storied trading floor, a far different image than that of Nasdaq, in reality, a lot of computer communications is going on in both markets. The notion of orders coming down to the auction on the exchange floor—with brokers scribbling orders on pads and scrambling around the exchange floor—is little more than a quaint idea from the past, at least when it comes to most of the small orders that individual investors place. In keeping with securities rules, trades are done at the best available price in the market, but for the most part they are handled electronically. They show up on a computer screen beside the specialist, and are completed online. The exchange is moving toward another system for small orders that will bypass its specialists entirely. With big orders, there is still a fair amount of scrambling and haggling on the floor, though many traders have traded in their paper order pads for hand-held electronic devices.

Nasdaq, too, has changed dramatically in its nearly 30-year history. When it was founded in 1971 as the National Association of Securities Dealers Automated Quotation system, it was little more than that: an electronic system that brokers used to pass around stock quotes on securities that weren't listed on an exchange. Back then, making a trade required a telephone call from one market maker to another. Companies whose stocks were quoted on Nasdaq didn't have to meet the same rigorous requirements that were imposed on exchange-listed stocks, and for years Nasdaq stocks were known as unlisted stocks. Nasdaq tried to put all that behind it during the 1990s after beefing up its listing requirements to help snuff out problems with penny-stock fraud. It even insisted that Nasdaq was no longer an acronym for its clunky birth name. From that point on, it was to be known as simply the Nasdaq Stock Market.

Another subdivision of the stock market, the OTC Bulletin Board (OTC stands for over the counter), closely resembles Nasdaq in its early days—and is run, in fact, by the Nasdaq market's parent, the National Association of Securities Dealers. The OTC Bulletin Board is simply a quotation service and has few regulatory requirements. Many legitimate companies' shares trade there, but it has also become host to many stock scams: for example, promoters touting fraudulent companies in an effort to profit from the subsequent gains in their shares. The NASD only recently started requiring companies whose shares are quoted on the OTC Bulletin Board to disclose basic information, such as earnings data. Many companies whose shares are listed on the OTC Bulletin Board are very small and highly risky. You must make an extra effort to learn about these companies before you invest: Don't jump into a low-priced stock looking for quick gains just because its price is low.

Tracking the Trade

There is little difference in the way an online trade and a traditional, off-line trade are handled. They both go to the same markets, where the same rules apply and the buyers and sellers of each kind of trade settle up their transactions using the same clearing process. There are some wrinkles, but for the most part, the biggest difference between an online trade and an off-line trade is simply the very first step. In an online trade, you type the order into a computer. In an off-line trade, you read the order to a broker, who then (usually) types it into a computer. It's as simple as that. That is where the time savings come in, and that is where the costs savings are realized for the online firms (no human giving advice or taking orders = $10 commission).

AFTER-HOURS TRADING

Trading stocks outside of the markets' regular hours (9:30 A.M. to 4 P.M. Eastern Time) is gaining an enormous amount of attention—but whether you do it through a traditional market's after-hours session or a private trading system, it is a risky proposition. After-hours trading is a different environment, and you don't have the same protections that you do during the regular trading day.

Because there are far fewer participants in the markets outside of regular trading hours, prices tend to be more volatile. When many investors are buying and selling, it is easier to match up the two sides of a trade without moving prices significantly; after hours, you must be prepared for a big price swing. In many cases, far better prices will be available during regular trading hours the next morning.

You'll need to shop around in the after-hours environment to be sure that you are getting the best available price for your trade. Different services will have different prices because they don't share information and orders: The market is fragmented. The Securities and Exchange Commission addressed this problem years ago when it pushed the markets to link up their communications and required them, during regular trading hours, to give investors the best available prices for their trades—regardless of which exchange the order was sent to.

There are other dangers. For instance, a major reason that investors are eager to trade after hours is so they can react to news that is released after the close of regular trading. Big professional investors have been able to do so for years, and small investors believe that the pros have been getting better prices because of that ability. But access to information is uneven: Professional investors have better information than individual investors, and that gives them a leg up in the after-hours market.

Consider: When a company releases its earnings report after the close, individual investors may decide to purchase shares based on the fact, say, that the earnings topped expectations. That level of information is quickly available to professionals and individuals alike through news outlets. But other details may not reach individuals as quickly as they get to the Wall Street pros. After releasing the results, the

(continues)

company may call analysts and warn them that its robust earnings won't last. Or an influential analyst may
spot a red flag in the good news, and make negative comments about the company. Such critical developments
are quickly relayed to professionals, but they can
take much longer to reach the press and the public.

The next step, in many trades, is for your brokerage firm to check if it already owns the stock you are interested in buying (or has stock available to sell to you). This is very often done electronically, especially for the small orders that individual investors tend to place. If the firm can—and wants to— do the trade itself, the order is sent to the exchange floor or to its Nasdaq market makers to be executed. If the firm can't—or doesn't want to—complete the trade itself, it tries to find a buyer (or seller) for you. Again, the trade is sent to the exchange floor or the firm's Nasdaq market makers. In both cases, a trader will try to find someone willing to take the other side of the trade.

Both exchange specialists and Nasdaq market makers are required to stand ready to be the buyer (or seller) of last resort if another party doesn't exist in the market. That doesn't mean that they must give you the price you want; they merely have to make a trade at a reasonable price, as determined by the rules of the market. (Firms, for instance, face limits on the amount they can mark up the price of a stock before selling it to you.)

There is a twist to all of this. Increasingly, stock trades are being sent to an electronic communications network—commonly called an ECN— to be matched up with a buyer or seller. Some firms tout this process as an additional time-saver for investors who don't want to lose seconds when placing a trade. Datek Online (**www.datek.com**), for instance, uses its own ECN (a company called Island) for many trades, and the firm promises that most orders will be executed in less than a minute. Other firms use ECNs such as Archipelago, Brut, and Instinet. (Instinet, a unit of Reuters Group PLC, is the oldest ECN, dating back to 1969.)

LIMIT ORDERS AND MARKET ORDERS

There are two main types of buy and sell orders: market orders, executed at the prevailing market price, and limit orders, executed only at the price you specify. If you learn nothing else from this book, learn the difference between the two. Some brokerage firms charge more for limit orders than for market orders. But the extra expense might be money well spent.

If you place a market order on a fast-moving stock, you could end up paying a lot more for it (or receiving a lot less, when selling) than you expected. You may press the "Trade" button at your online broker when the stock is trading at $25, but by the time the trade is executed, the stock may have jumped to $30. A limit order, on the other hand, locks in a price for you. If you specify $25, the order can only be completed at $25.

But there are pitfalls to limit orders, too. For instance, because they are targeted to a specific price, you may never get your order filled. A stock may move within a whisker of the price of your limit order to buy, but your trade will never go through. That could turn out to be a missed opportunity if the stock later rallies.

Another potential problem could leave you holding the bag if a stock suddenly drops. Suppose a stock is trading at $25.50, but you'd prefer to pay a bit less—so you enter a limit order to buy shares at $25. That is fine if the market drifts down to your price and stabilizes, but you'd be stung if there was suddenly bad news about the stock and its price plunged to,

(continues)

say, $22 before you could cancel your order. Your buy order would be filled as the stock moved lower—some lucky seller would be able to unload shares on you at $25 and you'd be down $3 a share before you knew it.

You can reduce some of the risks associated with limit orders if you choose a third type of order: a marketable limit order. This kind of trade offers protection if the market turns against you between the time you enter an order and when your trade is executed. Say a stock is trading at $25 and you'd like to buy it right away but are afraid it could jump to $30 (a price you find unacceptably high) before your market order is completed. You could place a buy order with a limit of $26. That way, your order will be executed at the market price, providing it isn't higher than $26.

A way to reduce, though not eliminate, the risk of having your limit order filled in the midst of a plunge in a stock's price is to specify your limit order as a day order, meaning that it will expire at the close of the trading day during which the order was placed. In contrast, a good-till-canceled order will remain in effect day after day.

Regardless of where a buyer and seller come together, once the order is executed, its price and size are reported within 90 seconds to a single computer system (run by an industry-sponsored company called Securities Industry Automation Corporation) in New York—Brooklyn, to be exact. The information is recorded for regulatory and bookkeeping purposes, and is immediately disseminated into the marketplace. That is where all stock quotes originate—whether read to you over the phone by a broker, retrieved from a Web site, or broadcast in a scroll on CNBC.

Trades are settled—the buyers get their stock and the sellers their cash—in what is called the clearing process. At the end of each trading day, brokerage firms sift through their trade records (electronically, of course) and compare notes to be sure everyone agrees that the trades and prices each recorded are accurate. The stock and cash are sent to a third party, called a clearing firm or clearinghouse, which acts as an intermediary, delivering the stock and cash to the buyers and sellers. Securities rules give firms three days to settle trades; no trade is officially complete until the end of the process. The settlement process, which used to take five days, has been sped up by automation, and the industry is now moving toward a one-day settlement process.

IS ONLINE TRADING SAFE?

When asked why he robbed banks, Willie Sutton, the notorious stickup artist of the 1930s, famously explained: "That's where the money is." Do online brokerages and traders need to fear modern-day Willie Suttons—cyber-bandits outfitted with modems rather than pistols? For a moment, let's put aside concerns about making a big investment decision to ask: Just how safe from hackers is an online account?

With more and more money pouring into online brokerage firms, the potential rewards for crooks are greater than ever before. Compared with an average day of business on most Internet retailing sites, online brokerage transactions are enormous. The money, Mr. Sutton might have said, is in online brokerages.

But online stickups and account break-ins probably aren't worth worrying about for the average Internet trader. Certainly those scenarios shouldn't be any more worrisome than getting robbed of a pocketful of cash while on the way to your broker's office, or having sensitive information stolen over the telephone when calling in an order. "The bottom line here is [that online trading is] actually more secure than a telephone conversation," said Vincent Phillips, vice president of Web systems at Charles Schwab in San Francisco.

How can that be?

First, think about how you make a trade over the phone with a traditional brokerage firm: You pick up the phone, dial your broker, and tell him or her that you want to sell, say, $80,000 worth of Microsoft stock. Every word you have uttered is open for eavesdropping. If you use a cordless phone, anyone with a garden-variety radio scanner could pick up what you said, including enough private information (a Social Security number, bank account information, a password) to access your account in the future. If the eavesdropper had access to the guts of the telephone network, he could also tap into the call through a switching station or a satellite downlink.

There are other weak links in the conversation. How do you know the guy on the other end of the line is really your broker? Sure, he sounds like the broker, but maybe he's some crook with a talent for impersonation who simply picked up the broker's phone. Or maybe the broker is furious because he's just been passed over for a promotion and he decides to get revenge on his rotten employer by transferring your $80,000 to his own offshore bank account.

Compared with all that, a trade with an online brokerage has the security of a presidential detail. When you log on to your brokerage firm's Web site (typing in a username and password), your browser performs the equivalent of a split-second background check on the firm. The browser makes sure Online Brokerage X really is Online Brokerage X, not some evil impostor waiting to intercept your private information. The browser does this by checking for a digital certificate—a kind of virtual ID card—on the brokerage firm's Web server, then matching it to a bit of software code contained within the browser. That code bears the signature of a certificate authority, the company that issued the certificate to the brokerage firm in the first place. Most digital certificates are issued by VeriSign of Mountain View, California, or some other third-party certificate authority that vouches for the identity of the firm.

After the site passes the first test, your browser and Online Brokerage X use something called a session key—a random piece of code generated by the interaction of a public key on your computer and a private key on the firm's server—to encrypt or scramble all the information that is exchanged during the session, using an encryption technology called Secure Sockets Layer. (Checking to make sure that your session is encrypted is easy: If you're using Netscape Navigator, look for a key symbol in the corner of your screen; if you're using Microsoft Internet Explorer, look for a lock. If the symbols are unbroken, your session is safely encrypted.)

The session key will range in length from 40 bits to 128 bits, with the longer-bit keys requiring more guesses from an eavesdropper trying to crack the encrypted code. We're talking about a lot of guesses. When it comes to predicting how long it will take to break a 128-bit session with today's code-cracking computers, most experts offer preposterously long periods of time (i.e., "When the sun is extinguished"). Even if some improbably powerful computer could be developed to compromise your transaction, the session would be long over before the task could be accomplished. But suppose for a moment that this mythical computer did manage to crack the session: Is your $80,000 sell order really worth the cost and energy of building such a computer?

Common-Sense Precautions

While most security experts agree there are more profitable lines of work than eavesdropping on online traders, that doesn't mean Internet investors are completely in the clear. There are a whole slew of tricks that a resourceful cyber-crook can use to break in to an online account, from hacking in to a brokerage firm's computers to conning unsuspecting investors into revealing their usernames and passwords over the phone. Most brokerage firms are obsessive about guarding sensitive information from intruders, but they can't spot every security hole, nor can they prevent heedless mistakes by their customers.

Consider the unsettling story of John Dennis. One day in April 1999, Mr. Dennis, an environmental planner in Ithaca, New York, found himself locked out of his E*Trade account for no apparent reason. Although he now regrets it, Mr. Dennis waited two days before calling the brokerage's customer service department to get a new password. What he found, when he finally logged on, made his stomach churn: Someone had authorized a funds transfer of $42,000 in cash from his E*Trade account to a bank in Riga, Latvia. Mr. Dennis's money had gone on holiday in the Baltics.

Fortunately, it wasn't a long-lived holiday. Mr. Dennis contacted the Federal Bureau of Investigation about his missing money, and before anyone could walk into the Riga bank to claim it, the $42,000 was transferred back to his E*Trade account. Mr. Dennis was mystified how the break-in happened, but he admitted to some lapses that may have been significant: In the two and a half years since he had opened the account, he hadn't changed his username or password once, a precaution that brokerage firms recommend customers take from time to time. He also checked his account from computers in Asia when he was traveling there on business. Mr. Dennis could have had his password snatched through a special program used by hackers to monitor keystrokes. He believes it's also possible the culprit managed to get into his account by using his Social Security number to convince E*Trade customer support to hand out a new password.

E*Trade told a slightly different version of events. Clifford Reeser, director of systems security at E*Trade, said the FBI noticed Mr. Dennis's money being transferred to Latvia. The FBI then notified E*Trade, which then told Mr. Dennis, Mr. Reeser said. E*Trade speculated that Mr. Dennis lost his password in his travels. While the company can ensure the security of data that passes between its Web site and an individual's computer, "past that point there's nothing one can do to protect the user from compromising their password," Mr. Reeser said.

Certainly, one of the easiest ways for someone to get into your brokerage account is simply to swipe your username and password. Protecting those two pieces of information, therefore, should be a top priority for online investors. That means avoiding high-risk behavior, like writing private account information on a yellow Post-it note marked "my E*Trade info" and attaching it to a computer monitor at work, or tucking such a note into your wallet. Protect your username and password the same way you protect the PIN number for your ATM card. (Incidentally, if you have such notes, it might not be a bad idea to tear them up before chucking them into the garbage: "Dumpster diving," or digging through garbage bins, is an old standby for hackers. Of course, change any secret codes that you can.)

Be on guard against more traditional cons too—the snooping techniques security experts call "social engineering." This can take many forms, but the most likely trick is an unsolicited call from someone claiming to be a customer service agent from your brokerage firm. In his most officious voice, the "agent" might ask you for your username and password, offering some plausible-sounding reason for the request. ("We need to do some routine maintenance on your account.")

Choosing an account password carefully is a wise security precaution. As a rule, picking anything that can be guessed easily—your middle name, the last four digits of a home telephone number, your zip code—is a no-no. To prevent mistakes like this, many online brokerages require users to create passwords that combine letters and numerals. Besides making it more difficult for someone to guess a password, this approach also complicates "shoulder surfing"—unwanted surveillance by, say, a coworker who takes unusual interest in your keystrokes as you log on to a brokerage account. The theory is that it's trickier for a snoop to memorize a password that is composed from different rows of the keyboard.

There are more acrobatic techniques a hacker can employ to get into a secure site. Although brokerage break-ins may not require crawling through ventilation shafts, there are always back doors, physical and virtual, that a crafty individual can exploit to get inside. Brokerage firms haven't made that easy, though. Schwab, for one, has two protective "fire walls" that prevent unwanted Internet intruders: One keeps users from breaking into its Web site, the other cordons off all private account information, which is kept in a separate computer system inaccessible from the Internet. For good measure, Schwab has even hired hackers—of the "white hat," or friendly, variety—to try to break in to its systems. Schwab's Vincent Phillips said the hackers found "a couple of issues around access control" within Schwab's physical facilities, but they didn't succeed in finding ways to access any sensitive data or transfer money.

But what if, despite all of the precautions, someone manages to break in to your online brokerage account?

Most firms vow to reimburse their customers if an intruder manages to steal funds by breaking in to customer accounts. After all, their reputation is riding on the security of their systems. But there are limits: If you lose your password through some careless mistake (remember the Post-it note on the computer screen), chances are you're going to get stuck with the bill if your money can't be recovered. The same holds true if your child logs on to your account and starts doing his or her best day trader impersonation.

While a teen trading Daddy's stocks would certainly cause some mischief, it's unlikely anyone transferring money to another bank account would get very far. Wire transfers are easily traceable by law enforcement and bank authorities. Many brokerage firms like Schwab only permit customers to wire funds to accounts they've specifically designated for transfers. To register those transfer accounts, Schwab requires something rather old-fashioned—the customer's signature on paper. Meanwhile, at Ameritrade Holdings, all large fund transfers to overseas banks are scrutinized to make sure they're authorized by the customer. "If there is anything there that is even remotely suspicious, it's flagged," said Tom Lewis, co-CEO of Ameritrade.

One of the best defenses against theft is to spot suspicious activity early and report it to the brokerage firm. Dan Burke, a senior brokerage analyst at Gomez Advisors, said that this is easier for online traders, whose sometimes hyperactive trading habits keep them in close contact with their accounts, than it is for other investors. "Most people check accounts continuously so they would notice if they saw $1,000 moving out of their accounts," said Mr. Burke.

Investors should also get an idea of how their brokerage firm is using their personal information. Most firms pledge to keep private investor data just that—private—instead of selling it to another company that might use it to market products to you. Some brokerages have taken an extra step by displaying seals of approval from various third-party firms such as CPA WebTrust and TRUSTe that audit the brokerage firms' security and privacy practices.

So Far, So Good

Whether through vigilance or luck, online brokerages so far have had a relatively clean record on security. Tales of theft on the order of John Dennis's experience are rare (and he, at least, got his money back). In comparison with commercial banking, Mr. Dennis's temporary losses were peanuts. In one high-profile case, a Russian man managed to steal about $400,000 in 1994 by hacking into Citicorp's computers. The man was sentenced to a three-year prison term.

How long before an online brokerage firm gets cracked in a really serious way? "There is a belief in many people's minds that it's just a question of time," said Mark Greene, vice president of security at International Business Machines. As brokerage firms proliferate, "the law of large numbers suggests there will be one bad apple someplace." Meanwhile, not all brokerage firms will opt—or be able—to dedicate the same amount of resources to security efforts.

The bad apples could be out there already. Law enforcement officials say businesses tend to dramatically underreport financial fraud crimes, fearing the news will inspire nasty jabs from competitors, bad publicity, and copycat attacks. Online brokerages could simply be adept at keeping a lid on news of break-ins.

The online trading phenomenon is still new enough that statistics about financial losses from fraud are hazy at best. In a 1999 survey of 521 U.S. businesses and government agencies by the Computer Security Institute in San Francisco, 27 respondents reported computer-related financial fraud resulting in losses of nearly $40 million. FBI statistics don't shed much more light on theft and cyber-attacks aimed at online brokerages. While it stated at one point that half of its 56 field offices were each investigating at least one Internet-investment-related fraud case, those cases included investment schemes aimed at defrauding investors and other crimes, as well as theft.

In the meantime, although security remains a worry for online investors, it no longer appears to be the dread-inspiring issue it once was. In a 1999 survey of 550 U.S. households, the Gartner Group's Dataquest division found that security fears were keeping 34% of respondents from trading online more frequently. At the same time, 80% of the respondents said they were concerned about doing any transactions on the Internet—but 75% of those people were making online purchases anyway.

HOW TO PICK AN ONLINE BROKER

Making an online stock trade is easy. Choosing an Internet broker isn't. For starters, there are a lot of them: An industry that barely existed only a few years ago now has scores of players. Those firms, in their short life span, have splintered into several categories. Some offer lots of services and even some advice, almost like traditional, full-service brokerage firms. Others concentrate on the stock trade itself, promising a fast execution, a cheap price, and little else.

Here is a rundown on some of the biggest, most popular online trading firms:

Charles Schwab
(www.schwab.com)

As the largest brick-and-mortar discount brokerage firm, it's perhaps a bit surprising that Schwab has such a commanding lead in market share among online firms too. Its basic $29.95 commission fee is among the highest charged by online firms, and the overall trend in the industry has clearly been toward lower fees. (Several firms offer $5 trades.)

Schwab, though, unveiled two tiers of lower commissions early in 2000 for its most active customers: Those who trade more than 60 times a quarter are charged $14.95 a trade, while those trading between 30 and 60 times a quarter are charged $19.95. The discount to active traders was a bit of a departure for Schwab. At the same time, it agreed to acquire CyBerCorp, a faster growing online firm that caters, in part, to day traders.

Online trading is a natural fit for Schwab, which built its business on do-it-yourself investors. Schwab was an early cheerleader for online trading as far back as the late 1980s. Later, when the Internet exploded in popularity, Schwab already had a base of customers and a strong brand name on which to build.

Schwab has always relied on its reputation to attract new clients, and the speed at which it has been able to sign up new customers (thanks to its large network of branches) has kept it firmly in the top spot. Though Schwab has by far the biggest share of the online-trading market, as measured by trades per day, its market share is slipping as more and more firms move online—and offer lower commissions.

There are few freebies on Schwab's site. Schwab's commission fee applies only to the first 1,000 shares in an order. (Several competitors allow up to 5,000 shares for the same price.) After that, there's an additional charge of three cents per share. And despite its roots in self-serve investing, Schwab offers a surprising number of online services typically found at more full-service firms. Extensive research reports from Credit Suisse First Boston and Hambrecht & Quist LLC are available through Schwab for a $29.95 monthly fee. Schwab also provides market commentary from its Capital Markets and Trading Group, as well as briefings from several other financial news sources. And many of its high-end accounts include free banking services, like check writing and debit cards.

One of the most valuable services offered by Schwab is the capacity to execute trades through alternate methods when the online system goes down. Schwab certainly hasn't been immune to the outages that have plagued most online firms. In the event of technical trouble, though, Schwab clients can execute trades at one of 300 Schwab branches around the country, or through the brokerage firm's automated telephone-order system.

E*Trade
(www.etrade.com)

"Someday we'll all invest this way," boast E*Trade's advertisements. That prophecy seems to be coming true quickly, as many firms offer commissions even far below E*Trade's levels: $14.95 for exchange listed stocks and $19.95 for Nasdaq issues, each up to 5,000 shares.

As the first "true" online firm—you won't find any E*Trade branches in strip malls—the company established itself early on as a place where do-it-yourself investors could execute trades with an easy-to-use interface, but without much hand holding. E*Trade's advertisements, which can be found just about everywhere, target computer users who may not have much experience with investing in the stock market.

E*Trade's roots can be traced to 1981, when it operated as a service bureau that provided online quotes and trading services to several traditional firms. In 1992, the firm evolved into an online brokerage, and offered trading through the dial-up services of America Online and CompuServe.

Part of E*Trade's success can be attributed to the strong partnerships it has built with other Web sites. E*Trade's site provides news and data from scores of sources, including TheStreet.com (**www.thestreet.com**) and Briefing.com (**www.briefing.com**), as well as lots of tools for viewing and analyzing your portfolio. The firm's research offerings include real-time updates from BancBoston Robertson Stephens (free for three months, $9.95 a month thereafter), and consensus estimates from analysts provided by Zacks Investment Research.

E*Trade also offers access to after-hours trading through Instinet, the largest electronics communication network (ECN), at its regular commission rates. And it offers a special service, called Power E*Trade, which provides deep discounts to clients who execute at least 30 trades in a calendar quarter. Trade at least 75 times a quarter and you qualify for Power E*Trade Plus, which offers "preferred access" to initial public offerings.

E*Trade provides the usual access to the most popular mutual funds, and recently launched several of its own funds, which track technology stocks, bonds, and the S&P 500. In 1999, it acquired TIR Holdings, a Cayman Islands trade-processing company that operates in thirty-five countries, and announced plans to offer trading in global stock markets. As E*Trade envisions it, a U.S. customer will be able to execute trades on an exchange in Italy just as easily as on the Nasdaq Stock Market.

TD Waterhouse Securities
(www.waterhouse.com)

TD Waterhouse is a subsidiary of TD Waterhouse Group, Inc., of which the Toronto-Dominion Bank is the largest shareholder. Unlike other traditional brokerage firms that have become dominant players in cyberspace, Waterhouse offers cutthroat Internet pricing: $12 a trade, up to 5,000 shares, regardless of whether it's a market or limit order. (Many other firms charge an extra $5 for limit orders, which are only executed at a specific price, rather than the prevailing market price.)

Waterhouse is up-front about why its commissions are so much lower than those of many of its competitors: The firm doesn't provide investment advice of any kind. Indeed, the service is decidedly no-frills.

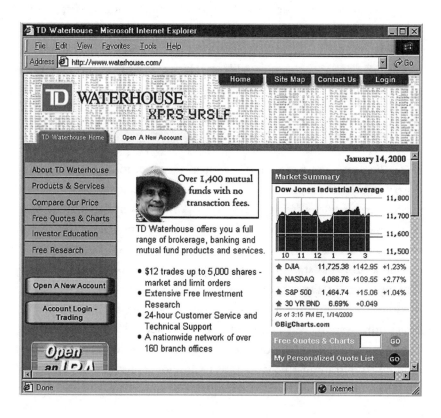

Unlike Schwab, Waterhouse has remained targeted toward investors who are looking for true self-serve investing. Its Web site contains all the typical sources of market data, including Zacks, Briefing.com, Quote.com (**www.quote.com**) and Morningstar (for mutual fund information). But most of those sources are also available on rivals' sites and for free elsewhere on the Web, and Waterhouse hasn't linked up with any research firms. The site does feature some basic lessons on investing—planning for retirement, or college expenses, for instance—but other than that, you're on your own. Still, all this seems just fine with Waterhouse's clients, whose ranks have been growing at a steady clip. (In 1999, it was close on the heels of No. 2 E*Trade, which has spent considerably more on marketing.)

Like other discount firms, Waterhouse gives you options in the event of a catastrophe. The firm has 160 branches across the country where "account officers" (essentially order-takers; they aren't there to give you advice) can handle trades, and, like most competitors, Waterhouse also allows trading over an automated telephone-ordering system. Waterhouse has full banking services, including free check writing and access to money through ATM machines, and offers several retirement accounts for individuals and businesses.

Datek
(www.datek.com)

Datek has emerged from a rocky past in the traditional brokerage industry as a top choice for active online traders. The firm guarantees fast executions on trades (within 60 seconds, or it's commission-free), and its stripped-down Web site is geared toward experienced traders who want quick access to information and trading screens.

Datek got its start in the fast-paced—but controversial—day-trading industry. Datek's old Datek Securities unit, which specialized in rapid-fire trading through the Nasdaq Stock Market's Small Order Execution System, was censured and fined several times during the 1990s by the National Association of Securities Dealers for infractions ranging from trading-rule violations to employees using foul language. The firm also had been on the losing side of numerous customer arbi-

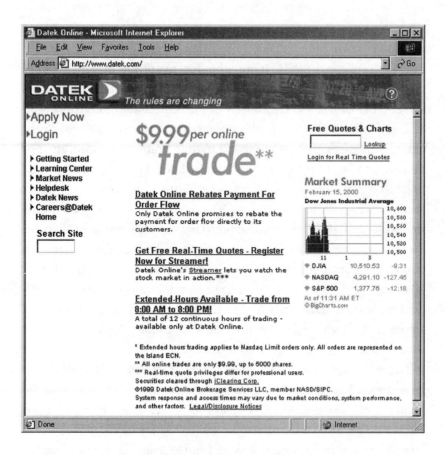

trations alleging violations such as unauthorized trading or failure to execute. The old securities unit has been sold to a small securities firm.

Datek scrapped early plans for an initial public stock offering in 1998 amid publicity over investigations by the Securities and Exchange Commission and the U.S. Attorney's office in Manhattan. Authorities were examining trading and lending practices at the old Datek Securities unit, Datek officials have said. The officials added that the firm was cooperating with authorities and didn't feel the activities of Datek had anything to do with the firm's current business. Also, in 1999 Datek was fined by the SEC for mishandling customers' funds. The firm termed the violation a bookkeeping error.

Datek has one of the lowest commission schedules of all of the major online firms ($9.99 for all orders, up to 5,000 shares), and provides deep discounts for large-volume trades, making it an attractive choice for active traders. Datek also offers some of the lowest interest rates on borrowed funds. It was the first major online firm to offer after-hours trading, through Island ECN. (Datek is the principal shareholder of Island.) Customers can execute trades as early as 8:00 A.M. and as late as 5:15 P.M., all for the same $9.95 commission. Eventually, Datek says, it plans to expand trading hours even more, and potentially to an around-the-clock schedule. Datek provides free, unlimited real-time quotes (some competitors charge for access beyond a certain allotment, such as 50 a month), and also offers a continuously updating quote streamer. The site also features "Express Server" service, a low-graphics version of its trading system, for traders who want to shave a few more seconds off the total time it takes to find a price quote and execute a trade. But be careful: Datek disables several safeguards for its Express Server users, including a screen that in other cases requires users to double-check and confirm their orders before they go through.

Datek doesn't have any branches for customers to use if the Web site goes down, but the broker does promise it will only charge you the regular $9.99 commission if you have to phone in an order during an outage. The site also offers streaming financial headlines from NewsAlert and reports on stocks and funds from Thomson Financial Network.

Fidelity
(www.fidelity.com)

Fidelity has long been a leader in the traditional mutual fund business, and has taken an equally aggressive stance in going after the online trading market. Fidelity, like Schwab, has reaped the benefits of its name recognition and large pool of financial services customers.

Fidelity's Web site is geared toward more experienced investors. Its "Active Trader" section, for customers who trade frequently and have at least $500,000 in assets, provides full account information on one screen, without bulky graphics to slow down access to trading. Fidelity has also launched several other services aimed at active traders, including one that permits trades using a pager or a handheld personal digital assistant.

Novices will find some help in the in-depth literature Fidelity provides on investing. You'll find details about IRA rules, strategies for investing in the stock market to maximize retirement gains, and access to financial planners. There is also quick access to Fidelity's annuity and life-insurance products.

And of course you'll find details on Fidelity's thousands of mutual fund products. Fidelity's popular mutual fund calculator is a handy tool whether you're a Fidelity customer or not. The calculator will help you select a mutual fund based on your criteria, and will show you which funds have performed best over the years. (The site includes research from Morningstar.)

Fidelity has linked up with Lehman Brothers to provide access to that firm's equity research, and even access to Lehman-led IPOs (although, with few exceptions, you'll need $500,000 in assets on account with Fidelity to participate in such offerings). Fidelity also offers earnings estimates from First Call/Thomson Financial, and stock data from Market Guide.

Ameritrade
(www.ameritrade.com)

Ameritrade's $8 commission charge for market orders is among the cheapest in the industry. (Ameritrade charges an extra $5 for limit orders, making Datek's $9.95 cheaper on those types of orders.)

Ameritrade's stock-trading interface is simple, and you won't find some of the in-depth information found at other sites. Still, the site offers the usual suite of investment tools: stock screening from Market Guide and analysts' earnings estimates from First Call/Thomson Financial. But Ameritrade also gives clients access to news from Dow Jones News Service, as well as the major press release news wires.

The service is clearly designed for the bargain hunter, which means you're going to pay extra for features not used by most clients. Ameritrade limits the number of real-time quotes you can receive (you get 100 for opening an account, and 100 for every trade you execute.) Alternately, you can pay $20 a month for unlimited real-time quotes.

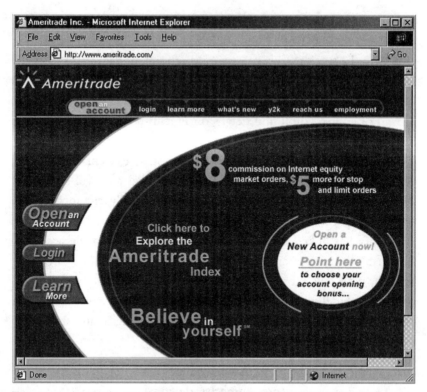

This screen shot is the property of Ameritrade Holding Corporation and is reprinted
with the permission of Ameritrade Holding Corporation. All rights in the copyrightable
content and trademarks are owned and reserved by Ameritrade. Ameritrade® is a
registered trademark of Ameritrade Holding Corporation.

Ameritrade only allows trading of listed securities on its Web site. To
trade a stock quoted on the NASD's OTC Bulletin Board service,
you'll have to call an Ameritrade broker (and pay an $18 commission).

Ameritrade's growth in the late 1990s was unmatched by any of
its competitors, despite a strategy by the company to actually slow
growth so that technology (and trading capacity) could be upgraded
to meet demand. Analysts say Ameritrade has benefited substantially
from large advertising campaigns by firms like E*Trade and Schwab.
Those firms may be drawing investors to the Net, but once they get
online, customers have been lured to Ameritrade with cheaper commission charges.

QUESTIONS TO ASK WHEN PICKING A BROKER

The biggest online firms capture the vast majority of online customers, but there are scores of other firms angling for business. With all the choices, the task of choosing the best broker for you may seem overwhelming. But you can whittle down the list considerably by asking yourself the following key questions:

What kind of investor am I?

First and foremost, figure out your investing needs. Investors tend to fall into one of three main categories, with specific requirements of their online broker: Some investors require a lot of advice, others simply want enough tools to make their own decisions, and a final group simply wants the best way to trade a lot.

If you are in the first group, check out the online components of full-service brokerages, including Merrill Lynch (**www.ml.com**) and Morgan Stanley Dean Witter (**www.online.msdw.com**). Do-it-yourself investors, who want charts, screening tools, research reports, and the like, should consider the online services offered by firms such as Charles Schwab (**www.schwab.com**), E*Trade Group (**www.etrade.com**), and TD Waterhouse Securities (**www.waterhouse.com**). If you plan to trade stocks actively, you'll be best served by firms that offer low commissions, fast executions, and lots of real-time data, such as Datek Online (**www.datek.com**).

Intense competition forces online brokers to continually improve their services. Products and services at most firms are always evolving, so it's a good idea to do periodic comparison shopping to make sure you're still well served.

How reliable is the broker's customer service?

One reason for using an online broker is to minimize contact over the telephone. But you should test firms' customer service when you're deciding which broker to use, because at some point you may need to call in when Internet access isn't available. Here is how to kick the tires a bit: E-mail a question or request to the brokerage firm and see how long it takes to get a response. Find out when representatives are available over the phone (not all of them offer around-the-clock service). Call them on both light and heavy trading days to see how quickly you get through.

You should also determine whether a firm offers alternatives to on-line trading. Many online firms experience outages on the Net from time to time, and although most firms have made strides to accommodate increased capacity, it's a good idea to have a reliable backup plan. See if the firm also takes orders over the phone, whether it charges more for called-in trades, and whether it has branch offices you could walk into in a pinch.

How high are the commissions?

Investors first flocked to the Internet for the low commission prices. Now, trading prices have pretty much stabilized, and can be had for as little as $5 and $7. But unless you plan to trade frequently, which can make commissions add up quickly, don't choose a broker based on commission price alone. Depending on what type of investor you are, extras like research and planning tools can far outweigh the few dollars you might save on trades.

Also, realize that your commissions may be higher than the low rates that firms advertise. For example, firms usually advertise their rates for market orders (those filled at the prevailing market price), but you may opt to use limit orders (which allow you to specify the price you will accept). Limit orders cost $3 to $5 more per trade at many firms. Bear in mind that online brokers also usually charge more than their advertised base price if you place a large order. Extra charges kick in above 1,000 shares at some firms, and above 5,000 shares at others. The best way to measure fees is to compare prices based on trades that are similar to the ones you usually make, rather than the base prices firms promote. And, of course, for many trades, the amount you pay in commissions will pale next to the amount lost in the spread earned by the broker. That can be the biggest trading cost of all.

How much money do I have to invest?

One way to narrow the field of online brokers is to find out what their initial balance requirements are: There's a lot of variation in this area. Suretrade (**www.suretrade.com**), a unit of FleetBoston Financial, for instance, has no initial minimum requirement, while Fidelity

Investments (**www.fidelity.com**) requires $5,000 to start trading. Brown & Co. (**www.brownco.com**) requires at least $15,000 to set up an account, and Merrill Lynch requires a $20,000 beginning balance in order to join its pay-per-trade online program. Many firms fall in the $2,000 to $10,000 range.

What types of investments are available?

Most online firms allow investors to trade stocks, mutual funds, and stock options, but you should investigate the specifics available from firms you are considering. Not all firms, for instance, allow trading in OTC Bulletin Board stocks, or bonds (in some cases you must call in your bond trades rather than placing them online). You may want to investigate whether the firms you are considering have access to initial public offerings of stock. A growing number do, but it remains very hard to get in on a hot new stock. Other things to consider: access to traditional bank services, such as check writing, ATM cards, and online bill payment.

What types of research tools are available?

If this is an important area for you, there are many things to consider. Competition over tools and other resources has been intense: Every time one firm adds a service, others tend to follow. Offerings include: real-time stock quotes, charting services, online portfolios (including some that update in real time), research reports from Wall Street firms, and calculators and worksheets that allow you to manage personal finances.

What is the firm's history and background?

When you have some firms in mind, find out how long each has been in business. Is it a division of a larger organization? Has it had any disciplinary problems that trouble you? How much insurance coverage does it provide for its accounts in case it runs into financial troubles?

News stories can be a useful resource in investigating companies. Search some news archives for the firm's name and see what you come up with. Online message boards can be a good place to gauge investor sentiment toward firms. Sites such as Silicon Investor (**www.siliconinvestor.com**) have message boards dedicated to specific online brokerage firms. (But beware: Online messages are more likely to focus on problems users have had, rather than the successes.) If the firm is publicly owned, you can get financial reports from the Securities and Exchange Commission (**www.sec.gov**).

How easy is the site to use?

When you have some brokers in mind, test out their Web sites and see how easily you can find the information you need. Are you able to access research and account information easily? Some brokerage firms provide demos that you can use before you sign up to take their sites—including the process of making a trade—for a test drive.

Are there any perks for big spenders?

If you have a substantial amount of money to invest, trade frequently, or both, it's worth finding out whether you'll be entitled to any special services. Charles Schwab, for instance, has premium services based on account size and trading frequency. Clients with large accounts and those who trade frequently can get in on things like conference calls with company executives. TD Waterhouse provides a dedicated toll-free phone number and discounted phone trades to customers who make at least 24 trades per year and have at least $50,000 in their accounts.

TWO

Initial Public Offerings

J eff Barrish didn't have a seven-figure portfolio or an uncle who's a stockbroker. Yet he managed to snag shares in two initial public offerings, then quickly turned around and sold them for an almost instant profit of $9,000. For Mr. Barrish and countless other ordinary individuals, online brokers have unlocked the door to the world of IPOs—a world that once was reserved for well-connected investors with deep pockets, such as mutual funds and other professional investors, or affluent individuals.

IPOs almost always rise in the first day of trading, and brokers have traditionally reserved shares for just their best customers. "I think of what could have been possible had I started looking at IPOs a few months earlier," said Mr. Barrish, a 50-year-old accountant from San Antonio, Texas. He had been playing the IPO game for less than two months when he managed to land IPO shares in Priceline.com Inc. and Value America Inc., two hot Internet offerings, through E*Trade. E*Trade is among a handful of Internet brokers bringing small investors to a party that traditionally was just a dream for many individuals. "There are some guys who have made out like bandits. This is a sweet deal for small investors."

The bull market of the 1990s, the emergence of online trading, and investors' fascination with Internet companies have fueled an IPO boom. Consider the lucky souls who got in on the IPO of Marketwatch.com, a San Francisco–based financial news Web site, whose shares rose 474% (to $97.50 from $17) on their first day of trading. Gains like that have made individual investors like Mr. Barrish IPO-giddy. In a recent poll of individuals by Gomez Advisors, 60% of respondents said IPO availability would influence their choice of an online brokerage. Many are salivating for a chance to get a piece of a hot offering.

Until recently, acquiring shares in any initial public offering—let alone a particularly hot new Internet IPO stock like Priceline.com or Marketwatch.com—was impossible for individuals unless they had a significant portfolio at a full-service brokerage and the right connections. But the Internet is breaking down the traditional barriers that have kept individuals out of IPOs.

Online brokerage firms, such as E*Trade (**www.etrade.com**), Wit Capital Group (**www.witcapital.com**), Charles Schwab (**www.schwab. com**), and others, have begun to make IPO dreams come true. These discount brokerage firms traditionally have been shut out of Wall Street IPO underwriting syndicates (the groups of brokerage firms that sell shares in IPOs) because they don't have investment bankers, research analysts, and armies of brokers to find and promote the deals. But amid the online trading boom, several firms have managed to secure deals with Wall Street underwriters willing to offer them small chunks of those firms' IPOs.

There are several forces driving the changes. First, investment banks that underwrite many of the big IPOs want to broaden their distribution channels to investors on Main Street, whose importance has increased as Internet investing becomes a household phenomenon. Many investment banks that underwrite IPOs don't have a network of brokers to peddle shares to individual investors; Goldman Sachs's desire to distribute its IPOs online was behind its purchase of a stake in Wit Capital, for instance.

Second, some companies that are going public—especially Internet companies—are pushing underwriters to place shares in the hands of individuals. Underwriters view the Net as a way to turn the spotlight on an IPO, and online brokers are an efficient way to reach individual investors and create an online buzz.

Then there are the online brokers themselves, who are finding it necessary to hold out IPOs as a carrot to lure new clients and differentiate themselves in the vast and highly competitive world of online trading. They can't ignore the growing demands of online investors who want more than just cheap trades. The chance, however slim, to get in on a soaring IPO can be a powerful incentive when trying to attract new clients.

GOING PUBLIC

An initial public offering, or IPO, is made the first time that a company issues shares of stock to the general public. The process is often known as going public. Companies use the money raised in an IPO to fund their continued expansion, and for other purposes. Many companies that sell shares in IPOs are start-ups—unseasoned companies without much of a track record. Sometimes these companies are unprofitable, and their futures can be very uncertain. That was particularly common during a couple of IPO booms that hit during the 1990s bull market. People who invest their money in an IPO are sometimes considered speculators, because they are making a risky bet that may well not pan out.

Nevertheless, not all companies that are going public are young, green, and risky. Some are well-established and profitable private companies (for example, investment bank Goldman Sachs) that have decided they need to tap financial markets to raise more money than is available through their other traditional sources. Others are spin-offs of blue-chip corporations that feel a subsidiary might fare better as a separate company (such as AT&T's sale to the public of its communications equipment business, now called Lucent Technologies).

A company that wants to raise money in the stock market usually does so through an investment bank, like Goldman Sachs or Merrill Lynch. The investment bank underwrites the offering by buying up all the shares from the company at a set price, in the hope of reselling them to investors at a profit. The investment bank prepares a prospectus, a legal document that serves as a billboard. The document provides a detailed analysis of the company, including financial information, a description of the business, the risks it faces, and information about its management, among other things. The prospectus, which must be filed with the Securities and Exchange Commission, is used to help sell the company to potential investors. It includes the number of shares the company is issuing and the offering price. Investment banks usually offer the shares at a 10–15% discount to what may be a fair value to ensure an opening-day stock-price increase—and to reward early investors.

The offering price is usually set late in the afternoon before the IPO's first day of trading. This process of establishing a price, which is done by the underwriter in consultation with the company issuing the stock, is often referred to simply as "the pricing." For closely watched IPOs, the price will be reported on financial wire services and Web sites—and maybe on TV. If you've expressed an interest in buying IPO shares, and will indeed receive some, your broker will let you know the price that has been set. Once the trading begins the next day you won't be able to buy shares at the offering price—unless that is the price at which the stock is available in the open market. A stock that hovers at its offering price once trading begins may not be worth buying.

Some IPOs can be sweet deals. But be careful: It's very risky and you can easily get burned. High-flying IPOs, which shoot to the skies when the gates open and allow some investors to reap a fortune, are the exception. Studies by academics and financial professionals also have found that a majority of IPOs usually underperform after a few months—either lagging gains of major market indexes, trailing their first-day highs, or even selling below their initial offering price. And there are some duds that crash and burn on the very first day.

Before you throw your money into the IPO ring, consider this: In the last three decades, "hot" IPOs—those which at least doubled after the first day—were outnumbered three to one by new issues that lost money, according to a review by Securities Data Company, a research firm. Jay Ritter of the University of Florida has other sobering statistics: Only one in every 100 IPOs doubles on its first day of trading, and about 25% give a zero or negative return. That means for every high-flying initial offering, many others sink like lead from the start or become sour in the long haul. A prime example is Boston Chicken. Its shares jumped from an initial offering price of $20 to $48 on the first day, November 8, 1993. Five years later, the stock was trading for less than $1 a share, and the company was forced to seek bankruptcy protection.

Most underwriters would quickly toss to online brokers the less appealing IPOs—the ones probably destined for failure—that they can't get their elite or most favored clients to buy. An informal review of initial public offerings made available to online investors from 1998 through January 1999 by four big online players showed that individual investors had a more than one in three possibility of getting burned. But even if you do get piece of a hot deal, your broker may discourage you from selling, or "flipping," your shares quickly to cash in on any initial run-up.

Flipping shares usually presents investors with the greatest opportunity to make money on IPOs because prices often soar initially, but may falter in the long run. Numerous academic studies, including one by Mr. Ritter of the University of Florida, have found that the long-run performance of IPOs is dismal. The average return on new issues between 1993 and 1998 that at least doubled the first day was 10.9%, compared to a return of 60% for the broader stock market. Further, in a review of 4,500 IPOs in the 1990s, Mr. Ritter found that the majority fell below their offering price after five years. Another study by data provider CommScan determined that many hot IPOs grow cold in their first year of trading. In most cases, you would be better off investing in a diversified portfolio of stocks, rather than putting your money in an IPO.

RESEARCHING IPOS

If the historical perspectives don't scare you and you're still eager to try your hand, remember this: Institutional investors don't buy an IPO without doing lots of homework on the company to make sure they are spending their money wisely. That should go for you, too. It's easy to throw reason out the window and become emotional when it comes to buying an IPO, given the headlines some highfliers have gotten for their huge gains. But it is better to let common sense be your guide.

You need to analyze the company whose IPO you are considering to ensure that it has the right fundamentals—a promising earnings outlook and a solid business plan—just like you would when making any other investment decision.

But before you get started, you first need to know which companies are going public and whether any of them whet your appetite. Getting that information shouldn't be difficult. Many newspapers and financial news sites carry news stories and other listings of planned IPOs. Some other sites devoted solely to IPO news and information—such as IPO Maven (**www.ipomaven.com**)—also will let you know what's in the pipeline, and will even alert you via e-mail when a new company announces plans to go public.

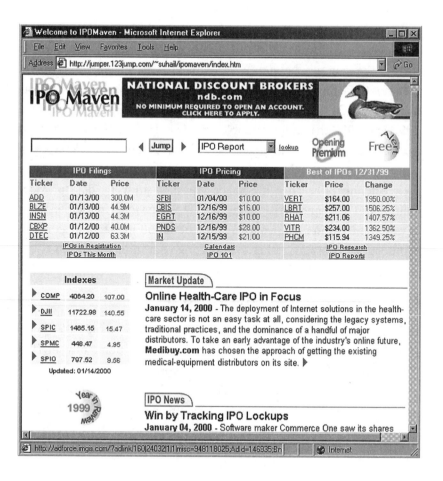

Once you find a company that you might be interested in, you are ready for the next step: Dig into the information that is available about the company. The first place to start is the prospectus, or registration statement, called an S-1, which the company is required to file with the Securities and Exchange Commission when it wants to sell shares to the public.

The prospectus provides insight into a company's financials, strategy, history, future goals, and management. It also spells out how much money is being raised and what it will be used for. Many ordinary investors don't bother to read the prospectus because they are buying into the hype over IPOs, not basing decisions on a review of a company's fundamentals. Some people also avoid the document because it is dense, littered with all sorts of jargon and other seemingly complex information that ordinary individuals might find a challenge. However, ignoring a prospectus before buying is a grave error. The SEC requires the fullest of disclosure in a prospectus to help protect investors. So why avoid it? This is where you will find all the dirt or good news about the company—and *from* the company itself. Sometimes the prospectus is the most up-front a company will ever be about itself. Investors can get a copy of the prospectus from the company or from one of the underwriters of the deal. Easier yet, you can download a copy from the Internet.

Online brokers who are planning to sell shares of the IPO usually post a copy of the prospectus on their Web sites. Copies can also be obtained over the Internet from the SEC's Edgar database. Edgar is an acronym for Electronic Data Gathering, Analysis, and Retrieval—the central database of the SEC, where all company prospectuses and other required reports are filed. Investors can view the prospectus of an IPO company by going directly to the SEC's Web site (**www.sec.gov**). The information is provided free of charge, but is usually delayed a day or two. If a prospectus arrives at the SEC on a Monday, it may not be online until Wednesday. About a dozen private data vendors also pay a fee to the SEC for access to Edgar filings and make the information available to investors over the Internet. Most of these sites are free and are more user-friendly than the SEC's. They also have tools that make the Edgar database easier to navigate and understand.

Some of the commercial Web sites that disseminate Edgar filings will give you access to data without a delay, for a fee. But even without instant access, investors still have more than enough time to analyze the documents, because it takes a company about two months, from the time that it files its first disclosure documents with the SEC to roll out its offering. Among the more popular of these private Edgar vendors are sites run by Partes (**www.freeedgar.com**), Primark (**www. primark.com**), and Edgar Online (**www.edgar-online.com**). Edgar Online, for example, will also provide you with e-mail alerts when companies file registration statements with the SEC as part of a subscription package that costs $9.95 a month.

Once you have gotten a copy of the prospectus, you should scrutinize it for information that will help you determine whether or not the IPO is worth the risk. Some companies selling stock to the public have little more than an ambitious business plan; the intelligent investor will look closely at the company's financials and other information. Perform the same due diligence and fundamental analysis you would when buying any other stock. Find the answers to the most basic questions of all: Is the company making money, or at least does it seem likely to do so at some reasonable point in the future? Are profits growing from quarter to quarter or year to year? Are the company's profit margins going up or going down from year to year? If the company passes these early tests, probe a little deeper: Does it depend heavily on only one or two products for its success? What would happen, then, if another company came along with a better product or service? Does it depend on only one or two customers? It might take the loss of just one of them to derail the company.

Pick a company with strong management. Look at its business strategy and its competition to gauge how successful it might be. Look at the business risks it faces. Don't let this be an immediate turnoff, though: All prospectuses will contain, in great detail, the risks a company faces, and sometimes they can leave you with an incorrect negative taste. Check out the company's management team and early financial backers. Do they have a successful track record? Have any of them had experience in similar businesses? Should you notice a well-recognized financial backer, such as a Microsoft, then that's a good sign. It's wise to stick with companies that have an experienced management team, well-known financial supporters, and a leadership position in their industries.

Pay attention to the company's major rivals, customers, and suppliers. A start-up that jumps into a highly competitive business dominated by a few companies might have a very tough time making inroads. Think, for example, how difficult it would be for a start-up to challenge a company like Microsoft.

While professional investors have a chance to talk to company management and pick up other important tidbits of information during what investment bankers call a road show, you don't. During the road show, investment bankers showcase the company and its management to various big investors around the country. Although companies aren't supposed to provide information that isn't included in the prospectus, they do sometimes give verbal earnings, revenues, and growth projections at road shows. That is information to which you won't be privy. Try to do some extra legwork to overcome that handicap. If you have a chance, check out the company's product. Log on to its Web site. Try to put yourself in the shoes of its customers. Are they selling something you would buy? How likely are you to become a repeat customer? The challenge here is to decide whether the company has a future. All of this legwork might sound like a tall order, but don't be turned off: It will pay off in the end—either by steering you to a winner or by helping you avoid a stinker.

If you find some of the legwork a bit challenging to do on your own, there are some professional sites on the Internet where you can get helpful advice and information. Some will highlight information in the prospectus that's pertinent, and will provide news and analysis on the company. Others will give you access to professionally prepared research reports on a particular company—although most often for a fee. Most will list aftermarket performances (aftermarket refers to trading in a stock in the days, weeks or months after its IPO), which can help you gauge, for example, which industry currently has the worst-performing IPOs. Aftermarket numbers also are useful in determining the success rate of various underwriters. You might want to avoid deals underwritten by firms whose past IPOs have a poor track record.

DISSECTING A PROSPECTUS

Here are some tips on poring over a prospectus and using the information to make smart decisions:

- The first section of a prospectus gives an overview of the deal, including a list of underwriters and, often, the estimated share price. It also tells you how many shares the officers and founders are selling. Look at the number of shares and the estimated price relative to the actual and potential earnings the company discloses. A $10 stock may look cheap, but if the company is selling 10 million shares, it had better be worth $100 million. You can also use these same numbers to figure out whether the stock seems pricey or fairly valued. To do that, take the stock price and divide it by the earnings-per-share figure to calculate the expected price-to-earnings ratio. A low ratio is good. Find other, similar companies and see how their price-to-earnings ratios compare. Use caution if the new company's PE will be much higher than the PE ratios of its peers.
- Next, you'll want to read the company section, which contains an in-depth description of the firm and its products and services. Later on, the business section presents the size of the market, research and development projections, the company's top customers, and market initiatives. Scrutinize this information not only to determine whether the

(continues)

company's valuation seems on target, but also to glean insight into growth opportunities.

- Then check out the section labeled "risk factors." The fact that some are mentioned is itself not necessarily a problem, because they are required by the SEC. But the list may contain some red flags. It may mention, for example, that the company has a history of loan defaults, that management doesn't expect the company to make money anytime soon, or that the management team is inexperienced.

- Pay close attention to the sections that explain how the money raised in the offering will be spent. You want to make sure that most, if not all, of the money is going to be used to help grow the company. Be careful if a significant portion is going to be used to pay down debts. That in itself may be a sign that the company hasn't been good at managing its debt.

- Always look at the list of the company's managers. The management is as important as the financials are. You want to make sure they are the right leaders and can execute the company's growth strategy successfully. Has the company's management been successful in previous ventures? What industries do they hail from? What are their track records? How old are they? A chief executive who has led several other companies into bankruptcy might not be a good person to have at the helm. A bunch of unseasoned managers just out of business school might also be a red flag.

- Who are the deal's underwriters? An IPO with big-name underwriters may perform better than one underwritten by a lesser-known firm. But be careful:

This is by no means always the case. Some big underwriters have brought flops to market, while some smaller firms have had some stunning deals. Market-data provider Quote.com (**www.quote.com**) is a good source for checking on how underwriters' IPOs have fared in the aftermarket.

- Check to see how the price of the offering has changed since the company first announced its plans for an IPO. This won't be stated explicitly in the prospectus, but you can determine if changes have been made by keeping track of amendments made to the prospectus or registration documents using the SEC's Edgar database. Forms must be filed with the SEC each time changes are made. Changes in the expected price for a deal also are sometimes reported on financial news wires or Web sites. When an offering price is cut, it usually means that professional investors to whom the underwriters have showcased the deal aren't going crazy to get a piece of the action—and maybe you shouldn't be either. Sometimes an IPO whose offering price is lowered will begin trading at or below that level. So if you're looking for an IPO that will get a big pop out the door or do well in the long run, this might not be the one.

RESOURCES

It's possible to make money on IPOs, but doing so requires far more research than do most investments, not to mention an understanding of the market. Where can you get some help?

There's no shortage of Web sites to help you. The IPO craze of the late 1990s spawned a number of sites, many of which contain some free information. The selection includes basic primers for the novice, listings of coming deals, information on companies from SEC filings, charts with aftermarket performances, news, and rankings of the hottest deals and the coldest ones. Unfortunately, only the most basic information is free. For the bells and whistles—such as research reports, e-mail alerts on new filings, and other important developments—there is usually a fee.

Many of the Web sites provide very much the same information packaged differently. Alert-IPO! (**www.ostman.com/alert-ipo**) charges $34.95 a year for its subscription package. You get daily reports on companies that have filed to go public, e-mailed to you within 24 to 48 hours, as well as weekly summaries and daily news on the IPO market. Some information on past IPOs is free. The company also allows you to track up to twenty IPOs in a personal file.

Another popular IPO site is run by Hoover's, a supplier of business information. At Hoover's IPO Central site (**www.ipocentral.com**), much of the information is free, but investors can subscribe to additional services ($14.95 per month or $124.95 per year). The site lists companies that have filed to go public, and provides historical information on the companies, lists their executives and major owners, highlights a deal each week, and provides aftermarket information. It also has links to news stories and press releases. Viewers without subscriptions have access to the following: delayed reports of filings at the site, a step-by-step guide to the IPO process, an IPO directory of filings since May 1996, related news and analysis, free e-mail alerts each Monday of the previous week's IPO filings, pricings, and the current week's scheduled pricings. But you must subscribe for access to Hoover's valuable database of company profiles and real-time access to SEC filings through Edgar Online. One nifty feature is the power search, which lets you sort by underwriter and check out the pricing and track record of its recent IPOs.

Other sites that provide information on IPO filings, pricings, company snapshots, and aftermarket information include IPO Data Systems (**www.ipodata.com**) for a subscription fee of $15 per month or $180 per year; and IPO Monitor (**www.ipomonitor.com**), which costs $29 a month or $290 a year. There is also IPO Maven (**www.ipomaven.com**), which is free and contains the most complete historical list of IPOs, going back to 1995. In addition, IPO Monitor provides research material from underwriters to its subscribers on demand.

If research help is what you want, a good place to turn is a Web site run by Renaissance Capital of Greenwich, Connecticut (**www. ipo-fund.com**). For $50 a pop, this site will give you detailed research reports on companies that have filed to go public. Renaissance Capital writes a research report for every IPO that may be of interest to institutional investors. It dissects the prospectus and interviews the company's key competitors to determine its prospects. It also provides an investment opinion, essential facts about the issuer, key investment risks, and financial and valuation ratios with comparisons to similar publicly held companies. Each report is six pages long. The site also includes free basic information, including a primer and a message board for discussions.

Another good site for reports is Multex Investor Network (**www. multexinvestor.com**), which sells research reports from over 200 financial firms, including some on IPOs. Investors can search Multex's database for reports by ticker symbol. Registration for Multex's site is free, but you pay for individual reports. Standard prices range from $10 for a one- to five-page report to $150 for 60 or more pages. Some providers charge different fees, including Renaissance Capital, IPO Maven, and Standard & Poor's.

GETTING IN ON THE ACTION

If you thought researching an IPO was difficult, wait until you try to buy shares in one. While online brokers have opened the IPO doors to small investors, the demand far exceeds what's available, and many people are still shut out. But at least individuals have much more of an opportunity now, as online brokers try to level the playing field and satisfy the seemingly insatiable appetite of cyber-investors for IPOs.

E*Trade, Wit Capital, Charles Schwab, and DLJdirect (**www. dljdirect.com**), the online arm of Donaldson, Lufkin & Jenrette, have led the charge in making shares of IPOs more accessible to individual investors over the Web. About two dozen other discount brokers, such as TD Waterhouse (**www.waterhouse.com**), Quick & Reilly (**www. qronline.com**), and Datek Online (**www.datek.com**), have agreements to distribute IPOs through Wit's service. And the number of firms pushing IPOs online is growing. Newcomers include W. R. Hambrecht (**www.wrhambrecht.com**) and Friedman Billings Ramsey (**www.fbr.com**).

But getting shares in an IPO isn't as simple as visiting these brokers' sites and placing an order. Some online brokers award IPO shares by lottery (E*Trade, Wit, and Friedman Billings). Others show preferential treatment when determining who gets shares in their IPOs. For example, Charles Schwab and DLJdirect make IPOs available to just their best customers—usually wealthy clients (accounts of at least $100,000 at DLJdirect) and those who trade frequently. Newcomer Hambrecht plans to dole out IPO shares through a computerized auction system that will reward the highest bidders. It doesn't hurt to have accounts at multiple brokerage firms to increase your chances of getting IPO shares. Small investors might want to look at Wit Capital, E*Trade, or one of the other brokers who have no minimum for IPOs, and a low or no minimum for opening a trading account. At Wit, for example, you can open an account with a low balance of $2,000.

MISSED OUT? WATCH OUT

Didn't get shares in the IPO you were pining for, but still want to own the stock? Be careful. You may be better off not buying shares on their first day of trading. That's because newly traded stocks so often peak on their first day, and then drift lower on subsequent days. You may be better off waiting a few days or weeks.

If you just can't wait, and want to buy the stock immediately after it begins trading, be sure to place a limit order, which allows you to specify the price you are willing to pay. Many people have been burned by placing market orders (filled at the prevailing market price, not a specific price) for IPO stocks. They usually get filled just minutes after the stock starts trading, when prices tend to be at a high.

When an IPO is particularly hot, the repercussions of a market order can be dramatic: An order for 100 shares of a $20-a-share IPO, which would cost $2,000 plus commission, could be filled at $60 or $80 a share—at a cost of $6,000 or $8,000.

Even if you are lucky enough to get in on an IPO through one of these brokers, remember: They all have policies that penalize those who flip their shares—that is, sell their shares for a profit—just after the IPO begins trading. Some brokers threaten to put flippers at the back of the line for future IPOs, or ban them from future offerings altogether (though there are questions about how rigorously those threats are carried out against good customers).

Brokers usually list available IPOs on their Web sites. Some also will send e-mail alerts to premium customers—those with significant balances or who are active traders. Or you might get that extra service for a fee. There are also professional monitors such as **www.catchipo.com** that will check your broker's site and send you e-mail alerts when an IPO becomes available.

Once you find an IPO that you want, you'll have to wait until your broker begins taking orders. (Usually, that's for a limited time.) Again, that's done through a message posted on the broker's Web site, or e-mailed to customers. The trick is to get your order submitted before the window of opportunity closes. At E*Trade, for example, customers usually have a window of two hours to submit orders. If you meet all the broker's criteria for IPO participation and your order is in, you can cross your fingers and hope to get some shares.

Here are some of the requirements for IPO participation at various online brokers:

E*Trade: The company is one of the biggest online brokerage firms, and was a pioneer in selling IPOs to individuals. E*Trade has a distribution agreement with BankBoston Corp.'s BancBoston Robertson Stephens & Co. unit, and underwrites its own deals. It also owns 28% of start-up online investment bank E*Offering, which plans to make 50% of its IPO shares available to individuals and give E*Trade customers first access. At E*Trade, shares are distributed through a lottery system. (The company shifted from a first-come, first-serve basis after many investors complained that the process was unfair.) The firm lists available IPOs on its Web site, and also sends e-mails with price and order solicitations to customers who trade at least 75 times a quarter. Customers then have an opportunity to submit an order for shares, which are typically sold in blocks of 100. E*Trade accepts indications of interests in all public offerings for at least two hours; longer, when the number of shares available allows. Again, customers with a history of flipping may be excluded from future offerings.

Wit Capital: This hybrid of start-up investment bank and retail brokerage has roots in the very first sale of stock over the Internet in 1995, when its founder successfully raised $1.7 million for his beer company. Today, Wit gets IPOs from various investment banks, in some cases acting as a co-underwriter, and distributes them to its "E Syndicate" of about two dozen discount brokerage houses, including its own discount brokerage arm. Wit allows investors to open an account with a minimum of $2,000. These customers are then given a chance to buy IPO shares through a lottery, and on a first-come, first-serve basis if any shares are left over. The firm discourages flipping. Investors who sell an IPO within 60 days could be barred from future offerings. Goldman Sachs owns 20% of Wit, a promising development for investors because the firm is one of Wall Street's major underwriters.

Charles Schwab: The huge online broker, with more than two million accounts, gets IPOs from a handful of big investment banks, including J. P. Morgan, Hambrecht & Quist Group, and Credit Suisse

First Boston. Unlike Wit, Schwab determines whether you qualify for an IPO in part based on the amount you trade and your total assets. Deals are offered only to members of the firm's two frequent-trader clubs, as well as wealthier investors in its Schwab Priority Gold group. As for flipping: Selling within 30 days may put you at the bottom of the list for any future deals. The firm lists its IPO offerings on the Internet, but investors have to phone in their orders to a broker.

DLJdirect: The discount brokerage firm receives shares when parent company Donaldson, Lufkin & Jenrette is the underwriter. Customers must have a minimum of $100,000 in their accounts to qualify. The firm also uses other criteria, such as the length of time a client has been with the brokerage. Customers can buy as few as 100 shares but the maximum is 300.

Fidelity Investments (www.fidelity.com): The firm gets a portion of the IPOs underwritten by Citigroup's Salomon Smith Barney brokerage unit. Only the firm's wealthiest and best clients can participate. That means you must have at least $500,000 in your account or make at least 36 stock and bond trades a year, or 72 options trades. The firm lists available IPOs on its Web site, but clients have to phone in their orders.

Friedman Billings Ramsey: Friedman Billings Ramsey is a stock underwriter that has just begun to test the Internet as a way to sell IPO shares. The firm says that on deals it manages or co-manages it will offer up to 50% of its stock allocation to online investors. Customers are alerted to the availability of an IPO via e-mail, and through postings on the firm's Web site. Shares will be awarded by lottery to those who submit their orders within a publicized time frame.

W. R. Hambrecht: The online brokerage, which was started by William Hambrecht, the founder of Silicon Valley investment bank Hambrecht & Quist, has taken the egalitarian approach to IPO access a step further. It sells IPO shares in an auction, allocating them to the highest bidders instead of to a broker's best customers.

So, should you make the leap?

Before buying shares of an IPO, make sure that it fits in with your investment goals and your tolerance for risk. After all, when it comes to risks, IPOs top the list, because so many companies going public for the first time are unseasoned and have no track record in the market. You should know why you want to own the stock, and how long you intend to keep it. If you want the IPO because you're looking for a quick gain, then make sure your homework tells you it is likely to soar right out the door. If you are looking for the next Microsoft, then make sure the long-term prospects are sound and favorable. It's easy to get carried away when reading about the stratospheric gains of other IPOs.

DIRECT STOCK OFFERINGS

Direct public offerings are exploding over the Internet. These are first-time sales of registered securities by small companies—typically raising less than $5 million—directly to investors. Think of a DPO as an initial public offering without the middleman—the underwriter, who conducts due diligence on the company, shepherds the offering through the regulatory process, and then makes the final sale to investors. For small companies, it's a do-it-yourself version of the traditional IPO.

Because DPOs don't involve an investment banker, they are typically riskier than IPOs. These stock offerings—be careful, some are investment scams—require investors to conduct much of the research that's normally done for an IPO by an investment bank and included in a prospectus promoting the deal. But DPOs offer ordinary individuals a better chance of getting in on a young company at the ground floor than do IPOs—simply because of the difficulties individual investors often face trying to buy into IPOs.

DPOs provide a great opportunity for big gains, should the company become a success. On the flip side, an investor can lose his entire investment if the company turns out to be a failure. Another worry for investors: DPOs aren't traded on the national markets, such as the New York Stock Exchange or the Nasdaq Stock Market, so it's difficult for an investor to trade in and out of these stocks. However, many DPO companies do try to provide investors with a means to trade their shares, either on regional exchanges, through the company itself, or on bulletin boards set up on the Internet with approval from federal securities regulators.

DPOs have been around since the mid-1970s, when they were first approved by the Securities and Exchange Commission. Back then, these offerings were sold through time-consuming sales pitches over the telephone and by mail. But the Internet—and regulatory changes in 1995 permitting the initial sale of securities by small companies in cyberspace—have increased the prominence of direct stock offerings and have led to a surge of such deals. For example, a Dallas industry newsletter, *SCOR Report* (an acronym for Small Cap Offering Registration), tracked 321 direct public offerings in 1998 that attempted to raise a collective $439 million. That's up from 33 DPOs in 1990, seeking to raise $12.6 million.

Along with the growth of DPOs over the Internet (the first was the sale of shares in a small company called Spring Street Brewery in 1996) have come several Web sites that provide information and other resources on DPOs to help investors. A sampling:

Virtual Wall Street (www.virtualwallstreet.com): This site provides extensive information and resources on DPOs. Here you can get the legal definition of a DPO and the different types of offerings available.

Direct Stock Market (www.dsm.com): This site, which requires investors to register, provides a listing of companies that are offering stock for sale directly to the public. Investors also can view a virtual road show over the Net.

Direct IPO (www.directipo.com): This is another listing service for companies offering stock directly to the public, and it also provides information and other resources for investors.

IPO Data Systems (www.ipodata.com): This site provides a listing and brief descriptions of companies offering stock for sale directly to the public, and provides links to those companies' Web sites.

SCOR Report (www.scor-report.com): This Web site for an industry newsletter covers small business finance, and also provides general and legal information about DPOs.

DIVIDEND REINVESTMENT PROGRAMS

Purchasing shares directly from a company is a cheap way for investors to get their feet wet on Wall Street. Most often this is done through dividend reinvestment plans, or DRIPs, which require you to buy just a single share of a company's stock to enroll. DRIPs are an excellent option if you would like to start out with a small position in a stock and add to it on a periodic basis. Plus, your dividends are automatically reinvested in more shares, and you don't have to pay brokerage commissions. More than 1,500 companies—including well-known names such as Intel, Coca-Cola, Johnson & Johnson, and Wendy's International—offer dividend reinvestment plans. Many foreign companies, such as BP Amoco PLC and DaimlerChrysler AG, also have programs.

DRIPs allow people to invest a dollar amount, rather than having to buy a specific number of shares. Traditionally, they have been favored by people who want to invest as little as $10 or $25 every month in individual stocks. In traditional plans, the first shares are bought through a broker, but after that, investments can be made directly with the company for free or, at most, $2.50 a trade. Recently, though, many companies have been revamping their programs to allow the initial shares to be bought directly from the company. About half the companies offering DRIPs—such as McDonald's and Campbell's Soup—let you buy initial shares directly. That's up from only about 50 at the beginning of 1995.

Many of these direct-purchase DRIPs have also added new services. For example, Home Depot and Compaq Computer recently started letting DRIP participants invest through their Web sites. Some DRIPs, including McDonald's and Fannie Mae, let investors review their accounts online. But in adding these new features, many DRIPs have raised or added fees, saying they have to pass on costs to the consumer. Many DRIPs now charge $5 a transaction, plus 10 cents a share. That could be a turnoff for some investors, with online trading commissions now below $10 in many cases; DRIPs made a lot more sense a few years ago, when commissions often ran into hundreds of dollars.

In addition, as more and more individual investors seek to make fast moves in and out of the stock market, DRIPs are beginning to seem too restrictive to some people. There usually is a lag—sometimes as much as five days or more—between the time an order to buy or sell is placed and when it is executed. Also, record keeping could be a burden. There are no consolidated statements for DRIPs; if you're in ten different DRIP plans, you get ten different statements. For a fee, however, some companies will consolidate your statements.

However, DRIPs are still attractive for many people, allowing them to build stakes in well-established blue-chip companies. For example, most of the 30 companies that make up the Dow Jones Industrial Average offer DRIP plans. As an added incentive, some companies allow investors to buy shares at a discount. For example, Time Warner gives DRIP participants a 5% discount on shares purchased with reinvested dividends.

Here are some places to go for more information:

Net Stock Direct (www.netstockdirect.com): This site provides a searchable database of 1,600 companies with direct stock investing plans. It allows investors to research the companies, view prospectuses online (or e-mail companies to have one sent in the mail), access information, and enroll in plans online. Investors can get a list of the top ten requested DRIPs, search for companies that offer plans online, and find those that have no fees.

Moneypaper (www.moneypaper.com): This is an online newsletter about direct stock investing. It provides comprehensive information, including tips for getting started and a list of companies that don't charge fees. It also helps investors set up DRIP accounts (for a fee).

National Association of Investors Corp. (www.naicstockservice.com): This site provides comprehensive information to help you get started with DRIPs. For a fee, NAIC will help you simplify your record keeping by providing a consolidated statement of all your plans and investments.

DRIP Investor (www.dripinvestor.com): This site, run by a company that has long produced a print newsletter on DRIP investing, includes selected columns and a message board on the topic.

THREE

Day Trading

T ara Rill, a schoolteacher in Gainesville, Florida, joined the growing number of people who have quit their jobs to become day traders. She spent about $4,000 on a new Dell computer and three monitors, opened an account with an online brokerage firm, and was in business.

It was fun and profitable, but after a few months, the stress of constantly buying stocks and selling them minutes or seconds later proved too much. Eventually, she took a step back. While continuing to trade online actively, she decided to invest in fewer stocks, and hold them longer.

"Mentally, I just couldn't handle day trading," Ms. Rill recalled. "I was making money overall, but timing the market is really difficult."

You bet. In fact, day trading has a lot in common with gambling. Regulators and advocates for individual investors warn that successful day trading is at least as much a matter of luck as skill, and say that many day-trading firms gloss over the risks inherent in such trading. "An active trader has to really think about what advantages he or she has over the rest of the market," said John Markese, president of the American Association of Individual Investors in Chicago. "The technology available now is impressive, but a lot of people have access to it. Really, the best way to make money actively trading is to get lucky."

This form of investing has grown exponentially in recent years. Dozens of brokerage firms have sprouted up across the country offering ordinary people office space and terminals from which to day trade. And many more people, such as Tara Rill, have set up shop on their personal computers to day trade from home. A large number don't take on the sophisticated setup Ms. Rill did. They just get an account with the cheapest online broker they can find, and troll the Net for ideas on how to make a quick buck.

No one knows for sure how many people are day trading these days, but clearly, the long bull market of the 1990s lured many people into taking the plunge. A. B. Watley, a brokerage firm that caters to day traders, said revenues in its 1999 fiscal year more than doubled from the year before, while the total number of transactions at its online unit rose nearly 300%.

But the long upward march of the Dow Jones Industrial Average masks a critical fact: Day trading is a very difficult—even financially perilous—way to make a living. Even before an unsuccessful day trader went on a killing spree in an Atlanta brokerage office in 1999, regulators had been collecting evidence to dispute the claims of day-trading advocates that day trading is suitable for most any investor. In a study by the North American Securities Administrators Association, a group of state-level securities regulators, a random sample of brokerage accounts at one Massachusetts day-trading concern found that nearly three quarters of them weren't profitable.

Industry representatives insist it's not so dire as that, but even they acknowledge that it's a tough business. "Most people lose money when they start," said Bill Lauderback, vice president of an industry group, the Electronic Traders Association. Most people lack the skills required to succeed—the ability of a professional trader to sense the market's ebb and flow and bet right more often than wrong.

HOW IT WORKS

There are several flavors of day trading, but all of them have this in common: The trader is trying to profit from a quick move in, and then out of, a stock that is often chosen with little if any regard for the company's business or financial position. Some day trading is tied to price movements triggered by company news, but in many cases, day traders don't even know the name of the company whose shares they are buying—they merely see a stock symbol and a trading opportunity.

Regulators are most concerned with day traders who work from the office of a day-trading firm, which sells them space and access to trading systems and services. These people, who have made day trading a full-time job, use special equipment to identify stocks on the move and take advantage of sometimes minute changes in stock prices. They buy at a low price, sell at a higher price, and pocket the difference—as little as pennies per share in some cases. The Electronic Traders Association estimated that there were 4,000 to 5,000 people doing this type of day trading in 1999. At the same time, state securities regulators had identified 62 day-trading firms nationally. (Not all of the clients of these day-trading shops work from the firms' offices. Many use the firms' sophisticated computer equipment from home via a high-speed network connection.)

There is another breed of day trader that is much more difficult to quantify. These are people who have adopted the day traders' mind-set, but haven't quit their day jobs. They also try to take advantage of "momentum" in the market, but while full-time day traders may make scores or hundreds of trades a day, these part-timers may make only a handful each day—or they may step out of the market for stretches of time. Because they don't have the equipment to detect and take advantage of fleeting trading opportunities, these people aim for bigger gains on each trade. A few pennies on each share won't do; they need a full dollar or much more. Their strategy is simple: Find a stock that is rising and seems like it will continue to do so. Buy in, hold that investment while it rises, and then bail out before the stock begins to slip back.

The concept sounds so simple that anyone could do it. Amid the powerful bull market of the past five years, it has been easy for a novice to come up with a hunch, take a flier on a stock, and score a quick profit. Once you win (ask any gambler), you are likely to try your hand again. Experts in behavioral finance say success can breed excessive— and unjustified—self-confidence, and this self-confidence pushes investors to trade even more. Some people quit their jobs and try to make a go of day trading full-time, while others merely dabble off and on, still holding down a regular job. Regulators don't classify any of the part-time momentum players as day traders (saving that term mostly for the investors sitting in the day-trading shops), but in the popular perception, that is just what these investors are.

It wasn't just a bull market that lured people into day trading—the ease, and somewhat anonymous nature, of online trading also played a role. In the past, if you had a hunch on a stock, you had to call your broker to place an order. When you were ready to bail out, you placed another call. If you bet wrong and had to lick your wounds, your broker knew. With online trading, you can move much more easily—jump to your browser, make the trades, and go back to what you were doing—without any embarrassment factor. If you bet wrong, no one has to know.

Of course, without the Internet, momentum day traders would have a harder time coming up with investing ideas. Momentum investors rely heavily on stock message boards, online chat rooms, and e-mail newsletters to come up with trades.

The cheapest and simplest way to find day-trading ideas is to simply scan the popular online message board sites—like Silicon Investor (**www.siliconinvestor.com**) and Raging Bull (**www.ragingbull.com**). Day traders prowl active boards, seeking leads to active stocks, which are good day-trading targets. News sometimes stirs things up on message boards, but there don't have to be any new developments, especially at a small company, for its stock to get a lot of sudden attention online and begin moving in the market.

For the most serious momentum day traders, though, the regular message board fare isn't enough. They rely on day-trading Web sites or e-mail bulletins to find stocks on the move—and sometimes pay handsomely for these services. Most of the services rely on technical analysis to identify picks. Technical analysts use trading patterns (in stock prices or trading volume) to try to divine stocks' future directions. Some analysts use complex, proprietary formulas, which the services claim have proven accurate.

Day-trading sites often include real-time chat rooms, where stock picks can be instantly communicated to hundreds or thousands of people. The site operators often lead the discussion, but users can chime in as well. Unlike a message board, where you must constantly push the "refresh" button on your Web browser to see if any new messages have been posted, new comments in chat rooms appear automatically on your screen. The effect is like a quickly moving online conversation—as if all of the users were sitting around a table making comments to and about one another.

Popular day-trading sites include Pristine Day Trader (**www.pristine. com**), ActiveTrade (**www.activetrade.net**), Day Traders On-line (**www. daytraders.com**), Digital Traders (**www.trading-places.net**), Momentum Trader (**www.mtrader.com**) and Sharkattack, a chat service on America Online's dial-up online service.

The Pristine Day Trader site is typical: At 8:30 A.M. Eastern time, a general chat begins among users of the site, and then—just before the market opens—the site's editors enter to announce their stock picks of the day. The discussion continues throughout the market day, with new messages posted every few seconds. News that can move stocks is posted, questions are answered, and hot stocks are constantly being offered up and analyzed. Pristine charges $525 a month, or $1,425 for a three-month subscription to the chat.

Sometimes day traders' chats themselves seem to move stocks. In March 1999, shares of CNET, a Web site company, surged inexplicably—jumping more than $23 at one point—before reversing course. There weren't any news developments to account for the activity, but the swings did occur in lockstep with the postings made on a chat in Digital Traders. At first the chat's leaders picked CNET shares, posting a note that said CNET "IS A MONSTER CALL!!!" The stock rallied for 90 minutes as chat participants cheered it on. But later came the message: "PULLBACK ALERT: CNET I WOULD TAKE PROFITS HERE." The rally died, and the stock fell back.

QUARTER HERE, EIGHTH THERE

Back at the day-trading firms, they don't care as much about online chats and bulletin boards. These traders use special software, services, and high-speed communications to route orders more directly into the

The following is an excerpt from the CNET chat at trading-places.net, indicating the time each message was written (far left) and the author (in brackets).

11:15:21 [skibum] TRADE ALERT: CNET made more profits than YHOO last quarter
11:15:33 [Wags] profits that's bad isn't it?
11:16:02 [skibum] TRADE ALERT: sorry about the hype, but when I find easy monstas, i like us to be in
11:16:37 [Merlin] WINNER ALERT: CONGRATZ TO ALL CNET PLAYERZ
11:16:56 [skibum] WINNER ALERT: CNET 129
11:17:12 [ACDC] money money money money
11:18:06 [runahead] cnet uncanny
11:18:19 [Merlin] WINNER ALERT: CNET UP 15
11:18:59 [spartacus] Ski, whats your target today on CNET :-)
11:19:05 [Posjim] out of second cnet 129 1/2
11:19:07 [sal] cnet easy 140 by tomorrow
11:20:02 [Excalibur] WINNER ALERT:stonz +1 CNET
11:20:49 [Mozart] Scalped cnet today fro 7 stix so far Ski!!
11:22:04 [Mozart] Looky money leavin yhoo & amzn and goin over to cnet !
11:22:44 [balfour] out half CNET position + 5
11:22:56 [Mozart] Kick-butt Ski!! :-)
11:24:56 [crstyn] cnet 's pullback was very brief
11:25:00 [sal] So who gets the 1000shares if CNET hits 200 before AMZN or YHOO ?
11:25:32 [Mozart] out cnet another stic!
11:25:38 [Posjim] ski, your doing great just holding CNET

(continues)

```
11:25:38 [Merlin] >WINNER ALERT:  CNET  130 (appears
8 times)
11:25:51 [Merlin] .. WINNER ALERT: SKIBUM THE MAN!!!
11:26:19 [crstyn] I pleaded w/my mom to buy  cnet
fri...nope she says
11:27:37 [crstyn] she says "can you trust daytraders
?"- lol
11:29:18 [Merlin] WINNER ALERT:  CNET  131 (appears
12 times)
```

market than is possible with a standard online-brokerage account. All of this shaves the amount of time it takes to complete a trade, allowing these traders to take advantage of smaller changes in prices. They often use software tools that allow them to find potential trades—a sudden jump in volume or flurry of activity by market makers are two red flags—and then they dart into and out of stocks, aiming to get their transactions completed almost instantaneously.

This type of day trading first caught on big in the early 1990s, when many traders used a form of arbitrage that took advantage of an automated trading system for the Nasdaq Stock Market called the Small Order Execution System, or SOES. That system, beefed up in the aftermath of the 1987 stock market crash, was designed to give brokers a means to ensure that small investors' orders were promptly executed, even amid market turmoil. Many market makers had stopped answering their phones and making trades during the crash, so SOES was created as a means to place automated trades without the attention of a market maker.

Day-trading firms soon found a way to use SOES to scalp small profits from differences in market makers' quotes—particularly when stocks were moving quickly and the market makers were slow at updating their quotations. These traders would find a market maker who, for instance, was quoting stock for sale cheaper than other market makers. They'd use SOES to quickly buy from that market maker and later sell the stock to another market maker at a profit. These day traders were dubbed "SOES bandits," and the securities industry later found a way to slow them down.

Today's day traders still use the SOES system, but not nearly as much as they used to. Harvey Houtkin, who runs All-Tech Investment Group and has called himself "the original SOES bandit," said 80% of trades at his day-trading firm used to be made via SOES. Today that number has fallen to just 20%.

Part of the drop-off in the use of SOES is tied to the securities industries' response to SOES bandits, but another important factor is the new tool that day traders were handed in the late 1990s when the Securities and Exchange Commission mandated changes in rules that govern the way Nasdaq orders are handled.

As with the creation of SOES, these changes came in the aftermath of a black eye for Nasdaq: The SEC mandated a new way for investors to get better prices from market makers following allegations that they had colluded to keep investors' costs high. (Nasdaq officials said some of the reforms were already in the works before—and would have been adopted even without—the allegations of improprieties.)

The new rules made it easier for individual investors to make trades at prices other than those offered by market makers. This rule change triggered enormous growth in the number and use of electronic communications networks, or ECNs. The speed and efficiency of ECNs, coupled with the bull market, breathed new life into day trading.

But none of this means that taking a seat at a day-trading firm is a sure way to riches. Indeed, the firms have been under investigation by securities regulators for inadequately disclosing risks to investors. Some people manage to make money using the high-tech systems, but most don't. One big reason is the high costs that some day-trading firms impose upon their traders. The firm gets a commission on each trade that the day trader makes, and that can quickly eat into any trading profits that are earned.

ARE YOU STILL INTERESTED?

If, after all this, you still think day trading is for you, here's how to get started:

If you elect to day trade from home, you should decide just how aggressive you intend to be, because that will greatly affect your start-up costs. If you don't plan on making dozens of trades every hour, an account with a major online brokerage may be all you need. Such online brokers as Datek Online (**www.datek.com**), SureTrade (**www. suretrade.com**), and A. B. Watley (**www.abwatley.com**) all promise to complete orders quickly, charge low transaction fees, and even offer interfaces specially designed to make trading fast. These rank among the best firms for hyperactive traders, according to Gomez Advisors.

Wherever you go, experts say that if you intend to trade aggressively, you should select a site that provides the most real-time information on a single screen. Especially important are real-time price quotes and a log of recent changes in a stock's price. You should also find a brokerage that executes and confirms trades quickly. And, of course, transaction costs are a big consideration. Firms that cater to active traders typically charge $5 to $10 a trade.

You may want "Level II" Nasdaq quotes, allowing you to see individual quotes from market makers all at once, just as a Wall Street broker would see them. Many online brokerages offer Level II quotes. E*Trade (**www.etrade.com**) offers free Level II quotes to people who trade 75 or more times every three months.

If trading actively via an online broker isn't enough for you, you can create your own day-trading system at home, or start trading from the office of a day-trading firm.

Either way, getting started is expensive. High-end at-home day trading requires a reasonably powerful computer, a fast network connection, and multiple monitors to view all the data. It is wise to get the fastest equipment you can find, because the opportunities to scalp a quick profit can literally vanish in seconds. Some day-trading brokerage firms, meanwhile, will require you to deposit at least $20,000 in an account with them before you can start trading.

Many day traders find it necessary to open margin accounts, meaning to buy securities with borrowed money. Margin trading can enhance your returns—or it can bury you, because even if you lose money on stocks bought on margin, you must still pay back your margin loan, plus interest. (If you don't have the money, you may have to sell stocks to come up with the cash.) Remember that if you buy stocks on margin, you can lose more than your invested capital.

Several firms offer the tools necessary to make day trading possible from your home; about $300 per month is the going rate. "Our main service is to allow you better access to the markets, put you on a level playing field with the market makers, and give you the ability to act *extremely fast*," says the Web site of a firm called 1800daytrade.com. It charges up to $299 per month for proprietary software that facilitates day trading, including point-and-click ordering, Level II quotes, real-time balance information, and fast order confirmation.

A. B. Watley offers a phone-line connection to its proprietary telecommunications network for a monthly charge of $300. Watley officials say their system is more reliable than an Internet connection, and helps minimize technical problems that can interfere with trading.

If you prefer the company of other traders, firms like All-Tech Investment Group Inc. (**www.attain.com**) offer their customers office space to trade on the firm's high-speed terminals. All-Tech has twenty-seven branch offices, mostly in the east and southeast. All-Tech systems can also be used at home; the firm markets its services to day traders and more mainstream investors.

Many such firms require that you take classes to learn the tricks of day trading. These classes may last as little as a day or as long as a month, and are usually held at the brokerage's headquarters—so be prepared to do some traveling. Prices range from free to quite expensive—and some regulators question just how useful the courses are, particularly since the brokerage has an obvious financial interest in seeing you become a hyperactive trader. "You really have to question whether they're offering unbiased advice," said Denise Voight Crawford, head of the Texas Securities Commission.

Harry Simpson, the chairman of A. B. Watley, is also dubious of the trading courses, which his firm doesn't offer. "The best those courses can offer is the basics of technical and fundamental analysis and warnings not to make trades when the markets are falling fast," he said. "But discipline is something you either have, or learn really quickly, or never get."

FOUR

Mutual Funds

For investors like Mary Ann Williams, a novice taking her first shaky steps in the world of online investing, the breathtaking array of mutual fund choices can be confusing, even paralyzing. She turned to the Internet to help move forward, but even that can seem daunting until you find the resource that is right for you. "Whenever I look at sites like Sage, on America Online, that say they're geared toward the beginner mutual fund investor, I find that the wording gets too deep. There's just too much to absorb and too many choices. It makes my head swim," she said.

A registered nurse and home health care worker, Ms. Williams spent hours online sifting through fund data and making various attempts to contact individuals and financial planners for advice through electronic message boards. She finally found what she needed on a Web site. "I found a list on one magazine's site that ranked funds by stars—with four stars being their best recommendation," she said. "Since I'm a real novice, all the lingo, the jargon, means absolutely nothing to me. But the four stars I understand!"

The opportunities have never been greater, but at the same time, deciding which mutual funds to buy has never been more difficult. The number of mutual funds available multiplied as a bull market for stocks stretched through most of the 1990s, and demand for funds grew. At the same time, fortunately, the Net emerged as a new tool for fund investors. Resources previously available only through a financial planner or broker are now available on any home PC. Just as with selecting a fund, investors must find the Internet tools that suit them best.

The Web can deliver the particulars on individual funds, what they invest in, and how those investments have performed: basic information investors need before deciding to buy or sell. It can be used to sort through—and screen—long lists of funds to pinpoint those that meet specific needs or goals; say, the best-performing fund among those that invest in Japanese stocks. The Web can even help investors figure out just what their financial goals are. Online calculators, for instance, may guide a young couple to less risky funds to help protect the nest egg they are building in order to buy their first home.

Once all the questions are answered and all the research is done, the Net can be used to put all of that information to work. Funds can be bought and sold using brokerage firms' Web sites, as well as sites run by some fund companies themselves. Some Web sites promise one-stop shopping, allowing investors to browse a vast array of funds offered by many different fund companies, in a "supermarket" setting.

Building a portfolio of funds isn't the end of the process. Investors can keep track of their funds, and other investments, using portfolio-tracking tools available on scores of Web sites. At any moment, they can log on and check the value of their investments, identify problems (perhaps that retirement fund just isn't growing fast enough to allow you to step out of the work force at age 55 after all), and refine goals (better aim for 62). There are other benefits throughout the process: Some sites, for instance, help out at tax time.

STARTING POINT

When you buy shares of a mutual fund, the fund company pools your money with that of other investors who share a common goal—for instance, taking on the risk of owning some speculative stocks, with the hope of building wealth for retirement. The fund company pools money from many investors to buy a portfolio of securities (stocks, bonds, and other assets) that will be managed by one or more professional advisers. In buying a share of a mutual fund, you effectively purchase a sliver of each security held in that fund's portfolio. Purchasing shares in mutual funds, rather than buying individual stocks or bonds directly, not only spreads out your investment risk but also is cheaper because you don't rack up heavy commission costs.

Fund companies issue shares of individual mutual funds at a cost that is calculated based on the funds' net asset values. Commonly called simply the NAV, the dollar value of a single mutual fund share is based on the value of the stocks, bonds, and other assets held by the fund divided by the number of shares outstanding. Fund NAVs are calculated at the end of each business day.

The benefits of mutual fund investing are many. Most important, it provides a way for small investors to access professional money management at a relatively low cost. Mutual funds give investors control over their money, allowing them to transfer funds as easily as picking up the telephone or clicking a computer mouse. Fund investing lets you spread out your investment risk, which may help to minimize the damage your portfolio will suffer in the event of a market slump. Finally, the heavily regulated fund industry is required to file frequent, detailed disclosure statements that let you evaluate how closely fund managers are meeting their objectives.

But getting started in fund investing and maintaining a portfolio of mutual funds can be overwhelming. The total number of stock mutual funds nearly doubled in the mid- to late 1990s, and assets held by all of those funds more than tripled to $3 trillion during the same period, according to Investment Company Institute, the fund industry trade group. As more companies convert their employer-sponsored savings plans to plans that require individuals to take responsibility for their own investment choices, choosing the right fund, or mix of funds, has become a critical retirement-planning decision for many Americans.

Most investors would be surprised to discover that the majority of funds available are not appropriate for their investment goals, and only a handful in each category has enjoyed the kind of market-beating performance over time that would merit a second look. Indeed, financial planners agree that the two hardest decisions novice investors face are deciding how much risk they're comfortable with (conservative, aggressive, somewhere in between), and figuring out what their investment goals are (a new home, college tuition, retirement income). After that, choosing the right funds to meet those investment goals can be relatively easy.

There are several factors you should consider before investing in funds:

- Should you invest in load or no-load funds?
- What fees and annual expenses do the funds charge?
- What kinds of investments do the funds hold, and how risky are those investments?
- Where do the funds rank in performance over the last three, five, and ten years?
- How much money do the funds manage, and what are their investment styles?
- Who is the fund manager, what is his or her background, and how long has he or she been managing this particular fund?
- What is the funds' minimum initial investment?

Load vs. No-Load Funds

When a mutual fund charges a sales load, that fee usually goes to pay for commissions to people who sell the fund's shares to you, as well as other marketing costs. Sales loads buy you a broker's services and advice. There are a variety of charges imposed by load funds, the most common of which are front-end load charges and back-end load charges. A front-end load is a sales charge, which by law cannot be higher than 8.5% of your investment, and which you pay when you buy shares. Conversely, a back-end, or deferred, load is a sales charge you pay when you sell your shares. It usually starts out at 5% or 6% if you sell in the first year and gets smaller each year after that until it reaches zero (say, in year six or seven of your investment). In addition, both front-end and back-end load funds charge 12b-1 fees of 0.25% to 1% a year, which are used to provide ongoing compensation to the broker who sold you the fund.

No-load funds do not charge sales loads. But even no-load funds charge ongoing expenses, including management fees. Funds list their expenses as equaling a percentage of the fund's assets, generally for the most recent fiscal year. Management fees for actively managed no-load funds (funds that cost nothing to invest in, but charge an annual management fee) average between 1% and 1.5%, while passively managed index funds tend to have much lower fees.

You can expect to pay higher expenses for certain types of funds that require intensive research and oversight, such as international stock funds or those that seek to time the market. And remember: While load funds may charge for professional services and advice, studies show that over time, funds that charge sales loads haven't performed better, on average, than no-load funds.

Index Funds

A search for "individual funds" on the Yahoo! Internet directory (**yahoo.com**) turns up links to hundreds of fund families with an online presence, all vying for your attention and, with any luck, your investment dollars. With that many choices, it's no wonder that index investing has become the most popular form of investment vehicle for the novice investor. Equity-index funds simply buy the same stocks, bonds, and other securities that make up a certain market index, in an effort to replicate the index's performance. The best-known index funds track the Standard & Poor's 500-stock index.

Novice investors, and those who haven't the time to closely track their investment holdings, often find that index investing best meets their needs for several reasons. Index funds are lower risk because investors attain the average market return. And by spreading their investment dollars across a number of index funds, investors can further lower their overall risk.

The investment goal of passively managed index funds is simply to match the market's performance, which allows the fund companies to charge very low annual maintenance fees—often as much as one per-

Yahoo! Fund Profile - U.S. Stock Funds Top Performers - Microsoft Internet Explorer

File   Edit   View   Favorites   Tools   Help

Address   http://biz.yahoo.com/p/tops/usstk.html   Go

YAHOO!FINANCE   Home - Yahoo! - Help   M(O)RNINGSTAR.com

> > You're ready.

[Fund Index | Funds By Family | Fund Top Performers | Screen Funds]

Mutual Fund Top Performers - U.S. Stock Funds   As of 14-Jan-00

Top Performers - 3 Month

Fund Name	Symbol	More Info	Return
PBHG New Opportunities	PBNOX	Profile , Chart , News	150.42%
PBHG Select Equity	PBHEX	Profile , Chart , News	129.62%
ProFunds UltraOTC Inv	UOPIX	Profile , Chart , News	112.06%
ProFunds UltraOTC Svc	UOPSX	Profile , Chart , News	111.62%
PBHG Technology & Communications	PBTCX	Profile , Chart , News	101.67%
HomeState Year 2000	HSYTX	Profile , Chart , News	91.85%
Dresdner RCM Biotechnology	N/A	N/A	87.61%
Millennium Growth	MGFQX	Profile , Chart	86.84%
Berger Information Technology Instl	BINFX	Profile , Chart , News	86.50%
Millennium Growth & Income	MGIQX	Profile , Chart	83.34%

Internet

centage point a year lower, on average, than actively managed funds. And many find index investing the appropriate choice because the funds' "buy and hold" investment formula results in fewer capital gains taxes. Sales are only made if a company's stock is removed from an index, or when investors request their money back.

The challenge for the index investor is to choose the right mix of market indexes to provide a strong annual performance at an appropriate level of risk. For instance, a conservative index investor might emphasize large U.S. stock and short-term bond indexes, while an aggressive investor might choose small, technology, and foreign stock indexes.

A good place to begin your search for the right mix of index funds is Indexfunds.com (**www.indexfundsonline.com**), an informational site published by IndexFunds of Austin, Texas. This site includes a good overview of the basics of index fund investing, including comparisons of index funds to actively managed funds. Indexfunds.com also offers a breakdown of index funds by sector and type, and provides a screening tool to help you determine the right fund for your portfolio.

Actively Managed Funds

The counterpoint to index funds, in many ways, is actively managed funds. Their portfolio managers don't simply try to match the performance of the stock market in general; they aim to beat it. So, rather than buying stocks that comprise whatever index they aim to mirror, active managers beat the bushes for stocks that will outperform the average stock. They spend a lot of time researching companies' fundamentals—that is, their earnings history and outlook, business plans, and the industry in which they operate. Fund managers pore over companies' financial statements, talk with their managements and customers, and solicit opinions from securities analysts.

All of this work is expensive, and that is why actively managed funds generally charge much higher fees than index funds. Investors who buy actively managed funds are betting that the fund managers' stock-picking expertise will generate returns that compensate for the higher expenses. But picking successful companies and buying and selling their shares at the right time is difficult, and most fund managers are unable to maintain a mutual fund portfolio that consistently beats the performance of the overall stock market. Indeed, in any one year, index funds typically beat 60% of comparable actively managed funds.

Actively managed funds, though, do offer some things that index funds don't: most notably, the ability to use mutual funds to make investments in, for instance, an industry group that is expected to excel. Say you expect great things from the semiconductor industry. An actively managed fund that invests in just that sector of the market may be a good way to put your hunch to work. The manager of a semiconductor sector fund would buy shares of the chip companies he or she feels have the best prospects. A fund that owns a portfolio of semiconductor stocks is less risky than buying individual chip stocks.

Closed-End Funds

Funds come in two basic types: open-end and closed-end. Most investors are primarily familiar with open-end funds. Open-end funds issue and redeem shares on demand, based on the fund's net asset value. The NAV is determined at the end of each trading session. By contrast, closed-end funds have a fixed number of shares outstanding, and do not redeem shares like open-ended funds. Such funds are usually listed on major stock exchanges and trade very much like stocks. Unlike a typical mutual fund, a closed-end fund's share price can trade above or below its net asset value. Closed-end funds often are incorrectly referred to as mutual funds, but they are actually investment trusts that are regulated by the Investment Company Act of 1940.

For a useful online source of information and daily quotes on closed-end funds, go to the Internet Closed-End Fund Investor Web site (**www.icefi.com**). The site includes online tutorials on investing in closed-end funds, data updated quarterly on roughly 500 closed-end funds from CDA/Wiesenberger, and an online discussion forum. For a $20 monthly fee, you also can access daily updates and performance data on the funds it covers. The site also provides links to Web sites with specific information on more than eighty individual closed-end funds.

Money-Market Funds

Money-market mutual funds act essentially like personal checking accounts, only the interest rates are much higher and your deposits are not insured by the government. Money-market funds invest in short-term debt instruments such as certificates of deposit, Treasury bills, and corporate bonds. Since money-market funds value the price of their individual shares at a constant price, usually $1, there is no chance for capital gains. Instead, your entire gain comes from the fund's yield, which is paid out monthly. As with no-load funds, be sure to seek out money-market funds with very low expense ratios, to make sure you're getting the most bang for your buck.

IBC Financial Data (**www.ibcdata.com**) offers practically one-stop shopping for investors seeking the right money-market fund. This publisher of mutual fund industry newsletters provides free money market-fund yield rankings for 2,400 funds on its site, and the data is updated weekly. It also includes a useful fund selector that will help you determine which fund is right for you, based on three criteria: safety, tax savings, and yield.

DIGGING IN AND DRILLING DOWN

Before you invest in any mutual fund, take the time to set your own investment goals and objectives and then plan an investment strategy to meet those goals. Remember, you are aiming to build a portfolio of funds that suits your needs and situation. You'll need to decide how much risk you can afford to take and what your time horizon will be. How much you'll need to invest, and how aggressive you'll have to be in putting your money to work, will depend on a number of factors: how much money you have available to invest; what financial goals you hope to attain with the funds you're investing; when you need to tap your investments; and, finally, how comfortable you are with risk.

Surprisingly, getting all that accomplished is a lot easier than it sounds.

If there's one area of financial planning for which the Internet is most useful, it's taking the hard work out of number crunching. Guidance on virtually every financial planning decision you'll need to make, from setting your goals (How much do I need to save for a new home/college tuition/retirement?) to achieving them (Should I be investing in aggressive mutual funds or stick with no-frills index funds?), can be found online. The best site on the Internet to start getting your financial house in order and setting your investment goals is Financenter.com (**www.financenter.com**). The site is jam-packed with calculators and worksheets that address nearly every financial planning question imaginable.

By calculating your retirement goals and the amount of time you've allotted to reach them, you will narrow the field of mutual funds that fits those guidelines. For instance, if you are saving for a retirement that's more than 20 years down the road, you may want to invest largely in stock funds, possibly overweighting those that favor fast-growing but risky companies. If you stick to more conservative bond and money-market funds, your investment may not grow fast enough to meet your investment goals. On the other hand, if you're a newly-wed hoping to buy your first home in the next five years, you'll want to stay away from risky, aggressive funds, because if the market is in slump when it comes time to sell, you may actually lose capital, and find that a house is out of reach.

Whether your investment profile points to a need for a more aggressive approach to investing or a more cautious one, the process of setting goals will sharply reduce the number of fund types you'll need to consider when you begin your fund research. Indeed, knowing *why* you need to invest will help to make the decision of *where* you should invest much less complicated.

Sorting Through the Funds

Once you've set a goal and calculated how much money you'll need to invest to meet that goal, it's time to start the search for those funds that best fit the bill. When winnowing down the types of funds you should be targeting and that suit your investment profile, you'll need to compare the following factors to help you narrow the field of funds: past performance, total return, costs, and risk.

Past Performance: Headline-grabbing performance figures blaring out from advertisements and fund-rating lists are often the first thing that catches a prospective investor's eye. A fund's past performance is important, but not for the reasons you might think. Studies have shown that funds that put in top-ranking performance in one year

It is important to get used to thinking about funds in terms of categories—that is, the types of investments they make and the level of risk that the fund managers take on with the investments they hold in the funds' portfolios. Funds' performances are often viewed in relation to their peers (other funds in the same category). That makes sense, because if you decide that a fund investing primarily in risky small stocks is right for you, you want to be sure that your small-stock fund is the best one around. Category types also are used extensively in the Internet-based tools you may use to help determine which funds to buy.

There are no hard and fast rules for how funds are divided into categories. Each research firm or online resource has its own names for its categories—sometimes called fund sectors or groups—and its own rules for assigning funds into categories. But in general, the names are descriptive. Of course you'll encounter broad terms such as conservative and aggressive, which describe the level of risk you face of losing some or all of the money you've invested. (Losing your money is a risk you face when buying any fund. They aren't insured by the federal government like bank deposits are.) Beyond the general descriptions of risk, funds are categorized by the assets they hold. The terms stock and bond are easy to understand, but you'll also see other terms, such as blend, mixed, and flexible, which mean the fund can hold a combination of investments.

Digging in further, you'll find that bond funds often are divided into categories based on the characteristics of the bonds they hold. So you may encounter categories such as taxable (including bonds issued by corporations, whose interest payments are taxed by the IRS), nontaxable (which will include municipal bonds, whose interest isn't taxed by the federal government), and myriad categories based on locations. (Note: States generally don't tax their residents on interest earned on bonds sold by the state itself.)

Stock funds are broken into scores of categories. The broadest groupings are based on the market value of the individual stocks held in the funds' portfolios, so you'll find words such as small, midsize, and large. Small stocks usually have a total stock market value of several billion dollars or less, while large stocks are often considered to be those with a total value of around $5 billion or more.

The investment philosophy of funds is another broad characteristic used to sort them. The term growth is used to describe funds that favor stocks of companies whose earnings and stock prices tend to grow quickly, but also are more volatile (companies must take risks to make big gains, and they end up stumbling at times). Value describes funds that buy shares of companies that have already stumbled, in hopes of profiting if those companies recover. Finally, you'll also encounter many stock-fund categories based on industry groups.

often log better-than-average returns in the subsequent year. But that seems to be the extent of any performance persistence. While past performance is not a reliable indicator of future returns, volatility of past returns *is* a good indicator of a fund's future volatility. If a fund you're considering seems to seesaw from the top to the bottom of ranking lists and back again over time, it's a good bet that that sort of volatility will continue in future years.

It is also important to look at past performance of the managers who run the funds you are considering. A fund that has been consistently hot wouldn't seem as appealing if the fund manager who was making the stock picks suddenly left. Finding this kind of data isn't as easy as finding data on fund performance. It is easy to check the five-year performance of Fidelity Magellan Fund, but not so easy to put your finger on the five-year performance of Robert Stansky, who has managed the fund since 1996. Still, many financial Web sites include information on how long a manager has been with a fund. Check that out at the same time you look at the funds' returns.

Total Return: Because the market is not static and fund values rise and fall each day, it's important to look not only at the share price, but also at the fund's total return. Total return measures not only gains and losses in the value of a fund's share price, but also takes into account the reinvestment of any income and capital-gains distributions. Most fund prospectuses show a yearly total return figure for the most recent ten-year period. Comparing year-to-year changes in total return is a good way to see how stable the fund's returns have been over time.

Costs: Figuring out how much a fund charges each year in fees and expenses can be a real headache, but it's a crucial factor in your investment choice, because costs lower your fund's overall return. A fund that charges an up-front load and high expenses has to put in a better performance than a low-cost fund, just to stay even. There are two main categories of costs to consider: sales loads and transaction fees, and ongoing annual fund expenses.

Risk: Every investment involves risk, and it's important to determine how much risk is appropriate for any fund that you are considering. Even funds of the same type can have significantly different levels of risks. For example, funds that have put in the best performances throughout the bull market of the 1990s, such as technology and Internet sector funds, usually are ranked very low in terms of risk-adjusted performance.

Put another way, investors were exposed to an extreme level of volatility in return for those stellar returns. Fund-rating services such as Morningstar and Value Line rank risk in terms of beta, a measurement of how volatile a fund is in comparison to a benchmark market indicator, such as the Standard & Poor's 500-stock index. A fund with a beta of higher than 1.0 (1.0 = the benchmark index) would be expected to outperform the market, while one below that figure would likely underperform. But a beta of greater than 1.0 also means the fund is volatile. In bad times, the value of these funds may fall much more than the major market indexes.

Other important things to consider when selecting a fund are manager tenure, performance in its best and worst years, and total net assets.

"Screening" Mutual Funds

It could take hours to plow through the pages of just a handful of mutual fund prospectuses to find the ones that are best for you, taking into consideration all of the factors outlined above. But luckily, resources found on the Internet do much of the work for you. Many fund Web sites offer interactive tools that collect data on thousands of funds and then let you "screen" or pinpoint the types of funds that most directly suit your needs. Say, for instance, you're interested in investing in a growth fund that has a low minimum initial investment and low expenses, yet ranks high in performance over the last five years. A screening tool will drill down into its database of growth funds and provide a ranking of the ones that come closest to matching those variables.

Here is how it works: Each screening tool is somewhat different—and some of the most powerful are tricky and may take some time to get used to—but the basic concepts are the same for all. Essentially, you fill out a form on a Web page that tells the screening tool just what you aim to find. The first question on many screens is a basic query as to what categories of funds you are interested in. Using a drop-down menu—those Web site mainstays that, with a click of a mouse, expand to reveal a list of options or choices—you may may select simply "stock

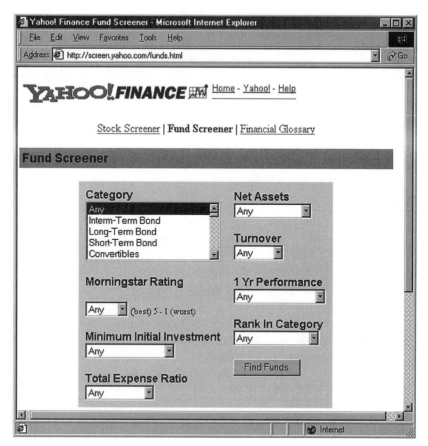

Reproduced with the permission of Yahoo! Inc. © 2000 by Yahoo! Inc. Yahoo! and the Yahoo! logo are trademarks of Yahoo! Inc.

funds." Or you may narrow your preference, selecting "growth," or narrower still, "small company growth."

From there, you specify other criteria that are important to you in selecting a specific small-company growth fund. Using a drop-down menu again, or perhaps a box on the Web site where you can simply type in your preferences, you may specify that you'd like to see only the small-company growth funds that gained more than 10% last year. In a separate box, you may specify that you want only funds that charge a modest sales charge—say, less than 1% of the amount you invest. And you may want a fund that allows a small initial investment. You may select "less than $1,000" from that menu.

Once all of your selections are made, the screening tool will begin its search. Behind the scenes, it taps into enormous databases of information held in computers at the Web-site operator. Poured into those databases is information from thousands of funds' prospectuses, annual reports, and other documents—the information that fund companies are required to disclose to the Securities and Exchange Commission on a regular basis—as well as data on fund performance and the performance of benchmark stock indexes. Within seconds, the computer sorts through the nuggets of information you are most interested in and returns a list of funds that meet your criteria.

If the list is too long, you may want to refine your search. If the search comes up empty, it may be time to adjust your goals (maybe you better aim for a somewhat smaller return or accept a somewhat larger sales charge). Once you have a manageable list, you can continue your research—and perhaps prepare to make a purchase. Some of the best sites also offer links to prospectus information on the funds, allowing you to perform an even more detailed comparison once you've narrowed your search to a few funds.

Screening tools are among the most popular and useful resources available to mutual fund investors on the Web. They put the power of research—which just several years ago was available only through financial planners and brokers—on the desktop of any investor with an Internet connection. Screening is offered at sites run by fund companies, brokerage firms, newspapers, magazines, and scores of research firms—including many upstarts that owe their existance to the Net. Many basic screens are free, but sites often require a subscription fee for the most sophisticated tools.

One of the best fund-screening tools can be found at Quote.com (**www.quote.com**). The screen sifts through more than 7,500 funds using data from Lipper Inc. and Morningstar, allowing investors to choose funds that meet any number of variables. If you've already trimmed your search to a handful of funds, and would like to compare just those using one particular variable, such as volatility, turnover (the rate at which a fund buys investment positions and then sells them), and one-, three-, and five-year return, try SmartMoney.com's Fund Analyzer (**www.smartmoney.com**).

Fund screens and analyzers can also highlight any overlap you may have in your portfolio. For example, if you find that the performance of your large-company growth fund closely tracks your technology fund, there may be a good reason—both could be holding large positions in widely held technology stocks, such as Microsoft or Intel. That kind of overlap in your investment portfolio can be risky, particularly in times of a protracted market slump. Currently, the SEC requires that mutual fund companies report on their funds' top ten holdings only once each quarter. A number of fund companies have set up Web sites that provide more timely fund data and rating information to users for free. But the best information generally isn't on the Web sites run by fund companies themselves.

BEST OF THE WEB

Investors' insatiable hunger for mutual fund information has spawned a cottage industry on the Internet: There are more than 500 sites devoted to mutual fund investors. In addition, most fund companies, brokerages, and banks have set up their own Web sites, where you can get basic information about the funds they offer, along with some rudimentary financial-planning tools. Often, visitors to these sites must sign up to access expanded services, such as educational materials and portfolio tracking tools.

Any number of investment-related sites provide data on fund company holdings for free, but, as in the real world, you tend to get what you pay for. For example, information provided on these sites might not be updated frequently enough for you to make informed investment decisions, or the fund evaluations and investment guidance provided may be influenced by the advertisers that sponsor the site.

But a number of sites are packed with useful information that can be tailored to your specific needs. What follows are some of the highest-quality Internet sites geared toward mutual fund investors, each specializing in a certain aspect of fund investing. On most, you'll find basic information about mutual fund investing, articles about the industry, individual fund information, and data and fund manager profiles, as well as chat and discussion areas.

Morningstar.com
(www.morningstar.com)

Chicago-based mutual fund tracking company Morningstar Inc. is hands down one of the best sites on the Internet for mutual fund research and commentary. Its Web site, Morningstar.com, is updated daily, and includes commentary on fund performance, portfolio makeovers, and in-depth data on thousands of individual funds—including its popular Stars ratings for individual funds. The site's helpful Quicktake feature lets you look up performance data, portfolio holdings, and other information on more than 7,000 funds. The site also includes a group of message boards where visitors can discuss broad in-

vestment strategies or share their thoughts on individual funds and fund families. The biggest drawback to this site is that its most useful tools and research can be accessed only by subscribing to its premium service ($9.95 per month, or $99 a year). The premium service features a number of targeted "X-ray" screening tools, one of which compares your portfolio's allocation to different investment strategies. (Is your balanced fund acting more like a growth fund?) Another helpful tool analyzes your fund portfolio's vulnerability to economic and political turmoil around the world, including in North America, Europe, Asia, and Latin America.

Standard & Poor's Personal Wealth
(www.personalwealth.com)

The Standard & Poor's site includes access to the company's vast databases of news, analysis, and fund recommendations. A fund search tool and educational area offers planning assistance to both novice and seasoned investors. Like Morningstar, the site includes a premium service ($9.95 a month, or $100 per year) that offers deeper financial-planning tools, the capacity to customize your own home page, and proprietary S&P investment recommendations.

Mutual Fund Investor's Center
(www.mfea.com)

Operated by the Mutual Fund Education Alliance, a Kansas City, Missouri, trade group for no-load funds, this is a great place to start if you're a beginner investor. What you won't get at this site is critical analysis of the no-load fund industry, so take advantage of the site's superior education and financial planning areas and steer clear of actual fund recommendations. Its Education Center is geared toward the basics: explaining how to read a prospectus, how to track fund listings, and the tax consequences to you when a fund makes a distribution. The site's Planning Center helps you understand better what type of investor you are, through questionnaires and worksheets. And a newly launched Retirement Center helps you figure out how much money you'll need to retire and explains the benefits of including mutual funds in tax-deferred plans such as Individual Retirement Accounts, 401(k) plans, and other employer-sponsored retirement-savings accounts.

Quicken.com
(www.quicken.com)

This site combines the strengths of Intuit Corp.'s Quicken personal-finance software program with the authoritative commentary of Morningstar and news from CNN's financial channel. The site includes fund analysis and evaluations from Morningstar, and a host of financial planning retirement-savings worksheets and calculators. Its "Fund Finder" lets you screen funds based on 15 criteria, including performance, investment style, and management fees. For example, you can build a list of top-performing large-growth funds with below-average fees.

Yahoo! Finance
(finance.yahoo.com)

The most widely used Internet search engine also features a wealth of financial information at this site. There's much to choose from here, including the ability to create and track your own portfolio, participate in electronic bulletin boards, and read news about mutual funds. While the novice investor will find the site's familiar interface and fund news and research more than adequate to meet their needs, sophisticated investors may find the site most useful as a jumping-off point to other financial resources on the Web.

Invest-o-rama!
(www.investorama.com)

Beginner investors may find this information-packed site a fun read, but more serious-minded investors could find themselves cringing at the site's excessive use of exclamation points (!!!!) in its commentary. There are also features for tracking portfolios, screening funds, charting, and research. Like Yahoo! Finance, this site is a great place to start your fund journey—its mutual fund category offers links to dozens of Web sites that cater to almost every type of investor. And those seeking the most extensive breakdown of mutual fund Web sites on the Internet need look no further than Invest-o-rama's Mutual Fund Analysis and Research center, a mind-numbing catalog of links accompanied by brief descriptions of the best the sites have to offer.

FundAlarm
(www.fundalarm.com)

Set far apart from the rest of the online fund community is FundAlarm, a quirky site geared toward advising investors on the right time to sell their mutual funds. But even if you're happy with your holdings, this site can help you identify funds to avoid. It ranks funds that have consistently failed to beat the market over time, and offers insightful, and often extremely amusing, criticism of funds and their managers in the site's Highlights and Commentary section.

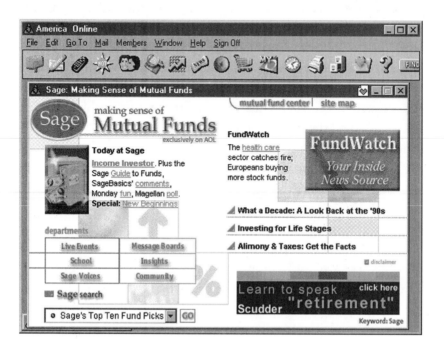

Sage at America Online

AOL, the Internet online service provider, features the excellent Sage mutual fund site available through the personal finance channel on AOL's dial-up service. The Sage School section of the site calls itself the place where "the love of investing meets the love of learning." It offers an easy-to-understand course on mutual funds, beginning with an article that answers the question: What is a mutual fund? The site offers descriptions of the different types and styles of funds available, hints on how to choose a fund, and how to develop good investment habits. The site's glossary of terms explains the most basic mutual fund terminology, and there is a chat room for beginning investors.

U.S. Securities and Exchange Commission
(www.sec.gov)

While not the prettiest site on the Web or the easiest to use, the Securities and Exchange Commission's Web site serves up just the facts. What it lacks in beauty, it makes up for in depth. Its Edgar (Electronic Data Gathering, Analysis, and Retrieval) database of all the documents that fund companies are required to file electronically with the SEC is an invaluable resource for a prospective investor. The reports date back to January 1994, or you can access the last week's, last two weeks', or last month's worth of activity. (New filings are delayed for two days on the SEC site, but several commercial services offer immediate access to filings as soon as they are entered into the Edgar system. The commercial services generally charge about $10 a month.) Aside from Edgar, the SEC site also includes investor assistance and education information, including tips for novice investors, and information from the watchdog agency's enforcement division, complete with investor alerts.

And, of course,

The Wall Street Journal Interactive Edition
(wsj.com)

The Interactive Journal offers detailed "Briefing Books" on thousands of funds, including performance information and background on fees, investment requirements, distributions, and major holdings—all from Lipper. In addition, the site offers interactive charting, daily updates on prices, and other performance measures for closed-end funds, quarterly special reports on U.S., European, and Asian funds, as well as all the news stories from the *Journal*'s daily coverage of the mutual fund industry.

Online Newsletters

Mutual fund newsletters track and publish statistics and returns for mutual funds, or make recommendations on fund purchases based on their unique investing strategies. Many build sample mutual fund investment portfolios, and recommend what to buy or sell in that portfolio depending on market conditions. Dozens of newsletters cover the mutual fund industry, and the choices can be overwhelming. If you already have a print favorite, chances are you'll find its electronic counterpart online.

Most online newsletters devoted to mutual funds are focused on a specific type of investment or trading technique. One publication might cater to investors looking for tips on investing in small-capitalization funds, while another might focus on helping subscribers increase their portfolios' performance through market timing. And some of the biggest fund families have spawned independent newsletters that seek to help shareholders make the right investment choices within a particular family. Fidelity Monitor (**www.fidelitymonitor.com**) is a monthly newsletter advisory service ($116 per year) that focuses exclusively on Fidelity mutual funds. Its goal is to help shareholders get the best performance from a mix of Fidelity funds while keeping loads and transaction fees to a minimum.

Because most online newsletters charge subscribers hefty annual fees, it would be prudent to get an objective opinion from an outside source on any newsletter you're considering subscribing to. And there's no better place on the Web for objective ratings of financial publications than the Hulbert Financial Digest Web site (**www. hulbertdigest.com**), the newsletter of investment newsletters, dealing with both stocks and mutual funds. The Hulbert Financial Digest provides ratings of more than 160 newsletters and 450 portfolios. Each month it reports the top five performing newsletters from this list (over various time periods), and includes a separate section dedicated only to mutual fund newsletters. Hulbert's updates allow you to compare your fund choices with funds that currently are most heavily recommended, or shunned, by the newsletter industry. But be warned: This type of comprehensive coverage comes at a price. You'll pay $59 for 12 monthly online issues of the Hulbert Financial Digest, which includes a complete newsletter directory and long-term performance ratings dating back to 1980. The newsletter is also available in print.

Online Bulletin Boards and Chats

The Internet is overflowing with sites where you can meet with other online investors to talk about your favorite investment, and sometimes even speak directly with an investment specialist in a live discussion forum. Participating in chat and bulletin board discussions can also be a therapeutic way of getting something off your chest. Whether you're frustrated at your funds' recent performance or angered by a recent blunder by your online broker, the boards offer a way to vent, interject new thoughts, or challenge the investment advice of others.

Bulletin boards and chats are virtual meeting places where people with common interests can communicate. The main difference between the two is in the timing of the conversation. With an electronic bulletin board, much like the corkboard variety, messages that are posted may remain in place for days, weeks, or months, and could elicit a posted response (and further discussion) at any time during that period. Time is more compressed in a chat, which can last anywhere from just several minutes up to several hours. Comments and responses are displayed almost immediately.

In their best form, bulletin boards and chats allow people to share information and help educate one another. But there is an ugly side, too. Just like in any conversation, arguments can develop, and online arguments are sometimes particularly bitter and nasty. Moreover, the anonymity that the Internet often affords means that online bulletin boards and chats have become a popular place for people trying to scam investors. (For more information on bulletin boards, chats—and scams—see "Message Boards" and "Scams and Deceptions," Chapters 7 and 8.)

Unfortunately, most financial sites that include live chat and bulletin board areas are usually geared toward the discussion of individual stock action. Morningstar is one of the few sites that have bulletin boards dedicated to specific funds, the way many other bulletin board sites dedicate boards to specific stocks. However, only a small number of individual funds—such as Fidelity's giant Magellan Fund—have their own boards, even on Morningstar. The Morningstar site also has broad-based discussion boards for different types of investors (novices, market-timers, etc.), and both it and Sage, the AOL service, have bulletin boards devoted to specific fund companies, where any fund in the family may be discussed.

MAKING THE TRADE

There's no reason to log off when you are finally ready to use all of the research and analysis that you have done on the Net. You can buy and sell shares of thousands of funds through Web sites run by online brokerage firms, and some fund companies themselves. But it isn't all as straightforward as buying or selling a stock online, where any brokerage firm can trade any stock listed on a public market and commissions are generally uniform within each firm. Not all mutual funds can be bought or sold at all brokerage firms, even the biggest and most well established. Further, commissions and fees can be confusing. Many brokerage firms charge commissions on purchases of funds that come without an initial sales charge, or load, when purchased directly from the fund family. In some cases, those fees can be high, at $20 or more per trade.

The variety of funds that are available, as well as the commissions that are charged on transactions, differ from one brokerage firm to another, so it pays to do some research on firms' Web sites before trying to place an order. Unlike the stock market, where transactions are funneled through a major stock exchange or the Nasdaq Stock Market, there is no open public market for mutual funds. So the fund availability from any given brokerage firm comes down to the relationships it has struck with fund firms. The firms that have most relationships, the greatest selection, and, they'd contend, the best prices, have come to be known as fund supermarkets.

But setting up an account at a fund firm, or an online brokerage firm, isn't as easy as pointing and clicking. An investor can't open an account online, because fund companies must have a customer's signature on file first. Savvy fund companies are at least trying to cut down on the waiting time by allowing prospective customers to download and print out a sign-up form, making it easier to fill out the form and mail in a check quickly.

Another obstacle in quickly setting up an online account is the transfer of funds. While customers can authorize an electronic transfer of funds from their savings or checking accounts, that process can take several days. And federal regulations bar customers from using a credit card to open an account. Once an account is established and the initial funds are in place, though, online trading can greatly speed subsequent mutual fund transactions—especially within a supermarket.

Shopping Fund Supermarkets

When King Kullen opened the first American grocery supermarket in 1930, consumers abandoned their local butcher, baker, and farmers market in favor of the selection, convenience, and lower prices offered at these new superstores. This same phenomenon has transformed the world of mutual fund investing with the introduction of the mutual fund supermarket. Fund supermarkets allow investors to pick from a host of mutual funds offered by hundreds of investment companies, with no commission costs, rather than jumping from site to site in order to evaluate and purchase funds from different fund companies. Across the industry, supermarkets represented 21% of fund sales in

1997, up from less than 13% in 1993, according to Boston's Financial Research Corporation.

Pioneered in 1984 by Charles Schwab, fund supermarkets were hailed as convenient distribution outlets that would help fund companies of all sizes compete. While the grand opening of Schwab's Mutual Fund One-Source (**www.schwab.com**) supermarket service featured less than 10 participating fund firms, it now offers the wares of hundreds of firms. Of course, the Schwab supermarket predates the explosive growth of Internet trading. In its early days, most investors shopped from Schwab over the telephone or by stopping by a branch office.

Following Schwab's lead, more mutual fund companies are moving to set up a presence on the Internet that will provide clients with one-stop shopping. Even traditional brick-and-mortar full-service institutions that in the past shunned the Internet are getting into the act in order to stem the flow of clients to the Internet. In March 1999, Merrill Lynch, which had been one of the Internet's biggest detractors on Wall Street, launched its own online fund supermarket, Mutual Fund Advisor Selects.

Investing the old way, an investor would have to call each fund's customer service number, tell the representative how many shares he wanted to redeem, and then wait up to a week before the check was mailed to his home. Once the check was deposited into his bank account, he would begin the process of opening up a new account at another fund company, and wait several more days for his application and check to be processed before the money was actually invested in the fund of his choice.

But by using Schwab's online fund supermarket, redeeming fund shares and purchasing new ones can be done within minutes—and at no cost, assuming you are buying one of the no-transaction-fee funds. You simply log on to the Schwab site, then type in the fund's symbol and the number of shares you would like to purchase. Shares are purchased at the fund's closing NAV price on the day an order is placed, allowing you to capitalize on the fund's performance immediately.

The shift taking place in the securities industry toward fund supermarkets makes it clear that they have become one of the most popular ways to invest online. Internet brokerage companies such as E*Trade (**www.etrade.com**) and Waterhouse Securities (**www.waterhouse.com**), which made their name on the Net by offering bargain-priced commissions on stock trades, are now offering a full complement of investment services, including their own family of funds and access to fund supermarkets.

Is Supermarket Investing Right for You?

If you're already made funds a staple of your investment portfolio, you're probably juggling a half dozen or more funds from a number of different fund families. If this is the case, consolidating your holdings through an online supermarket could simplify your life.

Fund supermarkets effectively let an investor create his or her own individual fund family from a variety of investment companies at the click of a button. An investor interested in a garden-variety index fund can pick up shares of Janus Twenty Fund—a portfolio of 20 stocks of large, fast-growing U.S. companies—in, say, "Aisle 4." Or for something with a more international flavor, he might step to "Aisle 7" for a helping of Janus WorldWide. At the "checkout counter," the order is rung up with no commission charge (though the fund family itself may still charge an initial investment fee, or load).

Many investors appreciate the convenience of being able to transfer cash from one fund to another without the three-to-five-day period you'd endure waiting to receive redeemed funds directly from fund companies, and the similar wait to set up an account at a new firm.

Buying all your funds through one supermarket also has the added benefit of minimizing the amount of paperwork you'll have to contend with throughout the year: Fund holdings are typically consolidated into one easy-to-read accounting statement, which in most cases can be accessed at any time on the Web site. Supermarkets also eliminate the hassle of coordinating your paperwork at tax time by mailing clients a single Form 1099 showing the previous year's share purchases and redemptions from each of your fund holdings.

But there are a number of drawbacks to supermarket-style investing. While there are no fees charged directly for purchasing funds through a supermarket, the convenience of quickly swapping in and out of funds does come at a cost. Supermarket operators like Schwab and Fidelity Investments (**www.fidelity.com**) have raised the fees they charge fund management companies to put the products on their "shelves," and the fund companies have been passing those charges directly to shareholders in the form of higher annual marketing and distribution fees. These fees are listed in a fund's prospectus as 12b-1 charges, named after the authorizing rule of the Investment Company Act of 1940.

While most sites claim that fund purchases come at no cost, some supermarket operators have even taken to charging additional fees to penalize investors for selling shares of a fund before a specified amount of time—say, six months. These charges are meant to combat flipping, or trading in and out of fund shares frequently in an attempt to time the market.

And many of the best-known fund families have opted against joining supermarkets on a no-transaction-fee basis. Vanguard Group (**www.vanguard.com**) and T. Rowe Price Associates Inc. (**www. troweprice.com**) are two of the biggest fund families that have refused. Before you decide to open an account at an online brokerage, make sure that it carries the type of funds, or fund families, you're interested in.

And, with supermarket investing, multiple types of investment accounts—a Roth individual retirement account, or more than one IRA—typically are not consolidated into one account statement. That is bad news for those who had hoped supermarket investing would free them from the dreaded tidal wave of monthly mailings.

A final consideration: Many fund supermarkets do not provide you with transaction histories from your old fund companies, so when tax time rolls around, you'll be on your own in determining the cost basis of fund shares originally purchased directly from a fund company.

Extra Services at the Supermarket

With grocery supermarkets, consumers often have a wide variety of choices available within a short driving distance, and price differences most times are negligible. So supermarket operators have had to expand their store sizes, shelf space, and product offerings—increasing the variety of name-brand foods and incorporating in-store banks and pharmacies—to entice shoppers to choose them over their competitors. Similarly, online fund supermarkets are scrambling to add services.

For instance, for a fee, both Schwab and Fidelity offer a network of financial planners who are knowledgeable about the thousands of load and no-load funds available on their sites, and can help suggest the proper mix. These and other fund supermarkets are adding the same types of interactive tools for screening and analyzing funds that are available so many other places on the Web.

E*Trade's site offers a free screening feature that lets users sort through the more than 3,000 funds it offers by seventeen criteria, including performance, how frequently the funds buy and sell investments, and manager tenure. Schwab and Scudder Funds (**www.scudder.com**) both offer useful asset-allocation worksheets that are based on the user's investment horizon, investment goals, and tolerance for risk.

Fidelity's financial-planning tools are rather sparse, including a simple questionnaire to help you determine the proper asset-allocation model for you, based on time horizon, current financial situation, and risk tolerance. The site also offers a fund evaluator, which uses data from Morningstar to compare more than 800 no-load funds.

Overall, your best bet is to start your search for the right mix of funds at a more comprehensive site, such as Morningstar, which provides the necessary screening tools to help you make an informed decision about what funds to choose. Then, when you've compiled a list of funds that meet your investment criteria, tour the various online supermarkets to determine which one offers all of the funds on your list at the most reasonable cost..

Using Fund Company Web Sites

In the past, fund companies were slow to embrace the Internet, wary of security issues and the substantial costs involved in adding major Web site enhancements.

But the pace has been picking up rapidly as more upstart Internet brokers convince droves of online investors to do their shopping at fund supermarkets. According to an October 1997 survey of 187 U.S. fund companies by the Investment Company Institute, half of those companies had created Web sites, but few had adopted the latest bells and whistles. The ICI represents about 95% of the mutual fund industry in terms of assets.

Still, most fund company Web sites provide a lot of marketing information, but little else. As recently as 1998, only one third of existing fund company Web sites allowed investors to download fund prospectuses, and roughly 20% provided service forms or account applications. While 25% of the mutual fund Web sites let investors access personal account information, only 11% of the sites allowed investors to move money among different funds within the family. And just 5% provided bulletin boards where clients can chat with mutual fund managers, executives, or one another.

Despite these dismal numbers, investors continue to cite a fund company's Web site as their preferred method for contacting their representatives and getting the latest information on the fund company's management and investment strategy. A survey conducted by Morningstar.com in mid-1998 of users of its Web site showed that 27% of respondents picked fund company Web sites as the most efficient way to communicate with a fund company, although many said they have a hard time finding what they need quickly.

Tellingly, an overwhelming number of respondents said they'd choose a fund company's Web site over a toll-free phone number late at night, when telephone customer service often is unavailable or understaffed. By contacting the fund company by e-mail, investors can get responses to their questions in writing, which tend to be more detailed, and often much more accurate, than responses given by representatives over the phone. One drawback, however, is that electronic communication between funds and clients still takes far too long to process. Many messages tend to go unanswered, and a 24-hour wait for a response is standard.

Big Fund Families Lead the Charge

There have been some significant improvements in many major fund family sites. Fidelity Investments, of course, runs a massive site where one can buy and sell its more than 150 mutual funds, or shop its FundsNetwork supermarket, offering hundreds of funds run by other firms. Dreyfus (**www.dreyfus.com**) offers account access for investors who want to view their balances. And it has added detailed fact sheets on all Dreyfus funds, including daily performance numbers.

The Janus Funds site (**www.janus.com**) allows users to trade funds electronically. The revamped site also includes links to daily performance figures, account histories, Morningstar rankings, and a monthly address from Jim Craig, Janus's chief investment officer. T. Rowe Price is another company whose site (**www.troweprice.com**) has been improving. You'll find Fund Fact sheets with a summary, performance data, and charts comparing each fund with its benchmark, as well as market reports and calculators.

At Safeco's site (**www.safecofunds.com**), investors can check fund returns and asset balance, and tap into real-time online customer service support. Vanguard, whose site (**www.vanguard.com**) ranks among the best fund company entries the Internet has to offer, features an asset-allocation program, Navigator Plus. Just input your personal information, and the program generates a customized investment allocation.

The Internet provides mutual fund companies with the unique opportunity to keep clients updated on changes in the market that may effect fund performance. For example, in times of increased market volatility, a fund company might try to ease concerns among new investors by keeping them updated with running market analysis. Or a fund site could give clients a heads up soon after changes are made in the fund's top 10 holdings.

But the sad truth is that relatively few fund companies take full advantage of the Internet's potential to reach clients. A survey of some of the largest fund companies' Web sites shows a wasteland of dated and quite often useless information, or data that can be found for free at hundreds of more comprehensive financial Web sites.

While most fund companies feature their latest quarterly reports, a surprising number of sites serve up data more than six months old. Even more frustrating is the trend among fund companies to offer crucial information about the fund, such as its prospectus and most recent annual performance data, in a mammoth downloadable file that requires Adobe Acrobat—a software program used to view computer files that are essentially a snapshot of a printed page—and, depending on the speed of your Internet connection, a lot of time to spare. Citing security reasons, few companies have been willing to allow their clients to access account information online.

One area where fund company sites appear to be of use to their customers is tax information, including details on mutual fund year-end distributions. Mutual Fund Education Alliance (**www.mfea.com**) maintains a list of fund companies that have posted their annual distributions, both estimated and actual, on their Web sites.

At Vanguard's Web site, shareholders have the option to "shut off paper" on their accounts, or stop postal mailings of fund materials and quarterly reports, and instead receive e-mailed notifications of when fund reports and other notices are available online.

KEEPING TRACK OF YOUR FUNDS

By keeping close tabs on your portfolio, you can figure out whether your investments are paying off—or whether you should sell some laggard holdings and maybe even change your investment strategy.

Keeping track of your mutual fund investments has never been easier, thanks to the Web. Mutual fund NAV quotes and portfolio-tracking tools, featured on practically every financial-planning and investment Web site, allow you to update your portfolio's value daily, so you can see day by day exactly how your investments are performing. Many sites offer online portfolio trackers free to investors who'll register with the site to use them, and for a small fee several sites offer trackers with features that for some may be worth the cost. Try out trackers on a couple of your favorite investment sites to find the one you like best.

Investor Guide (**www.investorguide.com**) includes a list of sites that feature exceptional portfolio-tracking resources available through various financial Web sites, via e-mail or by downloading proprietary software. Investor Guide also helpfully separates the free from the fee-based services, and gives a brief description of each tool. Sites that offer the option to receive an end-of-day e-mail summary of your portfolio can be valuable to investors who want a quick and easy update on their investments.

Another important aspect of keeping track comes when you buy, sell, or transfer shares and funds electronically. Every time you buy or sell shares in a fund, you should receive some form of confirmation from your fund company, either by e-mail or postal mail. Check carefully to be sure that each trade was completed according to your instructions. Check to see that the correct number of shares are bought or sold, and make sure the buying or selling price is charged as quoted. Be sure the commissions or fees are what your broker said they would be.

Most important, watch out for "unauthorized" trades in your account. If you receive a confirmation slip for a transaction that you didn't approve, call the fund company representative immediately. It may have been a mistake. If it happens more than once, or if your broker refuses to correct it, call the SEC or your state securities regulator. (You can learn more about seeking recourse when you feel you've been wronged by your broker or fund company in "Recourse," Chapter 9.)

FIVE

Bonds, Futures, and Options

Bonds, commodity futures, and options have been outcasts of the cyber-investing revolution. While stocks and mutual funds exploded in popularity, investors on the Net shied away from these investments—and brokerage firms were in no rush to offer online services. As a result, just a sliver of the hundreds of billions of dollars that are invested over the Internet go into bonds, futures, and options.

One big reason for the slow Internet start is that these investments can be tricky. Investing in stocks can be as simple as buying some shares, hoping for them to rise in value, and occasionally, perhaps, getting a dividend check in the mail. But with bonds, you have to worry about things such as "call" features, which could suddenly cash you out of your investment. With options, you may need complicated formulas to figure out if you are paying too much, and with commodity futures, you can be exposed to wild volatility triggered by hard-to-predict outside factors—such as the weather.

Moreover, investors have had little reason to look beyond stocks and funds. Stocks enjoyed a long-running bull market during the 1990s, just as the Internet was taking root in the investment world. In a time when the stock market was routinely delivering annual returns of more than 15%, investors didn't have much incentive to look into alternative investments. There's no need to move to the safety of bonds, or take a chance on options and futures, if stocks and funds are providing solid, reliable returns.

But that doesn't mean that alternative investments won't take on a greater presence on the Web, albeit slowly. Wall Street is expanding its Web offerings beyond stocks and funds, and investors—over time—are expected to take notice, especially during difficult times in the stock market. Do-it-yourself investors continue to become more savvy about the markets, and brokerage firms are getting better at delivering services over the Net.

BONDS: THE BASICS

When many people think of investing, the first thing that comes to mind is the stock market. After all, stocks are more appealing and are considered sexier than bonds. They are easier to understand and have historically outperformed bonds and other financial assets over the long haul. Still, while stocks can generate hearty profits, most financial advisers recommend at least a modest investment in bonds for long-term investors.

When an investor buys a bond, he or she is simply lending money to some other party, usually a corporation or government. The party receiving the money is known as the bond's issuer (a bond—or a stock, for that matter—is called an issue). The federal government sells bonds to investors so that it can get money to cover its expenses that are not covered by taxes and the like. Corporations borrow money from bond investors for new factories and equipment. City roads, airports, and schools are built with money municipal governments borrow from investors by issuing bonds.

A bond is a debt security, an I.O.U. It is a contract between the issuer and investor, much like a bank loan. It spells out the amount of money that is borrowed (the face value, or par value, of the bond), when it must be repaid (the date of maturity, usually between three months and 30 years), and the interest payment (called a coupon rate) the lender will receive (say 8%, or $80, per year on a $1,000 bond). Because the interest payments (the bond's investment return) are set, or fixed, by the bond's terms, bonds are sometimes called fixed-income investments.

Most individuals who invest in bonds don't trade them the way they do stocks. They buy and hold them until maturity. Bonds are especially attractive to investors nearing retirement or looking to preserve their wealth, because they are considered to be one of the safest forms of investments. Bonds provide a steady stream of income in the form of fixed interest payments. While many investors hold them to maturity, bonds do change hands in the market after they are issued.

However, not all bonds should be considered safe. Although they are quite often bought by investors for their perceived lower risk, bond values can fluctuate widely. Bonds can be hurt by inflation, rising interest rates, and the issuer's financial condition. Treasury bonds are considered the safest because they are backed by the U.S. government, which can raise taxes to pay off its debt to investors. Some bonds issued by corporations and municipalities can be just as risky as stocks because of the possibility the issuer may default—that is, become unable to pay its debts. Investors who buy these bonds are compensated for their risk with higher yields (the return on their investment). These high-yield bonds are sometimes called junk bonds.

To help determine how risky a particular bond is, you should pay attention to credit ratings. Several companies, known as ratings agencies, assess the ability of bond issuers to pay their debt—the same way credit agencies keep records that help banks and mortgage companies determine whether to loan you money for a car or house. These ratings agencies—Moody's Investors Service and Standard & Poor's Ratings Group are two of the most popular—assign a letter grade to each bond, from A to C. (Each letter has numerous increments.) Anything rated lower than Baa by Moody's or BBB by S&P is considered a junk bond.

Besides default risk and rising interest rates, the most overlooked bond-buying danger is complacency. Many investors buy a bond, put it in a safe-deposit box, and don't look at it again until it matures. But because interest rates and bond prices always change, the value of your bond portfolio will, too. It pays to keep track of the value of your bond holdings so you know where you stand. You may, for instance, find at some point that you need cash for an unexpected expense, and you would be in for a surprise if the bond you have decided to sell to raise the money has fallen sharply in value. You can avoid this situation by simply resolving to always hold your bonds until maturity, but of course, you may not always have that luxury. (Absent a default, at maturity, you get back the face amount of the bond, regardless of what the bond's value has been in the market over its life.)

Then there's tax danger. Because interest income is taxed at ordinary rates, it's best to put bonds in a tax-sheltered account and leave your interest payments there. (Stocks, which provide much of their returns from their increasing market value, primarily generate capital gains taxes, which are typically lower than ordinary income taxes.) Another overlooked danger: call provisions. Many bonds are sold with provisions that allow the issuer to pay off investors early. When interest rates fall, issuers often call their bonds (that is, pay off their loans early), forcing people who had invested in those bonds to scramble for a place to reinvest the cash they receive—often for a lower yield.

Generally speaking, there are two types of bond buyers. On the one hand, many people depend on bonds to provide a steady stream of income payments and simply want to protect the value of their original investment. (Stocks offer the chance for greater gains, but that comes with a greater risk of losing your original investment.) Other investors use bonds as a way to reduce the risk they face in their overall investment portfolio. They may put a lot of money in stocks—with hopes of nabbing profits from big gains in the market—but they hold some of their money in bonds, which provide a lesser return (in interest payments), but are less likely than stocks to have their value wiped out.

If you decide bonds are right for you, your next decision is choosing which maturities of bonds to buy. The traditional advice is to "ladder" your portfolio, and some Web brokerage firms offer tools to help you do this. Laddering simply means buying bonds maturing in a series of years—such as two-year, five-year, and then seven-year bonds—to guarantee a stream of interest payments that can be reinvested. Holding bonds with multiple maturities could allow you to get cash, if you find that you need it unexpectedly, without having to sell a bond, potentially at a loss, before its maturity.

Once you've decided what type of maturity to buy, you have to pick a bond. Those investors with a low tolerance for risk should stick to government-backed bonds issued by the Treasury Department (often referred to simply as Treasurys). Treasurys are also the easiest to buy, and help you avoid often onerous commissions charged on small-bond transactions. Through the Bureau of Public Debt's Treasury Direct program (**www.publicdebt.treas.gov**), individuals can participate in auctions of Treasury securities at no charge, unless their accounts are worth more than $100,000. If you sell a security before it matures, there's a $34 charge.

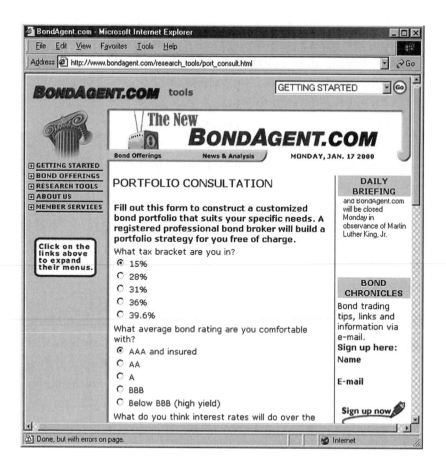

The Treasury Department also offers savings bonds, which can be purchased from banks or on the Bureau of Public Debt's Web site. Like Treasury bonds, savings bonds are backed by the U.S. government and accrue interest for up to thirty years. Their primary advantage for many people is the ease of making a purchase: You can buy them in denominations as small as $25 and can even purchase them via a payroll deduction.

Municipal bonds—sometimes called munis—should also play a part in many investors' bond portfolios, especially those of investors in higher tax brackets, because municipal bonds are free from federal and most often state taxes. For investors with a greater risk tolerance, corporate bonds may be the way to go. Their returns are taxable, but they typically provide higher yields than government bonds.

Bond Trading

Bonds make up the nation's largest securities market. About $350 billion of these fixed-income securities change hands daily in the market, dwarfing the $50 billion or so in stocks that trade each day. Nevertheless, the bond market still is shrouded in mystery. It is dominated almost completely by professional Wall Street dealers and institutional investors, such as insurance companies and pension funds, who buy and sell bonds in million-dollar amounts. Most deals are still negotiated over the telephone.

Bonds have lagged behind stocks in online trading precisely because of the bond market's mystery. Clear and up-to-the-minute price information is scarce because there is no central exchange on which bonds are traded, like there is for stocks. And prices vary widely. Thus, investors don't know if they are getting a good price when they buy or sell a bond. Also, brokerage commissions and other fees for stocks are clearly stated in confirmation slips and monthly statements. But bonds are different.

Someone who wants to buy or sell a bond calls a broker and asks for a price quote. The broker is free to name virtually any price, because there is no effective reporting mechanism that an investor can turn to for information about the price at which the bond has traded recently. To be sure that you are getting the best price available, you need to call numerous brokers and ask for a price. But that can be difficult on several levels. Not only is making repeated calls time-consuming, many firms won't provide a price unless you have an account. To make matters worse, the quotes are padded by built-in commissions—called markups or markdowns—that further obscure the price.

The absence of precise and timely information about prices has been a key obstacle to online bond trading, as have the market's decidedly low-tech roots. Some brokers still use pen and paper, rather than computers, to keep track of their inventory, and to update prices. While technology is pushing change, most trades still are conducted in the traditional fashion: using telephones and fax machines.

Also adding to the complexity of bringing bonds online is the quantity. While there are fewer than 15,000 stocks, the bond universe contains nearly 2 million issues, many of which trade infrequently. Moreover, bonds have many different characteristics, such as issuer, credit ratings, maturity date, and yield—all affecting the price. Even bonds from the same issuer aren't all the same.

Dan Burke, an analyst with Gomez Advisors, said all these unique variables make it that much more difficult to develop automated systems that would allow individuals to buy and sell bonds over the Internet as easily as stocks. But complex software and regulatory pressure are beginning to break down those barriers, leading to the development of some electronic bond-trading systems.

Electronic bond trading promises to make fixed-income investing more appealing to individual investors, make information about the market more readily available, lower trading costs, provide investors with better and more competitive prices, and improve efficiency for both investors and dealers. While these systems are removing some of the mystery of the bond market, there still is a long way to go before individuals will trade fixed-income securities online with as much enthusiasm as they have for trading stocks.

Although an increasing number of firms are developing online trading systems, these mostly cater to institutional clients instead of individual investors. These systems allow institutional investors to view an electronic list of bonds and quotes from one or more brokers and, in some cases, make automatic trades at prices that are posted. Most individuals who want to buy bonds still do so through a mutual fund or by contacting their broker. The broker then offers the investor something from the firm's own inventory or gets the bond from another Wall Street bond dealer.

Nevertheless, change is coming. A growing number of online brokers are focusing on individual investors' needs in the bond business, and useful sites for fixed-income investors are gaining users. Online brokers are hoping they can do for bonds what they did for stocks: make it cheaper and easier for investors to participate in the market. They also have their sights set on increasing business down the road as investors become risk-averse and look for additional investment opportunities.

BONDS: LOGGING ON

For individual investors who want to buy and sell bonds online, there still aren't that many choices for making actual trades and getting helpful information. Punch "stock investing" into an Internet search engine like Yahoo! and you're likely to be overwhelmed by the response. But type the words "bond investing" and you'll be lucky to find a handful of worthwhile Web pages.

Many bond sites on the Internet are geared toward institutional investors and professional brokers. They either restrict access to their powerful research and information and other analytical tools to licensed professionals, or, in most cases, those tools are simply too expensive for individuals. Many sites that allow electronic bond trading over the Internet (or through proprietary dial-up networks) require hefty minimum transactions, which many individuals won't be able to afford.

However, some sites are useful and accessible to individual investors. Some are hosted by brokerage firms, while others are watered-down versions of sites run for professional bond traders by commercial data vendors. These sites allow individuals access to information on bonds that only recently was available to just professionals, including delayed and real-time quotes from some dealers. Some are even paving the way for retail investors to execute transactions with the click of their computer mouse.

Research and Information

If you're are interested in investing in bonds on your own over the Internet, you should know where to look for basic information, research, tools, and other data that will put you in a much better position. General investing sites and other providers of financial news and information are good places to start. Try Briefing.com (**www.briefing.com**), TheStreet.com (**www.thestreet.com**), and The Wall Street Journal Interactive Edition (**www.wsj.com**). These three offer reports on market activity, broader trends on Wall Street and in the economy, and other basic information.

Many online and traditional brokerages also offer general information on bonds on their Web sites—even if they can't or don't allow investors to trade electronically just yet. Some offer research reports and analytic tools for fixed-income trading, although most restrict access to their paying clients or limit the amount of information available to guests. More on these Web sites later.

Here are some popular independent sites to get you going:

Investing in Bonds.com
(www.investinginbonds.com)

This free Web site, run by the Bond Market Association, a bond traders' industry group, is one of the best for novice investors. This site can help you understand bond basics, and it provides a broad array of information, including investing guides, research reports, historical data, and links to other sites.

The site also lists the previous day's prices for about 1,000 actively traded municipal bonds. Although this represents just a small fraction of the 1.5 million outstanding munis, the information could be very useful. It can help investors determine the prices of a municipal bond with characteristics similar to the bond that they are interested in buying. That can provide more leverage when negotiating a purchase price with a broker.

Investors can search a database by state, and can also sort issues by credit rating, maturity, trading volume, coupon, and identification number. And if those terms seem foreign, the Web site's primers could get you up to speed.

But even if you find a security in the database that exactly matches the one you want to buy or sell, don't expect a dealer to give you the same price you saw. After all, prices listed in the database are only a guide, and they reflect prices offered to professionals, who get a better deal because they buy large amounts.

The Bond Market Association also is working on a program to provide individual investors with end-of-day price information on investment-grade corporate bonds that trade at least four times a day. This information reflects wholesale prices that dealers charge one another; individual investors would pay more.

BondsOnline
(www.bondsonline.com)

This site, sponsored by Twenty-First Century Municipals Inc., an information company, offers a mix of news, free research, ratings, and other information on the fixed-income securities market (especially municipal bonds), which it collects from various professional suppliers. The site charges for information that it can't get for free from other providers.

BondsOnline also provides quotes for 12,000 bonds from the inventories of several brokerage firms. Treasury prices are real-time, and quotes for other bonds are updated throughout the day. Investors click on the type of bond they want and enter their criteria, such as ratings, maturity, and yield. The site will then return matches fitting that search. However, investors must call the broker if they are interested in buying.

The site also has links to other sites on the Net that provide daily price and yield information on Treasury securities. It offers primers on investing and provides a glossary that explains some of those obscure bond-market terms. Another interesting feature—especially helpful to novice investors—is the Bond Professor, which answers questions, posted by investors, about the fixed-income market.

Bondtrac
(www.bondtrac.com)

Bondtrac, which lists bond prices for professional bond traders, has put some of its information in the hands of individual investors through this Web site. Investors can view a list of about 8,000 corporate, municipal, and government-agency bonds that are available from more than 350 brokerage firms on any given day. The site doesn't provide price information, though. That is reserved for Bondtrac's professional users, such as institutional investors or bond brokers.

The site provides individuals with just descriptive information on the bonds—such as issuer, ratings, and yield. None of the bonds can be purchased over the Net. If you see a bond that you are interested in buying, you have to go through a broker—either your own or one listed on the Bondtrac site.

The service is a scaled-back version of a more ambitious effort that Bondtrac had run, showing a list of bonds, dealers that were selling them, and their price. The 30 firms that had listed on Bondtrac were aiming to drum up Main Street business, but that didn't pan out. Investors seemed to be using the data to get a better deal from their own broker rather than making purchases via the site, said Thomas Hannon, chief operating officer.

Bureau of the Public Debt Online
(www.publicdebt.treas.gov)

This site, run by the Bureau of the Public Debt, a unit of the Treasury Department, is a good source of information about U.S. Savings Bonds, Treasury securities, and more. Through the Treasury Direct program, investors can buy T-bills, notes, and bonds directly from the government without paying the sales commission a broker might charge. The minimum purchase is $1,000.

Bond-Quote Sites

Quote.com (**www.quote.com**) charges $9.95 a month for a package that provides Treasury prices updated every 15 minutes from Bear Stearns. The site offers some Treasury pricing from GovPX, a quotation service run by the biggest bond trading firms.

GovPX (**www.govpx.com**) itself offers a handful of Treasury quotes and some statistics on trading volume on its site, updated several times a day. For $200 a month, it offers a deep list of end-of-day quotes, delivered by electronic mail.

PC Trader (**www.pctrader.com**), a subscription-based quotes and market data service, offers its users access to the full feed of GovPX quotes, the same service used by many professional bond traders, for $165 a month.

BMI Quotes (**www.bmiquotes.com**) provides free pricing, updated intermittently through the day, on bellwether corporates, Treasury, and mortgage-related bonds.

Garban Information Systems (**www.garbaninfo.com**) offers free quotes for bellwether Treasury bonds, mortgage-backed securities, and money-market interest rates, updated periodically. It offers deeper quotes in real-time for a subscription fee.

BondVu (**www.bondvu.com**) offers real-time pricing for a broad range of bonds, for a subscription that starts at about $190 a month for a single user.

Credit Ratings Sites

Ratings agencies such as Moody's Investors Service (**www. moodys.com**), Standard & Poor's (**www.standardpoors.com**), and Fitch IBCA (**www.fitchibca.com**) offer information about how they arrive at ratings, as well as a rundown of some of their recent ratings decisions. Items available for free at the Moody's site include information on ratings actions taken in the past several days, a daily overview of conditions in the bond market, and some research reports.

Financenter Inc.
(www.financenter.com)

This site, which covers a wide range of personal finance and investing topics, offers calculators to help determine such things as the market value of a bond and the price you should pay for it, based on the yield you are seeking and other factors—including the number of months until maturity, current market rates, and the bond's coupon rate.

BUYING BONDS ONLINE

Several years into the boom in online trading, which took root in the stock market in the mid-1990s, electronic trading had yet to make any significant penetration in the bond market, accounting for less than 5% of the overall trading volume. Many online brokers purport to offer bond trading, but investors will be disappointed if they expect to see systems that mirror electronic stock trading, where orders to buy and sell are fully automated and don't require human intervention.

For the majority of firms, bond trading is done the old-fashioned way. Although a customer can get some information online, he or she must phone in buy and sell orders to a representative, who then tries to fill the request from the firm's own inventory or by calling around. And service is usually limited to actively traded Treasury bonds or exchange-listed corporate bonds. For others, online bond trading is no more than an e-mail service. Yes, customers can place an order electronically, but then the bond market's low-tech roots become apparent, as a broker takes over and tries to fill the order just as if it had been phoned in.

Only a handful of brokers offer any sort of automatic order execution to individual investors, and that service is still extremely limited. Electronic bond trading has been slow to reach the level of online stock investing, partially because it wasn't a high priority for either investors or brokers.

But firms are enhancing their electronic trading systems. E*Trade (**www.etrade.com**) and Morgan Stanley Dean Witter (**www.online. msdw.com**) have improved their bond trading systems. E*Trade's Bond Center is by far the most impressive, but other online brokers are planning to meet the challenge. Tower Group, a research firm in Needham, Massachusetts, predicts that 17% of all bond transactions will be electronic by 2001, and the number of firms working on bond trading systems is growing rapidly.

However, most of these systems are used by professional traders. Some feature bonds from a single dealer, and others list those from several firms. Yet others bring, or plan to bring, multiple dealers and investors together in trading networks where anonymous orders to buy and sell are cross-matched and automatically executed. TradeWeb LLC (**www.tradeweb.com**), for example, enables large investors to trade Treasurys with seven big brokerage firms: Salomon Smith Barney; Lehman Brothers Holdings; Goldman Sachs; Merrill Lynch; Credit Suisse First Boston; J. P. Morgan; and Barclays Capital.

While systems such as TradeWeb cater to professional investors, they are becoming the backbone of electronic bond trading for individuals. Bond Exchange (**www.bondexchange.com**), BondTrac (**www.bondtrac.com**), Bond Express (**www.bondexpress.com**), and others are helping brokerage firms develop online bond-trading centers for individual investors. E*Trade's bond center, for example, relies on software and a consolidated listing of bonds from Bond Exchange.

These developments aren't surprising. As cyber-investing moves into the mainstream, individuals are demanding a broader range of services, including the ability to shop for bonds online. Brokers are beginning to move to accommodate their desires, hoping that will help them attract new customers, as well as keep the old ones happy.

The strategy also might be prudent as American investors mature and focus more on preserving the wealth they have accumulated during the bull market for stocks that stretched through much of the 1990s. The typical online investor is young and aggressive. But as these investors mature and become wealthier, they are going to have less tolerance for risk and that probably means buying more bonds.

Forrester Research expects online fixed-income assets to grow to $306 billion in 2003, up from nearly zero in 1998. That will account for about 10% of overall online assets, which will grow to $3.1 trillion in 20 million accounts from 374 billion in 4 million accounts in 1998.

In deciding where to make your online bond trades there are several important factors you should consider. At the top of the list is the extent of your broker's online offerings: Does it offer access to a broad range of bonds—corporate and municipal bonds, for example, or just Treasury bonds?

Also, does your broker provide access to just its own inventory, or are you able to see a consolidated list of bonds and quotes from the inventories of multiple sources? Listings from multiple sources allow you to compare prices simultaneously across the market and select the most competitive. You'll also want to make sure that the inventory is extensive. It's better to be able to choose from a list of 8,000 bonds than from just 800. The more bonds that are available, the better chance there is that you'll be able to find a bond that meets your criteria—such as yield, years to maturity, and ratings—at a reasonable price.

Just as it helped pioneer online stock trading, E*Trade is leading the charge in bringing electronic bond trading to retail investors over the Internet. It was the first broker to allow cyber-investors to buy a wide range of bonds, including corporates, municipals, and Treasurys over the Internet. The firm has access to the inventories of 400 different firms that provide a listing through the Bond Exchange system. Investors often can get live quotes, and usually have 7,000 to 8,000 bonds to choose from.

The E*Trade Bond Center has many easy-to-use features that help guide an investor through the process. Investors can search for bonds from a database of 1.5 million listings by type, rating, maturity, industry, and coupon rate. But only a small fraction are available for immediate execution. The system features an array of analytic tools, too, as well as commentary (including weekly updates from *The Financial Times* and Interactive Data), credit rating information, and a bond calculator to help you compare bond yields and prices.

It costs a minimum of $1,000 to open an account to trade bonds at E*Trade. The cost for each transaction is $40 for municipal and corporate bond orders below $10,000 and for Treasury bond orders of less than $20,000. Like other firms, E*Trade tacks on a separate commission, or markup, when it must go to another brokerage firm to find the bond you are interested in buying. The amount of this added cost is determined by the size of the order.

BondAgent.com (**www.bondagent.com**) was the first bonds-only online brokerage firm. The Web site offers access to about 10,000 municipal, corporate, Treasury, and zero coupon bonds. Customers can search for bonds by using a range of criteria, such as maturity, yield, and issuer. BondAgent provides free research, news, bond calculators, and a learning center. Customers can also get free, customized advice to build a bond portfolio. The minimum amount for opening an account is $10,000. The firm doesn't charge commissions on purchases of 25 or more bonds. It makes money through a markup or markdown on the bonds. For orders of less than 25 bonds, customers pay a $25 fee.

Many other brokers are planning comprehensive bond trading services, including Charles Schwab (**www.schwab.com**) and Morgan Stanley Dean Witter.

Morgan Stanley currently allows investors to buy Treasurys and the 100 most active munis from the inventory of its parent company. The firm launched Treasury trading in 1998, and added munis in 1999. Investors can see live quotes from Morgan Stanley and place trades against them. The firm offers live trading 24 hours a day—something even stock investors can't do—and real-time prices. It plans to broaden its offerings and add corporate bonds as well as offerings from other firms. Transaction prices range from $14.95 to $49.95 based on the number of bonds involved.

Schwab offers online trading on exchange-listed corporate bonds and actively traded Treasurys at 20% off the normal transaction fees it charges for using a broker. Schwab charges $49 for Treasury transactions done through a broker, and charges broker fees ranging from $3 to $5 per bond for listed corporate bonds, depending on the quantity. The minimum fee on a corporate-bond trade is $35.

TRADING COMMODITIES ONLINE

Investing in commodities and financial futures is about as extreme as you can get on the risk scale. By definition, a futures contract is an agreement to buy or sell a specific amount of a commodity or a financial instrument for a set price at a future time. Investors are required to make only a small deposit to control a large amount of a commodity. That small deposit, usually about 10% of what the commodity would be worth on delivery, is called a margin payment. So, for example, an investor could control $30,000 worth of gold for just $3,000. That leverage is what makes futures investing exciting, but also dangerous.

In the case of a contact for gold futures, the investor essentially is agreeing to buy or sell, say, 100 ounces of gold in a designated future month for $300 an ounce. Because this is done with just a small amount of money up front (in the parlance of Wall Street, this is known as a highly leveraged trade), the potential gains can seem very attractive. If the price of gold surged by $100 an ounce, for example, an investor who bought a gold contract would see its value jump by $10,000. On the other hand, if the price of gold fell by $100 an ounce, the investor would face a huge loss, wiping out the entire $3,000 up-front deposit and forcing him to dig into his pockets for another $7,000.

There are many examples in everyday life of the basic principles of futures buying. Let's say you go to a clothing boutique to buy a certain a suit that you saw on display for $299. Unfortunately, the boutique doesn't have your size. The salesman says he can get it for you in a month. You want to make sure that you get the suit for the price you saw today. You put down a 10% deposit to guarantee the transaction and the salesman writes up a receipt. You (the buyer) have just entered into a futures deal with the store (the seller). The store has agreed to sell you one suit (the commodity) for $299 (the set price) next month (the future date). Even if the price goes up, you still will pay only $299 (your 10% deposit plus the balance) when you pick up your suit. (If the suit goes on sale before you pick it up, it is a different story. Some stores would give you the sale price on the suit, but in the futures market you wouldn't get such a break: You pay the full price even if the market falls before you take delivery.)

Nuts and Bolts

Investing in futures contracts can be very challenging for the novice. These are derivatives—complex investments whose values are based on the performance of another underlying product. (That product doesn't have to be a good, like wheat or crude oil, which many people imagine when they think of commodities. Many futures are based on, or derivative of, financial assets, such as Treasury bonds or the stocks in the Standard & Poor's-500 stock index.) An investor who buys corn futures is betting that the price of corn will rise during the life of the contract. An investor who sells corn futures is betting the opposite.

Online investors tend to make their own decisions and do their own research. With commodities and futures they are taking on a lot. The price of the commodity on which the futures contract is based—and thus the price of the futures contract itself—can be affected by a wide variety of uncontrollable domestic and international forces. The price of currency futures, for example, could be battered by global economic and political changes. Crop futures could be hurt by changes in the weather, bumper crops abroad, infestation by pests, or various government forecasts about supply and demand. An online investor who wants to play this game without any help from a broker would have to be very dedicated to doing some tough research and keeping up with all the changing forces that impact the commodity markets.

In the U.S., most futures trading takes place on an exchange floor, where traders gather at specific spots designed for each commodity. These are called pits because—traditionally—that was how they were shaped, with multiple tiers allowing traders to better see and interact with one another. Prices are quoted, and buy and sell orders are matched up verbally. This shouting match is known as the "open outcry" system. For actively traded commodities, the pits can be rowdy, or even hostile. Traders have been know to take an occasional pen jab from other traders jockeying for position on the trading floor. (Remember, there is a lot of money at stake here.) Futures trading, though, is beginning to move off exchange floors and on to computerized trading systems that will allow traders to make deals from their offices, rather than from the pit. For years, a lot of activity has occurred outside of regular business hours by using electronic trading systems.

The futures market is different than the stock market in several ways. For one thing, exchanges typically have different trading hours for different commodities, and they can be confusing for investors used to the New York Stock Exchange's fixed schedule. At the New York Mercantile Exchange, for instance, heating oil futures trade between 9:50 A.M. and 3:10 P.M., while gold futures trade between 8:20 A.M. and 2:45 P.M.

Futures prices are a little different than prices for stocks, too. For instance, while stock investors often focus on the price of the last trade that was made in a stock each day (those are the prices in most newspapers, for instance), futures investors look at settlement prices at the end of each day. The settlement price isn't necessary the last trade of the day. Because there is often a flurry of activity in the pits just before the close of trading each day, it can be difficult to determine which trade was last, and whether it was representative of the prevailing price that was available at the time. So, settlement prices are set each day by a committee (believe it or not) that looks at all of the trades that occurred in the final minutes of trading and sets what it believes is a fair settlement price based on trading volume. A price that was paid for just a handful of contracts will lose out to one that involved hundreds.

Another common term in the futures market that may be unfamiliar to stock investors is open interest. Like a "shares outstanding" number in the stock market (the total number of shares that a company has), open interest shows the total number of contacts that exist for each monthly commodity future. In general terms, open interest tends to be highest for the contracts that expire the soonest because those are the contracts that attract the most interest. Unlike a stock's shares outstanding, a futures contract's open interest changes all of the time. Only a company can alter the number of shares outstanding that it has, but any broker can change a futures contract's open interest. That's because when a broker sells you a contract, he is often simply creating a new contract—increasing open interest by one. If, on the other hand, you decide to sell a contract short (in a bet that the commodity will lose value) you yourself—through your broker, of course—are creating a new contract and boosting open interest.

As a buyer or seller of a futures contract, you are legally obligated to fulfill the deal unless you close out the contract before the settlement date, which typically is within a year for nonfinancial futures. Some currency futures, such as Eurodollar contracts, can have a duration as long as five years. Most participants in the futures market usually close out their contracts—for a profit or a loss—before the settlement date. They don't take or make delivery of the actual product—say, 5,000 bushels of corn. Only about 3% of futures deals result in actual delivery. Closing out a position simply means buying or selling. If you own a futures contract, for instance, you can sell it via your broker on a futures exchange.

Futures players are either hedgers or speculators. A speculator hopes to profit from the changing price of a commodity without actually expecting to take or make delivery on a contract. A corn futures speculator, for example, doesn't care what happens to the actual corn on which the contract is based. He or she simply cares about the price of the contract. A speculator accepts risk in hopes that the price goes the direction he or she bet. On the other hand, a hedger transfers risk. For the hedger, a futures contract is an insurance policy against a change in price. A hedger is either a producer (such as a wheat or cattle farmer) seeking protection against a future fall in price, or a business that uses the raw commodity and is looking for protection against a rise in the price (such as a bakery or a sausage factory). Hedging allows them to offset the risk of fluctuating prices. They essentially transfer their risks to others with a futures contract. A wheat farmer, for example, who wants to protect himself from the risk that prices might fall between the time he plants his crop today and brings it to market in five months would sell futures contracts. The wheat farmer essentially agrees to deliver his crop to the buyer in five months for the current price. If the price of wheat falls, he is protected because he has already locked in today's better rate with the futures contracts.

The individual investor who enters the futures market is doing so as a speculator. He or she hopes to score big gains by betting on the direction of prices. Indeed, fortunes have been made sometimes in seconds trading futures. News of troubles in the Middle East, for instance, can send crude-oil futures skyrocketing. But on the flip side, some investors have lost their shirts just as quickly. So, before taking the plunge, consider carefully whether you can stomach the risks. Be aware that you could lose a lot of money if the market moves against you: Futures trading requires you to make predictions about the future. For an example of how fraught with trouble futures predictions are, look no further than the TV weatherman. How many times have you made plans based on his predictions, only to have them rained out? The risky and unpredictable nature of forecasts is why many individuals have avoided the commodity futures market. Some studies have suggested that most individuals who venture into this market lose money.

Nevertheless, online futures trading by individuals is growing. Individuals are being drawn to the Internet to trade futures for many of the same reasons they invest in stocks online. It is cheaper than going through a full-service broker. Some online brokers offer trades for less than $10, compared with $200 at traditional brokers. Online trading also is fast and convenient, done with the click of a computer mouse. Many contracts can be bought round-the-clock over the Internet— something that can't be said for stocks just yet. Individuals also are warming to futures because of the reams of information becoming available online to help them—not to mention the growing number of online futures brokerage firms. More than 30 brokers (though not the popular stock trading firms) were offering Web futures trading by the fall of 1999.

And as interest grows among individuals—including those who trade online—exchanges are making big strides to accommodate them, by offering contracts designed to appeal to a retail audience. The Chicago Mercantile Exchange, for example, is offering "e-mini" S&P 500 and Nasdaq 100 futures contracts. These are bite-size versions of futures contracts that are extremely popular with professional investors, but at a more affordable price for individuals. E-mini futures are worth about a fifth of their larger cousins. (The *e* in e-mini comes from the fact that they are traded electronically, rather than in a pit full of screaming traders.) If a big S&P contract is valued at $350,000, the e-mini would be worth $70,000. With a 10% deposit requirement, an investor would have to put up just $7,000 on the e-mini versus $35,000 for the standard contract. Not to be left out, the Chicago Board of Trade also is offering a futures index contract pegged to the Dow Jones Industrial Average that's designed to appeal to individuals. The contract is worth $10 for every point in the industrial average. Say the industrial average was trading around 11,000: A futures contract on the average, worth nearly $110,000 and with a margin requirement of a bit more than 5%, could be bought with a deposit of about $6,000.

Commodities: Research

Before you buy your first futures contract, you ought to know more about the market and how it works. What better place to go than the eight exchanges where U.S. futures contracts are traded? They provide a wealth of educational material and other information on futures trading, and answers to some general questions you might have. Some of the best and most informative exchange sites are those run by the Chicago Board of Trade (**www.cbot.com**), the Chicago Mercantile Exchange (**www. cme.com**), and the New York Mercantile Exchange (**www.nymex.com**). These sites can get you on the road to understanding and trading futures.

At the Web site of the Chicago Board of Trade, the world's largest futures exchange, investors can learn about futures trading through online tutorials and seminars. The site also provides information about courses that are offered by the CBOT's educational arm, the Commodities Institute. These courses, though not offered online, are for beginning as well as experienced investors. The CBOT specializes in trading contracts on agricultural products such as wheat, corn, soybeans, and oats; financial instruments such as Treasury bonds and municipal bonds; precious metals such as gold; and stock indexes such as the Dow Jones Industrial Average.

The CBOT, like other exchanges, provides substantial information online about its specific futures products. At the CBOT site, a beginning investor can find, for example, basic information on agricultural futures and how they work. You can also learn the nuts and bolts of trading futures on the Dow Jones Industrial Average, including trading strategies ranging from basic to advanced. Want to know how to open an account? The CBOT provides that information, too. There also is a glossary of futures terms. You can learn, for example, the difference between a long and short position, two basic futures strategies.

The Chicago Mercantile Exchange, which offers contracts for livestock, meat, stock indexes, currency, and interest rates, provides a very comprehensive and easy-to-understand guide to commodities trading.

Separately, the exchange's education department also provides instant Web lessons that introduce newcomers to futures. The lessons are short, and each one introduces a new concept or set of facts. For example, Lesson 1 explains the basics of a futures contract, and Lesson 13 how to read quotes. And if you need to learn more, you can take the exchange's "Introduction to Futures Trading" online correspondence course. The course covers the basics of futures trading, and includes e-mail contact with instructors, an interactive bulletin board, online quizzes, a final exam, and a certificate of completion. There is also a link to an online glossary of futures terms in five different languages.

Other exchange sites that offer helpful, free information: the New York Board of Trade (**www.nybot.com**); Kansas City Board of Trade (**www.kcbt.com**); Mid-America Commodity Exchange (**www.midam.com**); and Minneapolis Grain Exchange (**www.mgex.com**).

The Futures Industry Institute (**www.fiafii.org**) is another information resource for the beginning trader. The institute, an affiliate of the industry trade group, the Futures Industry Association, offers an online tutorial to the futures markets that explains almost everything a beginner would want to know. You can also download its futures industry fact book, which provides current information on more than 1,000 futures and options contracts, and the exchanges on which they trade.

One of the most comprehensive and continually updated sources of information about the futures industry is Futures Online (**www.futuresmag.com**), the online version of *Futures Magazine*. The site provides almost everything you need to know about the business or steers you to other appropriate sources. At the site you can find links to education sites, exchanges, regulators, brokerage firms, and other industry groups. There is also lots of news and information, and more importantly for the beginning futures investor, there is an online learning center.

Another useful site for information is Virtual University of Investing (**www.virtual-u.com**). It offers some free educational information and introductory courses. Free beginner courses range from Commodity 101 (What are commodities?) and Commodity 104 (How much money do I need to start trading commodities?) to Commodity 109 (an explanation of how to profit from a decline in prices). More advanced courses, which include trading strategies, are available for a fee. And to get familiar with the market, you can follow along while Virtual University trades a mock $100,000 account. There is also a comprehensive list of links to other sources of futures information on the Internet.

The Commodity Futures Trading Commission (**www.cftc.gov**), the federal regulatory agency for futures trading, also provides general information about futures trading. The online "What You Should Know Before You Trade" brochure also gives investors some basic guidance.

Some futures brokers also provide a wealth of educational information on their Web sites. One of the most comprehensive and easy-to-grasp tutorials on futures trading can be found at the Web site of commodities broker World Link Futures (**www.worldlinkfutures. com**). The trading-for-beginners course is laid out in four parts: It includes an explanation of the basics, how the market works, types of orders you can make, and even provides trading tips for beginners. World Link also provides a more advanced series of educational articles for its clients, and has links to lots of other information sources.

While these sites can get you started, there are many more similar resources on the Internet if you want to do some digging around on your own.

Basics: Account Requirements and Quotes

The minimum account balance for futures trading varies from broker to broker, but typically you'll need at least $2,000 to begin. Some brokers might allow you to open an account and trade a contract with just the initial minimum deposit required by the exchange. On some contracts, that minimum could be just a few hundred dollars, but that would be a rare exception. Some brokers also may require you to meet certain minimum net worth standards, and may also look at your annual income. Most won't accept investors with a net worth of less than $50,000. World Link Futures, for example, recommends a minimum net worth of $100,000. And professionals advise that you should put no more than 10% of your assets into the futures market. So if you are worth $100,000, that means you should have no more than $10,000 tied up in futures. More important, you should never put more into futures than you can afford to lose.

The initial minimum margin requirements for the various futures contracts traded on U.S. exchanges aren't difficult to find. The exchanges list the minimum margin requirements for contracts that they carry. The margin, or down payment, usually ranges from 5% to 20% of a contract, depending on factors such as price or trading volatility. The more volatile a contract, the higher the margin. Most brokers' sites also list the contracts and the minimum margins required as a down payment. Some brokers may require you to put up a bigger cash deposit than is required by the exchanges.

You will always be required to maintain a certain minimum amount of cash in your account to carry the futures position from day to day. Each day, money is deducted from or added to your account, depending on how your futures contract performs. If your losses pull the money in your account below the minimum amount required to carry the position, you may receive a "margin call" from your broker. A margin call requires you to put more money into your account to meet minimum levels and prevent the broker from closing out your futures position. It may be unwise to respond to a margin call by putting up more money. Sometimes the best thing to do in this situation is to swallow your losses and allow your broker to close out your position.

An important key to successful futures trading is finding the appropriate information and analysis. Futures, whether they are agricultural and livestock commodities or financial instruments, can be affected by a multitude of factors. Weather, the economy, political climates, changes in supply and demand of a commodity, inflation, and the level of interest rates all play a role in one futures market or another. Bad weather, for example, could hurt agricultural crops and send their cash and futures prices soaring; good weather could have the opposite effect. Inflation and rising interest rates could tank bond futures. Getting this information in a timely manner is important.

For commodity futures prices, investors can start by going directly to the futures exchanges. The exchanges provide access to delayed price information at no charge on the futures contracts they list. At the CBOT's Web site, for example, investors can get 10-minute-delayed snapshots of quotes, as well as daily settlement prices on contracts for grains, soybeans, metals, Treasury bonds, and the Dow Jones Industrial Average. Online futures brokers also provide access to price quotes from the exchanges or through affiliations with independent price data vendors. Delayed quotes are usually free. For an extra charge, investors can get real-time snapshots of prices, and in some cases, streaming quotes (continually updated on your computer screen). Getting these quote services through a broker is usually cheaper than going through an independent data provider.

For example, Linnco Futures Group (**www.lfgllc.com**) offers its brokerage clients real-time quotes for $69 a month, plus applicable exchange fees that can range from $7.50 to $60. More sophisticated quote services are much more expensive. PC Trader (**www. pctrader.com**), a unit of Jones Financial Network, says it offers two deluxe packages that are useful to ordinary investors and day traders, which cost about $350 to $400 a month. Data Broadcasting Corporation (**www.dbc.com**), another quote service, offers various subscription packages under the brand name eSignal that include a choice of delayed, real-time, or streaming quotes. Fees are in the hundreds of dollars a month, with exchange charges.

Delayed futures quotes are good enough for many individual investors. In addition to the futures exchanges themselves, a comprehensive package of delayed quotes is available for free from Ino.com (**www.ino.com**). Lists of just the most actively traded futures contracts are provided by financial sites such as Futures.Net (**www.futures.net**), and news organizations such as CNNfn (**www.cnnfn.com**) and Bloomberg News (**www.bloomberg.com**). Pick the one that best suits your needs and budget.

Digging In

There are Web sites to meet the wide-ranging needs of futures investors. The exchanges, for starters, go far beyond basic information and price quotes. They offer a smorgasbord of data and related services, such as statistics, charts, market commentary, and links to other sites of interest. CBOT, for example, provides comprehensive data on crop production, supply, and demand. Traders also can get calendars of economic and other statistical reports expected to be released each month, and market commentary from the exchange's own analysts and other sources. The exchange's MarketPlex information center is an indispensable source, providing access to detailed weather forecasts (from four different sources) and analysis, charts and studies on various commodities, government reports and links, and free news from Bridge news service. MarketPlex also features live Internet radio broadcasts from the trading floor, which analyze how government crop production and supply/demand reports will affect the market as they are released. It also permits access to premium information for a fee.

Commodities brokers also provide comprehensive data and other information on their Web sites. That includes charting software, statistics, news, market analysis, government and other reports, access to weather information, and links to other sites that provide useful data. Again, some of the information is free for everyone, while some is available only to brokerage clients, and some only for a subscription fee. Brokerage firm Lind-Waldock (**www.lind-waldock.com**), for example, provides free end-of-day charts on futures contracts (which are useful in helping an investor determine price trends), free delayed quotes, news from online news site TheStreet.com (**www.thestreet.com**), and weather news. Alaron Trading (**www.alaron.com**) gives you quotes and charts, daily research, news from Bridge, free reports, and trading booklets. Other brokers provide just as much, sometimes more. There will be more later on how to find these brokers and their sites.

For agricultural commodities, various factors can influence prices. These factors include the amount of planted acreage, crop yield, government farm policy and reports, exports, the weather, and basic consumer demand. For financial futures, government policies, business conditions, Federal Reserve actions, and consumer preferences in saving and spending are among the factors. If you are looking for this type of information, your best bet is to head to government agencies or semi-official agencies, which track most of these statistics and churn out numerous reports closely watched by the market.

If you are trading agricultural products, one of the best places is the Web site for the U.S. Department of Agriculture (**www.usda.gov**), where you will find a wealth of information, including agriculture reports from the department and various other agencies, as well as extensive national and international weather and links to other sources. You can find a schedule of past and coming reports from the Economic Research Service, the Foreign Agricultural Service, the National Agricultural Statistics Service, and the World Agricultural Outlook Board. The bottom line: Here is where you can get all the minute details about crops, livestock, and weather that can affect futures prices. You can find out, for example, the number of cattle that were being raised or slaughtered in a given month. You can get weekly export sales reports on grains, or an early warning on the possible impact of agricultural obligations on U.S. supplies and prices. Weather and crop bulletins can help you assess whether supplies of corn, for example, will be bountiful at harvest (bad news for futures prices) or limited (which could push up prices).

The USDA Economics and Statistics System (**usda.mannlib. cornell.edu**) is a searchable database of nearly 300 reports from USDA. These materials cover U.S. and international agriculture, and related topics. The National Agricultural Statistics Service of the USDA (**www.usda.gov/nass**) provides access to daily reports and other data covering virtually every facet of U.S. agriculture—production and supplies of food and fiber, prices paid and received by farmers, and farm labor and wages. In addition, NASS's forty-five State Statistical Offices publish data about many of the same topics on a local level. You can get a list of the reports in alphabetical order or view a release schedule by date.

Other government statistics agencies also have Web sites with information that is pertinent to the futures market. A good place to find and access these sites is through Fedstats (**www.fedstats.gov**), operated by the Federal Interagency Council on Statistical Policy, which provides easy access to the full range of statistics and information produced by government agencies for public use. Even the White House (**www. whitehouse.gov**) provides access to statistics through its online economic statistics briefing room. Some of the government agency sites futures investors would be specifically interested in visiting are those for the Commerce Department (**www.commerce.gov**) and the Federal Reserve (**www.federalreserve.gov**), whose monetary policies affect interest rates, and thus financial futures.

Of course, weather also plays an important part in the commodities market because it affects crop yields. If you feel the need to go beyond what your broker, government, or other futures-related sites provide, there are many independent weather forecasting Internet sites to tap. Here are just a few samples: National Weather Service (**www.nws. noaa.gov**); the Weather Channel (**www.weather.com**); and Freese-Notis Weather (**www.weather.net**), which also provides daily commodity trading advice.

Charts are an important tool for the commodities trader: They can be used to spot trends in the market so that you can determine, for example, the direction of prices. Charts can help you decide whether to go long (buying a contract in a bet that prices will rise) or to go short (selling a contract in a bet that prices will fall), or whether to get out of a position altogether. Most, if not all, commodity brokers provide charting software on their Web sites for their clients' convenience, as do the exchanges. But there are also many independent charting services—some free, others not. Some of the places to go for free charts: Futuresource (**www.futuresource.com**), which requires you to sign up as a member; Ino Global Markets (**www.ino.com**), and TradingCharts.com Inc. (**www.tfc-charts.w2d.com**), which allows you to create a personalized charts menu to track specific futures. You can also get charts, for a subscription fee, from Prophet Financial Systems Inc. (**www.prophetfinance.com**). It charges $24.95 a month for its high-level service.

No commodity trader invests without a reliable source of market news. Before the explosion of the Internet, individuals had to wait for the next day's newspaper to read today's news, while professional traders with computer terminals on their desks had constant access to up-to-the-minute news from various wire services. But now the Internet has leveled the playing field: Individuals can now get news on their computers just like professionals. They can access the news through the Web sites of traditional news companies, or even get the same wire feeds that professionals receive—but usually for a fee. Sometimes, a broker might provide access to the paid news services to its clients for free. For a list of wire services and business news sites from major newspapers, you can head to World News (**www.worldnews.com**). Investors also can access market news providers, directly for a fee or as part of a subscription package from other data companies. Future-Source.com provides access to news from Bridge News and Futures World News, a real-time news service for futures traders. Limited news is free, but for the bells and whistles, you must pay a subscription fee. Data Broadcasting Corp. (**www.dbc.com**) provides access to real-time news from Dow Jones, IFN, Futures World News, and more—again, for a subscription fee.

COMMODITIES: PICKING A BROKER

When it comes to trading futures online, don't turn to your traditional Web stockbroker. These firms, so far, have avoided the business altogether because, on Main Street, futures aren't as appealing as stocks are. These are derivative investments that often clobber even the professional trader. Nevertheless, you needn't worry: If you're interested, futures boutiques have stepped in to fill the vacuum left by the popular online brokerage firms. And while Internet futures trading may not have taken off yet like stock trading, thanks to vigorous marketing by some of these niche players, it is slowly developing a following on Main Street.

More than 30 futures brokers now offer individuals a chance to trade commodities over the Internet. And as the Internet heralds sweeping changes in the investing arena, industry executives expect online futures trading to explode as individuals look to diversify their portfolios and become more comfortable with taking risks. Right now, general statistics on the number of individual investors trading futures online are hard to come by, but there are some hints of strong growth.

The CBOT says electronic trading on its exchange has been growing by leaps and bounds, although this includes both individual and professional traders. Through November 1999, for example, the volume of electronic orders to the CBOT surged 307% over the year-ago period. Each day, about 21% of all orders are made electronically.

For Steven A. Greenberg, president of Alaron Trading Corp., a Chicago futures brokerage firm that offers online trading to individual investors, Internet trading is the fastest-growing segment of his business—accounting for about 25% of trading as of November 1999. Alaron had about 4,000 online accounts in late 1999, up from 350 at the start of the year. Alaron is one of the key players in the online futures business. Some others are: Lind-Waldock & Co. of Chicago (**www. lind-waldock.com**), the largest discount futures broker; Jack Carl Futures of Chicago (**www.jackcarl.com**), a division of ED&F Man International Inc.; and LFG Linnco Futures Group (**www.lfgllc.com**).

When picking a broker, you should choose the one that offers the services, types of tools, data, accounts, and commissions that most suit your needs. If you are an active trader and prefer real-time quotes, then pick a broker that offers that service. Of course, if you plan to get your own real-time information elsewhere on the Web, that doesn't matter. Remember, a good brokerage firm is going to be crucial to your trading successes. Some firms allow you to execute online trades all on your own, without any intrusion from a broker (a truly bare-bones discount online account where the only service provided is order execution). Some provide a degree of hand holding—suggesting trades, providing analysis and advice on when to take or pass on a trade. These enhanced services cost more than a self-directed account, but are significantly cheaper than trading through a full-service broker. The choice is up to you, but remember: The truly self-directed account is the cheapest, but if you make a bad trade you are on your own.

Commissions at some discount online firms are as low as $5 a trade. Some brokers have a wide range of commissions, depending on the frequency of trading and markets traded. At Lind-Waldock, for example, commission rates range from $5 to $35 per trade. Unlike stocks, where you pay one commission to buy and another to sell, fu-

BEFORE YOU START

Before opening your account, you might want to visit the National Futures Association Web site (**www.nfa. futures.org**) for disciplinary information on broker- age firms and their employees. The information covers more than 50,000 futures firms and salespeople. Its "Background Affiliation Status Information Center" al- lows investors to obtain detailed disciplinary records.

Before you make your first trade, you may also want to take the futures market for a test run. Most futures firms and some exchanges allow you to make "paper trades," or test trades. This allows traders to run through normally entered trades during the day, experience trading con- ditions, and track profits and losses. The Chicago Merc, for example, offers two simulated trading services: one for $24.95 if you want to go it alone, and the other for $34.95, if you want help from a broker.

As you head to the futures market, be cautious. Re- member that with futures, you're obligated to honor a contract. If the market moves against you, you have to put up more cash to maintain your position, possi- bly making your downside unlimited.

tures traders charge one commission to open and close a position. This is usually known as a round turn. When you are quoted a com- mission by a futures broker, find out whether that is for each side of the trade or whether it is a round-turn fee. If the commission is for each side of the trade, then you would have to double it to get the full round-turn rate. You can visit various brokers to find out their com- missions, but in today's Internet age, there are easier ways to find out.

Futures Magazine provides a handy list of online brokers and their commission fees at **www.futuresmag.com/industry/references/ references.html.** Remember, low commissions at some brokerage firms may be offset by expensive fees for other premium subscription services, such as real-time quotes. So make sure you do your homework and find the brokerage that offers you the biggest bang and best service for your buck. However, don't let cheap trading costs be your only driver. Make sure your brokerage firm, for example, has an efficient trading system and allows you to place trades over the phone if its computers crash.

Here are a few brokers and what they offer:

Alaron Trading
(www.alaron.com)

For about $15 a pop (or round turn), investors can trade everything from S&P 500 futures to cattle futures—and, yes, pork bellies too. If you want some hand holding, it will cost you about $40 to trade through a broker-assisted account. Alaron also provides free daily research, commentary, and special reports from its in-house team of analysts. You also get delayed news from Future World News and real-time snapshot quotes and charts. Alaron has no minimum account balance: It relies on exchange minimum margins. However, the "unofficial" minimum for opening an account is $3,000. Most of Alaron's customers have a minimum net worth of between $100,000 and $250,000 and have annual earnings exceeding $50,000 a year.

Jack Carl Futures
(www.jackcarl.com)

The firm offers introductory commission rates of $12 to $30 per round turn, and the site offers a lot of free content, including news headlines, historical price charts, market commentary, and economic reports. As with most sites, the sophisticated stuff (such as streaming quotes and real-time news) costs extra.

Lind-Waldock
(www.lind-waldock.com)

The minimum deposit required to open an account is $5,000, and commission rates typically range from $5 to $35 for a round turn. Rates are influenced by a number of factors, including the frequency of trading and markets traded. You get many bells and whistles: free delayed quotes and end-of-day charts, access to weather and delayed news from Futures World News, and live commentary from the trading floor.

ZAP Futures
(www.zapfutures.com)

This division of Linnco Futures Group requires $10,000 to open an account. Commission rates range from $20 to $24 per round turn depending on the size of your account, and the number and types of trades you make. More active traders get the lowest rates. Higher-end customers also get free streaming quotes, charts, graphics, and news through DBC's Signal Online, the content provider for many brokerage firms. Others pay a discount rate to get this service. ZAP also offers high-end clients analytic programs that will make "buy" or "sell" recommendations. Everyone gets free delayed quotes, charts, and research. ZAP also provides continuous commentary from trading pits at the Chicago Mercantile Exchange, giving traders a feel for the action.

TRADING OPTIONS ONLINE

Options trading is heating up among individual investors even though it can be very complicated and risky. Options are attractive because of the opportunity to make big gains on relatively small investments. Options investing, like futures, uses leveraged capital to bet on the future direction of a security's value. For a small premium—the option price—investors acquire the right to buy or sell a security for a locked-in price within a specified time frame (typically three to nine months). Stock options are the most popular, but investors also can buy options on market indexes, Treasury securities, foreign currencies, and a range of futures contracts.

Like futures, options are derivatives—complicated investments whose value is based on some other underlying security. But though futures and options are usually discussed in the same breath, these investment cousins have distinct differences. A futures contract is an obligation to buy or sell a specific amount of a security for a pre-set price at a set date in the future. An option is the right—without obligation—to acquire or sell the underlying security. Option buyers don't have to go through with the deal; if they don't, their only loss is the generally small premium that they paid for the option.

Most individuals who invest in options buy stock contracts, avoiding more complex securities such as those tied to futures, foreign currencies, and bonds. Individuals prefer stock options because they are easier to analyze and trade than, say, pork bellies or the Japanese yen. They also are very familiar to stock investors: Their prices are linked to those of stocks, so if you understand why a stock may rise or fall in value, you are already a long way down the road of understanding options. Moreover, many of the traditional electronic brokerages where ordinary investors buy and sell stocks also offer options trading—and usually just the basic securities and strategies. In many cases, that means buying or selling puts and calls on stocks. A single put option is the right to sell 100 shares of stock while a call option is the right to buy 100 shares.

Options give investors an opportunity to bet on price movements without committing huge amounts of capital. There are many strategies for using options—some are conservative and others are very speculative and risky. Investors can use options conservatively as insurance against a drop in the price of a stock they own or to limit their downside risk when acquiring a position in a stock that they expect to rise. Speculators like options because options allow them to place big bets with just a little bit of money up front. Moreover, options prices can be very volatile, so if you bet correctly on the movement of a stock's price, you can be richly rewarded, very quickly. Of course, a bad bet can sour quickly, too.

Options Plays

Buying single calls or puts is the most basic play in options investing. The call and put distinction determines whether an investor has the right to buy or sell the underlying stock. A call is the right to buy 100 shares of a stock at a specific price, known as the "strike price." Investors who buy calls are bullish. They are betting that the stock price will appreciate to a value above the strike price of their option contract before its expiration date, allowing them to buy the shares for less than the then-current market value.

A put option is the right to sell 100 shares of a stock. Investors who buy puts are bearish. They are betting that the price of a stock will fall below the strike price of their option contract before its expiration date, allowing them to sell the shares for more than the then-current market value. When buying either type of option, an investor's loss is limited to the price—again, known as the premium—he paid for the option. If the stock doesn't move beyond the strike price of the option, it expires worthless.

Investors can also sell puts and calls—a process that is known as "writing" an option. The difference between buying and selling an option is your commitment. The buyer of an option pays a premium for the right to buy or sell stock at a preset price or strike price within a specific period. A buyer is not obligated to carry through with the transaction and can simply trade the option or let it expire. On the other hand, option sellers, or writers, are obligated to carry out their end of the bargain if they are called to do so. Someone who writes a call is essentially agreeing to stand ready to sell shares to another investor (the option buyer) at the predetermined price before the expiration date. A put writer is agreeing to be ready to buy the shares. The option writers are paid the premium for accepting the risk of being called upon to buy or deliver the underlying shares at unfavorable market prices. If the market moves in their favor, they win the bet and earn some income in the form of the premium.

Investors can also use puts and calls in various combinations to create more complex trading strategies, which sometimes are known by odd names, such as straddles and strangles.

A straddle involves buying a put and call option on the same underlying stock with the same strike price and expiration date. People use this strategy if they expect the stock (or whatever instrument upon which the option is based) to move sharply before the options' expiration date, but they aren't sure which direction it will go. This can be useful, for instance, when a company is expected to release news that is highly anticipated by investors, but could go either way for the company (could be good news, could be bad). As a result, the stock could race higher, or it could tumble: A straddle position is profitable either way. Of course, it is worthless if the stock doesn't move significantly: Say the news release is delayed until after the options expire, or the news is less than definitive, and the stock price remains stagnant.

A strangle involves buying a call and put with different strike prices. The concept here is generally the same as for a straddle, except it costs less—and is more likely to go bust. It costs less because in a strangle you typically buy options with strike prices further away from the current price of the stock than you would with a straddle. The further an option's strike price is from the value of the stock, the less it costs and the more likely it is to expire worthless, because the stock is less likely to move enough to reach one of the option's strike prices.

While simply buying a put or call option involves little risk (all you can lose is the money you paid for the option if it expires worthless), other options strategies are extremely risky. Losses can be enormous. The riskiest is writing, or selling, "naked calls." Naked calls are agreements to sell stock that you don't already own. If the price of the stock rises you lose the bet. In that case, you will have to buy the stock at its then-current market price, and sell it to the option's buyer for less. Your losses on a naked call could be significant because there is no telling how high the stock will go. Many online brokerages don't allow their customers to engage in risky strategies—especially writing naked calls. Those that allow risky bets require hefty minimum account balances, some as high as $25,000.

The Value of Your Option

The entire mind-set of options traders is at odds with that of stock investors. Time, the friend of the long-term stock investor, is usually a ruthless enemy for options buyers. Time is a key component in determining the value of an option. The further away the expiration date, the more expensive an option will be, because the underlying stock price has more time to make the desired move. This feature is called the time value of the option. The time value "decays" as the option approaches expiration. Price decay is especially steep in options that expire in less than 30 days, but such short-lived options are popular among inexperienced investors—a major reason many investors lose money in options.

Several other factors also have an impact on the premium. One, as mentioned earlier, is the relationship between the underlying stock price and the option's strike price. This is known as an option's intrinsic value, and it fluctuates with the changing value of the underlying stock. The options market has its own terminology for this relationship. A stock option whose strike price is trading at a rate favorable to the underlying security is described as being in the money. An option whose strike price is trading at an unfavorable rate is described as out of the money.

An in-the-money call option, for example, would have a strike price that is lower than the current price of the underlying stock. For example: If you buy a call option with a strike price of $50 and the company's current stock price is $55, it is in the money because that option would allow you to buy a $55 stock for just $50 a share. Any strike price over $55 would be out of the money. In this example, the option with a $50 strike price has an intrinsic value of $5. The option with a strike above $55 has no intrinsic value.

For put options to be in the money, the strike price has to be above the current price of the underlying stock. A strike price below the current stock price is out of money. This is because a put option gives the holder the right to sell the asset at the strike price. The strike price would have to be above the current stock price for the trade to be favorable for the option buyer.

Trying to take all of this into account to determine whether an option is a good value is no easy feat. Indeed, two professors, Myron Scholes and Robert Merton, were awarded the Nobel Prize for economics in 1997 for their work developing and putting to use a model for pricing options. That model—known as the Black-Scholes model—is ubiquitous on Wall Street and is widely credited with clearing the way for the huge growth that the options industry has had in the past 25 years. (The name Black refers to mathematician Fischer Black, who did early work with Professor Scholes in the 1970s.)

Learning More on the Net

For basic education and other resources on investing in stock options, individuals can turn first to Web sites run by the exchanges where options are traded. The Chicago Board Options Exchange (**www.cboe.com**) is the biggest options exchange. The CBOE and its Options Institute arm offer some of the best and most comprehensive material. At this site, novice investors can click on the link to the CBOE's education center to learn the basics of investing in options. It also provides an online strategy workshop and interactive worksheets. If you are stumped by options terms, there is an online glossary that can provide explanations. For the more experienced investor, the CBOE offers a tutorial on more advanced concepts. You can also find information at sites run by the American Stock Exchange (**www.amex.com**); the Philadelphia Stock Exchange (**www.phlx.com**); and the Pacific Stock Exchange (**www.pacificex.com**).

Brokerage firms and other independent sites also provide helpful learning material. E*Trade Group (**www.etrade.com**), for example, provides an options primer on the terms and concepts in its online learning center. Investors can learn more about basic strategies: spreads, straddles, and hedges, among other things. There are several other independent sites that provide primers for novice, as well as more advanced, investors. One of the best is OptionSource.com (**www.optionsource.com**), run by Schaeffer's Investment Research, a Cincinnati options-research firm. Click on the education tab at this site, and it will take you through a comprehensive online tutorial on the basics of options investing. You also can study more advanced topics on options strategies and attend live cyber-seminars with options experts. The Options Industry Council (**www.optionscentral.com**), an industry trade group, also provides access to educational material, and an online schedule of free educational seminars across the country.

Options exchanges, brokers, and many independent sites provide access to quotes, analysis, and other tools for options investors. At the CBOE site, for example, investors can access a wealth of free information at its Trader's Tools section, including delayed quotes, charts, news, market data, and free company research from Zacks Investment Research. CBOE also provides an options calculator that allows investors work out the cost of a particular option. Other calculators are available on many sites, including OptionsSource.com.

Online Options Brokers

Finding a broker that offers options trading isn't difficult; most online brokers provide this service. However, before signing up, you should find out what strategies your broker allows its customers to use, and what the minimum requirements are. While most brokers allow investors to trade simple puts and calls, some don't allow more complex and risky strategies.

E*Trade, for example, doesn't allow its clients to trade naked options, but it does allow them to use some complex strategies. Accounts must be preapproved for options trading, and the minimum requirements range from $2,000 to $25,000 depending on risks involved. At Ameritrade (**www.ameritrade.com**), investors can trade simple options as well as spreads, straddles, and strangles.

Typically, commissions for trading stock options are higher than for trading stocks and can vary considerably from broker to broker. While some brokers offer a flat rate, others charge a flat rate plus an extra fee per contract of about $2 or $3. The cheapest charge is around $20 for a typical trade (10 contracts that cost about $2 apiece), according to Gomez Advisors. The same trade could cost more than $50 or $60 at other sites, including popular stock brokerage firms DLJdirect, a unit of Donaldson, Lufkin & Jenrette (**www.dljdirect.com**), and National Discount Brokers (**www.ndb.com**). Gomez posts detailed and updated information about brokers on its Web site (**www.gomezadvisors.com**).

Meanwhile, before you start trading, you may want to check out the CBOE's options toolbox, a free software package that allows you to simulate market conditions and test trade options. Ameritrade also allows investors to get some practice with its free "Darwin: Survival of the Fittest" options-trading simulation game. Customers can download the software for free from the broker's site.

Part Two

SIX

Tools of the Trade

Mention the words "online investing" to someone and, odds are, the first thing that will come to mind is placing a trade: You sign on to the Net, tap your order into a Web browser and—snap—a few moments later you have bought or sold a stock. But there is another part to online investing that is just as revolutionary as the electronic trade. It is the wealth of information and resources that abounds on the Net, everything from stock quotes and news stories, to Wall Street research reports and corporate documents—from primers that explain the basics of investing, to sophisticated spreadsheets that let you track the value of your portfolio minute-to-minute.

All of these things empower individual investors. To the desktop (or living room) of anyone with a PC and an Internet connection, they bring a package of information much like the resources that only professional investors had little more than five years ago. Sure, market pros still have the best resources and the most up-to-the-second information, and they can profit handsomely from that. But the playing field has been leveled markedly. Investors no longer have to call their broker, or wait for the morning newspaper, to see how their stocks did. They don't need an expensive brokerage account, or to trudge to the library to read research. They don't have to take out their calculators to figure the value of their stock and bond holdings.

Just as important, investors don't have to take out their checkbook or credit card to use many top-flight investing resources on the Net. Stock quotes are free on hundreds of Web sites, and reams of financial information about companies are available at no charge on scores of sites. Of course, the most sophisticated and timely information does come at a cost—usually in the form of a subscription fee to a financial Web site (often just $10 or so a month) or as a perk for the commissions you pay to your online brokerage firm. But investors can do quite well, and make some informed decisions, even if they stick with the freebies. Need more evidence of how radically investing research has changed? Consider stock charts.

Charts that track the value of a stock over time are a valuable way to quickly grasp how a stock has performed and make a good guess about its prospects. As recently as 1994, you had to use an expensive computer service that might cost more than $1,000 a year to see a stock chart that included the latest data. For individuals, one of the best bets was a weekly or monthly chartbook service, a magazine-like publication that would string together pages and pages of static information. And even those weren't cheap. In 1994, one popular chartbook published by Standard & Poor's cost $589 a year.

Today, stock charts are everywhere and absolutely free. Virtually every major portal site includes no-frills interactive stock charting, and even quite sophisticated charting—on specialized Web sites like BigCharts (**www.bigcharts.com**)—comes at no cost. With the Web, creating and delivering charts has become so efficient that companies like BigCharts believe they can prosper simply by selling advertisements on their Web pages, and selling their service to other sites.

Looking for other tools of the trade? You can view detailed financial information about companies on Market Guide Investor (**www. marketguide.com**), dig into corporate documents at the Securities and Exchange Commission site (**www.sec.gov**), and gather basic information about mutual funds at Morningstar (**www.morningstar.com**). Then, if you've opted to invest, you can check quotes and create a detailed spreadsheet to track the value of your portfolio at Yahoo! Finance (**finance.yahoo.com**)—all without spending a penny more than the cost of your Internet connection.

Yahoo! Finance - tech stocks - Microsoft Internet Explorer

File Edit View Favorites Tools Help

Address http://finance.yahoo.com/p?v&k=pf_1   Go

YAHOO! FINANCE Home - Yahoo! - Help

Telebank pays top yields. Now view accounts on Yahoo!

Get Quotes Basic symbol lookup

Welcome, wsjinteractive My Yahoo View - Customize - Sign Out

Portfolios manage - create : **tech stocks** [edit] | Java Mgr

Portfolio for wsjinteractive - Tech Stocks

Banking in California? Sign up to view your Bank of America accounts on Yahoo! Click to trade or open an account. - Important Disclaimer

Views: **Basic** [edit] - DayWatch - Performance - Fundamentals - Detailed - [Create New View]

Mon Jan 17 10:02am ET - U.S. Markets Closed for Martin Luther King, Jr. Day.

Symbol	Last Trade		Change		Volume	More Info
AOL	Jan 14	$63\,^1/_4$	$-2\,^1/_4$	-3.44%	37,620,300	Chart, News, SEC, Msgs Profile, Research, Insider
CMGI	Jan 14	$121\,^{15}/_{16}$	$-7\,^{13}/_{16}$	-6.02%	14,354,400	Chart, News, SEC, Msgs Profile, Research, Insider
COMS	Jan 14	$46\,^5/_{16}$	$+2\,^3/_8$	+5.41%	6,983,900	Chart, News, SEC, Msgs Profile, Research, Insider
CSCO	Jan 14	$107\,^9/_{16}$	$+1\,^3/_8$	+1.29%	21,811,500	Chart, News, SEC, Msgs Profile, Research, Insider
EBAY	Jan 14	$133\,^{13}/_{16}$	-4	-2.90%	2,917,800	Chart, News, SEC, Msgs Profile, Research, Insider
INTC	Jan 14	$103\,^1/_{16}$	$+12$	+13.18%	92,202,600	Chart, News, SEC, Msgs Profile, Research, Insider

Internet

Of course, not everything is free. Investment information is one of the few things, so far, that businesses have found people are willing to pay for on the Internet. But these charges are tiny compared with what investors faced just a few years ago. In the past, to get quick access to the research reports that Wall Street analysts prepare, one needed to have a lot of money—perhaps hundreds of thousands of dollars—in a brokerage account. Today, investors who use Charles Schwab, a discount brokerage firm, can read research reports from analysts at prestigious firms, as long as they keep a modest balance in a $29.95-a-trade brokerage account.

Some things, meanwhile, are cheap or free for a reason. The quality of research and other tools on the Net varies widely. For example, investment advice and research is widely available on Internet message boards and stock-picking Web sites. But in some cases, the people posting the information have no more expertise than you do, and in other cases they are paid stock promoters, or others with an interest in boosting a stock's price. (See Chapter 7 for a detailed discussion of message boards and Chapter 8 for a rundown on investing scams and deceptions.)

GOING IT ALONE

Martin Van Acker had been using a full-service broker to place trades and get advice on stock picks for eight years before he discovered, on a fluke, what the Internet could offer investors. In his work as an accountant, he had begun to use the Net to analyze companies and compare them with their competitors. Before long, the 43-year-old Naperville, Illinois, resident realized that a lot of the resources he had found would also be helpful in researching investments for himself. He spent more and more time poking around financial Web sites, and "it just kind of snowballed," he says.

Today, Mr. Van Acker makes most of his investing decisions independently, and spends five or six hours a week online doing research. Why take on that responsibility and devote so much time? Fees, mostly. Mr. Van Acker says his old broker helped him consistently beat the performance of the Dow Jones Industrial Average, but he couldn't justify paying the firm several thousand dollars a year in service fees. "Doing it on your own costs a small fraction [of that], maybe one tenth," he says. And so far, Mr. Van Acker says he's gotten higher returns than his broker did. "I've done much better. I've been more aggressive and taken more risk, but so far it's worked out," he says.

Thousands of investors have followed a path similar to Mr. Van Acker's. They have become what the brokerage industry calls "self-directed." They do their own homework, choose their own invest-ments and—most of the time—place their trades through an online broker. Plenty of investors had begun to move in this direction before the Web emerged—the discount brokerage industry has been eating away at full-service firms since 1975, when brokerage commissions were deregulated, allowing prices to fall. But the real drop in commis-sions didn't come, and investors didn't have easy access to the infor-mation they needed to choose investments, until online trading and financial Web sites burst on to the scene.

For years, you were beholden to your broker for almost all of your investing information. Everything from stock quotes to getting infor-mation on companies and investing tips often meant making a call to, or taking a call from, your broker. It is a great arrangement for the bro-kers: Get a client on the phone, start talking and, soon enough, they'll make a trade and you get a commission—which could total several hundred dollars. Of course, investors could benefit, too, from brokers' professional advice and experience.

That still exists today, though brokers tend to call themselves in-vestment advisers, and more and more accounts are moving away from commissions toward an annual fee that is based on how much money is in the account. Most of this is done through the traditional full-service firms, like Merrill Lynch and Morgan Stanley Dean Wit-ter. Those firms are present on the Web, but aren't abandoning their traditional business. So, while they offer online trading, they don't do so at a deep discount, and they don't promote self-directed in-vesting, but try to foster broker-client relationships. They post research, stock quotes, and investment calculators on the Web, but the best is restricted to clients. They view these tools as a complement to, not a replacement for, their brokers' advice.

The boom in self-directed investing also owes part of its roots to the fact that corporations have been moving away from traditional pension plans since the late 1980s. Old pension plans required little involvement from employees: They worked for years with the promise that their employer would provide a certain level of pay during their retirement years. Companies made investments as they saw fit to cover those pension obligations, and as long as companies kept their promises, employees gave little thought to retirement investments. But those pension plans were expensive, and sometimes employers didn't keep up with their obligations. Companies began to move toward different pension schemes, such as 401(k) plans, that require employees to take a role in funding their retirements and selecting the investments they choose to hold. Investing, something that once was reserved mostly for the wealthy, began to grab the attention of more and more Americans.

Just as Wall Street's audience was growing (and perhaps, in part, because it was growing), the U.S. stock market entered its biggest bull market of all time—one that stretched across much of the 1990s. Investing became a hobby, and financial news and information became an obsession. It started with cable television stations like CNBC, doling out a steady stream of updates on the markets and investing ideas from Wall Street pros—and an endless crawl of stock prices along the bottom of television screens. The enthusiasm for investment information began to jump to the Internet in the mid-1990s, as the World Wide Web emerged as an easy-to-use and widely accessible window on Wall Street. The Web promised a storehouse of investing resources.

One needn't be an investing junkie to benefit from the Internet's resources. To the contrary, the Net's resources include plenty of information for people who know little or nothing about Wall Street, or managing their own finances. For them, introductory guides and primers abound. One can find enough of this kind of free stuff on the Web to make many books on investing and finance unnecessary (though, of course, you didn't read that here). Web site operators are more than happy to teach you the basics of stocks, bonds, and mutual funds: The more people they can initiate into the investing community, the more customers those sites will have for their services.

For the Novice

If you are new to the Web or investing or both, the idea of do-it-yourself investing may be intimidating. You may think that choosing investments is something best reserved for people with more experience, but the Internet is actually a great place for beginning investors to learn the basics. Many Web sites produced by reputable organizations provide tutorials on financial information from the ground up, and they're a terrific starting point.

One of the best-known sites for home-grown investing, Motley Fool (**www.fool.com**), is also one of the best for learning the ropes. The contents of the site, long a staple of America Online, are now much more than the financial message boards that first made it popular. The site's Fool's School section, for instance, starts with such basic information as defining a stock, a bond, and a mutual fund. The site goes on to discuss how to pick a broker and to review definitions of growth stocks, index funds, and selling stock short. David and Tom Gardner, who cre-

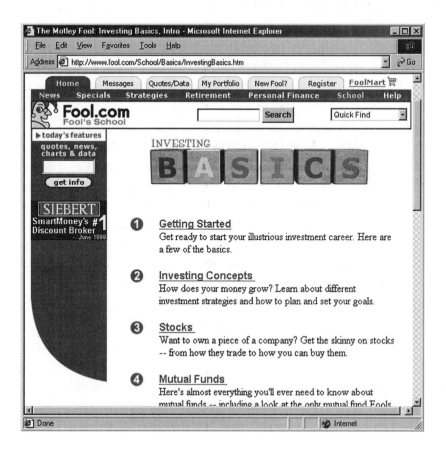

ated Motley Fool, have built a brand around their theories of investing, which they lay out in something called "The 13 Steps to Investing Foolishly." They have moved well beyond their beginnings on the Net, hosting a regular radio program, and writing books on investing. The Gardners' take on investing isn't universally accepted, but the site offers a wealth of information—if you can put up with the constant plays on the word *fool* and images of the Gardners' fools hats.

There are many other baseline investing sites. America Online's Money Basics subsection, produced in conjunction with Smart-Money.com (**www.smartmoney.com**) and available on the AOL on-line service, lays out the fundamentals of stock, bond, and mutual fund investing. Zacks Investment Research, a firm best known for providing data on securities analysts' earnings estimates and stock recommenda-tions, includes a free, detailed tutorial about investing on one of its Web sites (**www.zacks.com/invest101**). The Nasdaq Stock Market's site (**www.nasdaq.com**) has an area called Investor Resources, which includes an introduction to investing, and guides on how to assess your finances, diversify a portfolio, and choose a broker. Many of the online brokers have financial planning tools, but their advice is likely to steer you toward the firm's own products.

The Securities and Exchange Commission (**www.sec.gov**), in addi-tion to providing corporate documents—such as detailed annual re-ports—offers a lot of basic information and warnings to new investors on its site. It includes an online brochure that lays out the basics of a savings and investing plan in the form of a road map. The brochure be-gins with instructions for deciding what your financial goals are, and goes on to explain how to avoid problems such as unscrupulous brokers and online investing scams. The SEC site also includes a quiz that you can take to test your "money smarts" after you have studied the basics.

Once you know the basics and are ready to graduate to some-thing just a bit more sophisticated, Armchair Millionaire (**www.armchairmillionaire.com**) is a good place to go, and its friendly tone and simple language make it appealing. It's geared toward mutual funds and long-term, conservative investors, offering a commonsense approach to personal finance. The site, for instance, lays out what it calls "Five Steps to Financial Freedom"—a set of fundamental notions to help beginners get a handle on how to grow an investment portfolio. The site's recurring theme—no surprise—is how to amass $1 million in savings, and how long it will take you to get there. No magic solutions are offered, just basics—such as remembering to save in tax-deferred accounts (like a 401(k), which is funded from pretax earnings and isn't taxed until retirement); forcing yourself to put aside some of your take-home pay each month (it uses 10% as a starting point); and concentrating your long-term investments in a variety of stock mutual funds (it suggests spreading money equally in funds that invest in big stocks, small stocks, and non-U.S. stocks).

Microsoft's MoneyCentral Web site (**www.moneycentral.com**) includes a section on getting started with investing, featuring a "Research Wizard" that pulls together different types of information about companies and funds in a straightforward, easy-to-understand way. For instance, when it discusses a stock's historical quotes, it refers to them in plain language: How much have other investors been willing to pay for the stock in the past?

Many of the Web sites that offer investment basics, of course, also include information on more advanced topics. Intuit's Quicken.com site (**www.quicken.com**), associated with the company's popular personal finance software, includes a section called the "Self Reliant Investor." It addresses topics such as interpreting the meaning of insider sales and how to make sense of things like a company's price-to-sales or price-to-earnings ratios. The former is the company's stock price divided by its per-share sales, and the latter is its stock price divided by its per-share earnings. Both are called valuation measures. The higher the number, the greater the potential that the stock is trading too high relative to the company's financial position, making the stock very risky.

CALCULATORS AND WORKSHEETS

Time to put all of that new-found investing knowledge to work. You know what a stock is, how it is traded—and maybe even how to do some elementary stock analysis. Now it's time to evaluate your own finances and decide what types of investments make the most sense for you. How much of your money should you keep in stocks and how much in bonds, for instance, if you are planning for a retirement that is still 35 years away? What if it is only 10 years away? How much money should you sock away each month to buy a home or to be ready to pay for your two-year-old twins' college education?

These are just some of the questions that can be put to the calculators and worksheets that are available on scores of investing Web sites. These tools, which typically present a series of questions that must be answered using an online form (similar to the mutual fund screening tools described in Chapter 4), are the closest the Internet has come to providing personalized advice and feedback. It's not surprising that Web sites can dole out stock quotes and process trades like brokers traditionally did—both those two functions are largely mechanical. Worksheets and calculators are where the Web comes closest to mimicking human interaction. John types in information about his situation and goals, and the site replies, "Well, John, a person in your situation should invest . . ." Yes, some worksheets will call you by name—if you choose to share it with them.

But just as a broker can give bad advice, so, too, can a worksheet. Investors may be well served running their questions through the tools on several sites to get a sort of online second opinion. Different online worksheets have been known to give different answers to the same question. Of course, although computers can act like humans, they can't give truly individualized advice or weigh all of the variables as can a human adviser. A good broker, for instance, will develop an understanding of your tolerance for risk, which can allow him or her to make investment recommendations that are far more precise to your needs than any computer program can. Even the most comprehensive Web site won't be able to answer all of your questions. (Then again, no computer has ever churned a customer's account or recommended bad investments just to reap commissions. The same certainly can't be said for human brokers.)

CALCULATOR CONFUSION

It's not a huge sum, but $12,000 isn't chump change, either. That's the dollar difference between the answers given by Fidelity Investments' Web site (www.fidelity.com) and Kiplinger.com (www.kiplinger.com), when the same question was put to each of their college-cost calculators.

Both calculators were used to figure the cost of a four-year education, starting in the year 2010 at a school that presently charges $20,000 a year in tuition. Both calculators were given assumptions that the money invested to pay the tuition bill would return 7% a year and that the inflation rate for tuition would be 5% a year. Fidelity put the total cost at $136,827, while Kiplinger put it at $149,498.

Asset allocation—how much money you put into each of the various investment types, such as stocks, bonds, or "cash"—is an important starting point for any investing plan, and it is a task that is well-suited for calculators. People of different ages and with varying levels of comfort in taking on risk should allocate separate amounts within their total portfolio to different types of investments. For example, stocks tend to post the biggest average gains, but they also are the riskiest (meaning that in any given time period they could fall very sharply in value). As a result, people who are many years away from retirement often opt to invest a big part of their money in stocks, because they want their money to grow as much as possible, and they have the time to ride out periodic slumps in the market. People who are just a few years from retirement, or those who can't stand the thought of investment losses, meanwhile, often put far less money into stocks. Although stocks may offer better returns, these investors aren't suited to the risk that the market will take a big tumble.

Sites such as SmartMoney.com (**www.smartmoney.com**) offer straight-forward tools for coming up with a rough asset-allocation plan. At the SmartMoney allocator, you use your computer mouse to drag a pointer across several scales on one page of the Web site. You set your number of years to retirement age, the size of your portfolio, your annual spending amount, and your income tax bracket. Also, you estimate your tolerance for volatility in the market (if you agonize over market swings, you drag the pointer to the low end of the scale; if you are unfazed by a 1000-point drop in the Dow Jones Industrial Average, you drag it to the high end), and your general feelings about the outlook for the stock market and economy (setting the pointer between "weak" and

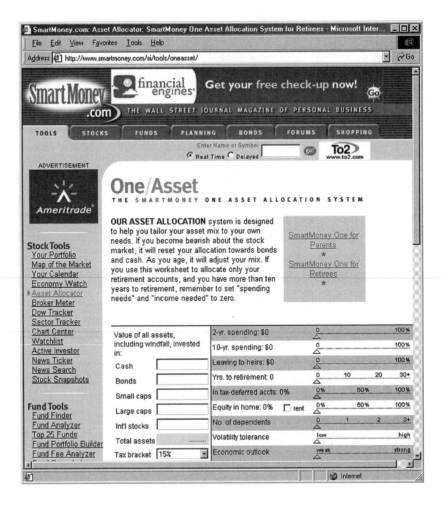

"strong"). As you make all of these adjustments, a pie chart at the bottom of the screen suggests what percentage of your investments should be in blue-chip stocks, small stocks, non-U.S. stocks, bonds, and cash.

(Cash doesn't mean money in your wallet—or even under your mattress. It refers to money kept in an account that has little or no risk, and is very liquid [meaning it can be withdrawn at any time]. Cash includes money in bank savings accounts or money-market funds. These cash holdings earn a small investment return.)

Asset allocation is just one type of calculator available on the Web. Hundreds of other calculators and worksheets can be found to help with everything from savings and investing, to getting a loan and choosing the type of insurance coverage that is right for you.

But calculators also can be confusing, and they sometimes require you to provide some detailed financial information. For example, a worksheet on the Financenter (**www.financenter.com**) Web site, designed to help you determine if you are saving enough to meet your needs in retirement, asks you to estimate what your monthly living expenses will be at retirement. It goes on to explain that people tend to spend more in their early retirement years, for things like travel, and that expenses then typically level off for a period. They usually climb again in late retirement—because of increased medical expenses, among other things. But that isn't much to go on in filling in this crucial part of the calculator, and users may find that the financial consultant they thought they could avoid by using the calculator actually is needed just to answer the calculator's questions.

Moreover, calculators often ask you to provide answers that you couldn't possibly have. Financenter.com, and many other sites, ask you how old you might be when you die. Quicken.com's retirement planner calculator (**www.quicken.com**) asks you to estimate the annual rate of inflation between now and your retirement. (Though it does offer some help, with a chart of the annual inflation rate for more than 70 years and the fact that the average inflation rate has been about 3% a year.) Another common, but difficult, question is asked by SmartMoney.com: How much do you expect your investments to return for the rest of your life?

Even with their shortcomings, online calculators and worksheets can be valuable, if only as a starting point. You may decide to get some general ideas and background online—and that may suffice for a while. At some point, you may decide to solicit some personal, professional advice. "[Calculators] aren't meant to be an end-all and a be-all. They're a tool to get good ideas," says Marni Patterson, marketing communications manager for Financenter. "Use them to get your ducks in a row, then go to a financial planner."

Some of the most useful calculators are the simplest. They don't try to answer grand questions that have lifelong implications, but rather are designed to provide straightforward answers. For example, Quicken.com includes a calculator that helps you determine the tax implications of selling an investment for a long-term or short-term capital gain. Say, for example, you picked a winning stock that has grown in value to $12,500 from $10,000 in just eleven months. Quicken's calculator shows that if you sell right away, you will end up with a tax bill of $700 (assuming a 28% tax rate) because your profit will be classified by the Internal Revenue Service as a short-term gain. On the other hand, if you wait until you've held the investment for a full year (and the stock holds its value), it would be classified as a long-term gain, and the tax bill would be just $500. Of course, the calculator can't tell you if a swing in the stock market will wipe out your profit during that extra month, but it does allow you to do a quick analysis that can help you make an informed decision.

Another simple but useful calculator that can be found on Lycos (**www.lycos.com**) and many other Web sites allows you to determine how much you'll pay each month for your home mortgage. In the past, you would need to flip through the pages of a loan-amortization schedule to figure out how large your mortgage payment would be for various size loans or at different interest rates. But with an online calculator, you simply plug in numbers and push a button to find, for instance, that a 30-year, $150,000 mortgage at a 7% interest rate yields a $998-a-month payment, while the same loan at 8% requires a monthly payment of $1,101.

The SEC's Web site includes a useful calculator that allows investors to figure out just how much they will pay in mutual fund fees over time. The calculator allows investors to compare the costs of owning various funds, depending on their annual expense levels. It shows, for instance, that a $10,000 investment in a no-load stock fund (which doesn't require a sales charge when investors buy shares) will result in $4,000 in fees (and lost earnings) over a 15-year period, assuming the fund charges a 0.50% annual fee. A similar no-load fund with an annual fee of just 0.35% would result in fees and lost earnings of just $2,800 over the same time period. Such results drive home the fact that investors should examine fees, and not just investment style or past performance, when selecting a mutual fund investment.

There are myriad calculators on the Web, and it pays to surf many sites to see what they offer that would be of interest to you. Financenter. com is one of the most comprehensive. It has over 100 calculators organized into major categories, including homes, autos, investing, saving, retirement, and insurance. Online brokerage firms also offer calculators, but some of these are only available to the firms' clients. Morgan Stanley Dean Witter (**www.online.msdw.com**) has a long list of free calculators dealing with a variety of subjects. TD Waterhouse (**www.waterhouse.com**) and Quick & Reilly (**www.qronline.com**) offer calculators geared to selecting an Individual Retirement Account.

INVESTMENT RESEARCH

Stock and mutual fund research is where the rubber meets the road. You know you need to invest and save, and you may already know how much you ought to plunk down in stocks, bonds, funds, and cash. The next step is deciding exactly what to buy. Using the Web, you can make a decision on what stocks and which companies have the best prospects. Many sites give an overview of companies' finances, with detailed data on earnings and the like. The SEC site and others that tap into the agency's Edgar system (short for Electronic Data Gathering, Analysis, and Retrieval) give you easy access to huge stores of documents that companies themselves produce. Independent research firms and some online brokerage firms let you tap into company analysis prepared by Wall Street analysts. (A summary of analysts' views on companies is also available on many sites.)

Packages of information on mutual funds are also within easy reach on the Net, using Web sites such as Morningstar.com (**www.morningstar.com**) and the Sage service (offered through America Online). Details on mutual fund research are presented in Chapter 4. As for bonds, the Web is just now becoming a force for trading and research. There are a handful of sites available, as described in Chapter 5.

The stock and company research sources available on the Web give investors information that puts them almost in the same league as Wall Street pros. Sites that give an overview of company financials, analysts' stock recommendations, and earnings forecasts are comparable with what big-time investors use today—though the information may not be quite as detailed or up-to-date. For instance, when an analyst at a major securities firm changes his or her earnings forecast for a company, that news is almost instantly available on Wall Street though a service called First Call, owned by Thomson Financial and a group of big brokerage firms. But not all of those detailed and instant reports are released by First Call outside of Wall Street. Rather, it releases just a subset of that information on the Web, and often delays its release.

Meanwhile, Main Street investors still don't have access to the breadth of analysts' research anywhere near that of Wall Street professionals. Reports from several Wall Street firms are available through online brokers, such as the access to internal research that Merrill Lynch and Donaldson, Lufkin & Jenrette give to clients of their online investing services. But the best way to get all of the information you crave, as soon as it's available, is still to have relationships with brokers at many big firms, because it is still something reserved for professional investors.

Nonetheless, ready access to any of this type of information and research is something as new as the Internet. A several-day delay in the release of company documents by the SEC, an overview of brokerage recommendations, earnings forecasts, and the full text of even a smattering of professionally prepared research reports are items that small-time individual investors didn't have before the emergence of the Net. At best, they could have gotten some of these things by making a trip to their regional branch office of the Securities and Exchange Commission or a good local library.

Web Portals and Other Overviews

A good place to start your research is one of the many Web portal sites. These free sites, such as Yahoo! Finance (**finance.yahoo.com**), Excite (**www.excite.com**), Lycos (**www.lycos.com**), and America Online (**www.aol.com**), serve as gateways to the Net. They are built around so-called search engines that allow you to scan the Net for the information you need, but also include a lot of general information. Many of them have a personal finance, money, or investing section.

In addition to offering links to the major investing resources elsewhere on the Web, portals also post lots of investing information on their own sites. Most portals include things like financial news, highlights from companies' financial statements, and summaries of analysts' views on companies' earnings and shares. Some of the portals have other features that make them stand out. Excite, for instance, allows users to create a customized version of the site that includes news alerts about companies they track.

Of course, the news on Excite, like other portal sites', is often lacking in analysis and depth. Some sites simply distribute press releases that come directly from companies, which naturally present just one side of every story. Companies are free to boast about earnings or new products with no skepticism or input from third parties.

Yahoo! Finance, the investing portion of the popular Yahoo! portal site, is well known for its hugely popular stock message boards (see Chapter 7). But it also has a vast amount of data on individual companies—everything from data pulled from companies' earnings statements and balance sheets to a rundown on stock sales by company insiders, analysts' ratings, and earnings estimates. Other sites have similar information, and many times the information is provided to the portal by research firms, which in turn have their own sites.

For example, Media General Financial Services (**www.mgfs.com**) and Market Guide (**www.marketguide.com**) supply many sites with earnings information and the like, which they compile from SEC filings, and both also provide that same information, for free, on their own sites. Likewise, Thomson Financial (**www.thomsoninvest.net**)

and Zacks Investment Research (**www.zacks.com**) provide summaries of analysts' reports and recommendations to many other sites, and maintain their own outposts on the Web. Both of those sites, though, charge fees for access to their most timely and detailed information.

Hoover's Online (**www.hoovers.com**) is in a similar position. The company started out publishing profiles of companies in a book, and now provides that type of information to many Web sites. It distributes similar information on its own Web site, including more detailed narrative on companies (publicly traded and privately held, U.S. and overseas), biographies of their top executives, and a rundown of their competitors—some for free, some not. The writing is entertaining: Its description of the Associated Press, for example, is written in the familiar style of an AP news story.

Company Documents

For some people, a summary of a company's financial information isn't enough. They want to go to the full reports that the corporation has filed, by law, with the Securities and Exchange Commission. The SEC's Web site makes this as easy as typing the company's name into the Edgar database. And there is much more filed away in Edgar than earnings reports. Annual reports outlining the latest developments at companies are also available, as are the disclosure documents that corporations must submit when they plan a public stock offering. The offering documents, in the form of a "registration statement" or "prospectus," contain intimate details about companies, including the pay of their executives, and a rundown of the risks their businesses face from competitors.

The SEC Web site, though, has some shortcomings. For one, filings are withheld from the site for at least one day—meaning that the key document that contains a bombshell about a company's prospects won't be available immediately. For most people, such a delay isn't a problem, but others may find that the site leaves them feeling behind. For them, there are other Web sites run by private companies that allow access to the same Edgar database without the delay, but for a fee. At

Edgar Online (**www.edgar-online.com**), for instance, subscriptions start at about $10 a month. Some people find non-SEC Edgar sites easier to use. For instance, some sites more clearly explain the purposes of the various filings that are included in the database. Form 10-Q is a quarterly earnings report, form 10-K is an annual report, and form S-1 is the disclosure document for an initial public offering.

Web sites run by companies themselves can also be useful resources. Most include background information on the company's business and products, as well as copies of its recent announcements and SEC filings—though sometimes links to company filings simply direct you into the SEC site. But you need to exercise caution when using company sites for research, because disreputable companies can post slick Web sites as a means to boost their stock price. So while you wouldn't expect to find misleading information on IBM's Web site (**www.ibm.com**), you may be misled on the site of a penny-stock company.

Meanwhile, some sites allow you to order copies of companies' annual reports that are delivered by mail. One such service is run by Public Register's Annual Report Service (**www.prars.com**), while another, which has ties to several newspapers, including *The Wall Street Journal,* is Investor Communications Business Inc. (**www.icbinc.com**).

Wall Street Research Reports

When professional investors on Wall Street are trying to decide whether to buy or sell a stock, they rely quite heavily on the opinions of securities analysts. These individuals are paid to study companies, quite handsomely in many cases, and they often have access to much more than the official documents that corporations release. Analysts often meet with executives of firms to quiz them about how their businesses are doing. They may visit factories and offices, and investigate competitors to try to identify potential trouble points.

Analysts are divided into two camps, known in industry parlance as buy side and sell side. Buy-side analysts work for the investment firms that are considering making an investment, while sell-side analysts work for the brokerage firms that are aiming to handle the trades. Because buy-side analysts don't have any interest in whether a trade is made or not, their opinions are often considered less biased than the analysts who work for brokers. But a lot of talented people are attracted to the sell-side community by the lucrative pay that can be found there, and many of them are highly respected. Their comments about stocks often move prices, sometimes significantly.

A considerable effort is exerted on Wall Street to be among the first to learn about changes in analysts' views—their estimates of companies' earnings, and their investment ratings of companies' stocks ("buy," "hold," "sell," etc.). The first people to learn that a prominent analyst has, say, raised a rating on a company's stock can buy shares before its price jumps. Sell-side analysts themselves call some of their firm's best clients, typically the managers of important mutual funds or pension funds. (The client who gives the firm the most business gets the first call—that's how influential data provider First Call got its name.)

Despite the inroads to Wall Street research that the Internet has opened for individual investors, folks on Main Street still can't hope to get news about analysts' ratings and earnings-estimate changes quickly enough to make a trade before companies' stocks move. Word travels quickly on Wall Street, and stocks sometimes move several dollars in value within minutes after analysts first make their comments. Individual investors can get news about analysts on many financial news or information Web sites, and from some brokerage firm sites, but those updates can come hours after the analyst first made his or her thoughts known, and well after the company's stock has moved.

Nonetheless, individual investors can still benefit a lot from their delayed access to analysts' research. Summaries of analysts' recommendations and earnings forecasts, available on portals and many other financial sites, are useful starting points, and the full text of analysts' reports can provide an exhaustive look at a company, its industry, and its prospects. These kinds of details can be invaluable for investors aiming to make a long-term investment. There are ways to find a lot of this research on the Web, though it often comes at a cost, and is typically available from sell-side analysts. The buy side typically doesn't release its research—it has nothing to gain from sharing with others the intelligence its analysts have uncovered.

Brokerage firms often use their Web sites to release reports that have been prepared by their own analysts—or analysts at other firms with which they have partnerships—but the information is only available to clients. Different firms have varying minimum requirements for allowing access to the reports. Charles Schwab, for instance, allows clients with account balances under $100,000 to read reports from Credit Suisse First Boston and Hambrecht & Quist for a monthly fee. Donaldson, Lufkin & Jenrette allows clients of its DLJdirect online unit access to reports by DLJ analysts if they have at least $100,000 in their account. Merrill Lynch and Salomon Smith Barney, among others, also allow clients to receive research over the Net—though non-clients sometimes can view research for a short trial period if they register as users of the firms' sites. Registered users are required to provide personal information to the site.

Several Web sites allow investors to order copies of reports from a wide range of brokerage houses and independent research firms—such as Standard & Poor's—over the Internet. Zacks Investment Research (**www.zacks.com**) has reports from 250 companies while Multex (**www.multexinvestor.com**) has reports from more than 250 firms. Some reports are available for free, but most are provided on a pay-per-view basis. Multex, for instance, prices reports at anywhere from $4 to $150 apiece. Most reports are at least several days old when they are released on Multex (some are released more quickly, but those typically don't come from big, influential Wall Street firms). Multex offers quicker access to reports from a different Web site (**www.multex.com**), but users must be approved by the firm that wrote the research. The same prerequisites required to get the research directly from the firm apply to those trying to read it via Multex: You must be a big institutional investor (managing a portfolio of, say, $100 million), a research analyst at a major firm, or a valuable prospective client.

Research firms, and their distribution partners like Multex, generally are more open with their analysts' views on the markets as a whole. Many firms provide reports from their market strategists—the gurus who are frequently quoted in the financial press—whose job it is to an-

alyze and make predictions about the outlook for the stock or bond market as a whole. These reports, from major firms like Merrill Lynch and Lehman Brothers, can be useful in gauging the overall investing environment, an important starting point when deciding when and if to buy a stock, mutual fund, or bond. But the reports usually don't recommend specific investments.

Finally, not everything that is labeled as research is worth reading. As with everything on the Web, you must consider the source of the research reports you read. Some analysts are highly respected for their skills on Wall Street, and others are ignored. (For help in sorting this out, *Institutional Investor* magazine [**www.iimagazine.com**] and *The Wall Street Journal* [**wsj.com**] both publish reports each year on the best analysts in the business—though plenty of good analysts never make these lists.) The biggest risk in using a research report is coming across one that was written by a promoter for the company featured in the report. These pay-for-promotion reports abound on the Net, usually on Web sites run by stock promoters. These sites, and the authors of promotional research reports, are required to disclose their compensation agreements. Look for a "disclaimer" statement on the research or Web site when gathering research. Most times, these disclosures can be found there, but of course, not all Web site operators follow the law. (For more on Web site scams and deceptions, see Chapter 8.)

FINANCIAL NEWS

The popularity that cable television station CNBC attained as the bull market extended through the 1990s illustrated that consumers' appetite for financial information just wasn't being satisfied by daily newspapers, and weekly or monthly business magazines. Investors wanted immediate information on the markets and the news that was moving stocks, and those demands also spurred the development of scores of financial news Web sites. These sites—as with sites that offer investment calculators, worksheets, and investment research—have become yet another empowering tool for investors. Again, information that was readily available only to professional investors, or through a commission-hungry broker, 10 years ago is ubiquitous now.

But quality varies. On many portal sites, companies' press releases pass for news, and while press releases can be a useful way to learn about official announcements—like earnings reports, dividend declarations, and product introductions—they don't offer much perspective, and certainly no objective analysis. Some sites publish stories that were written and researched by reporters, but again, not all of these offerings are created equally. Some upstart sites—particularly some of the free ones—don't attract particularly seasoned reporters and editors, and they sometimes have a tough time getting access to information or sticking to traditional journalistic tenets of objectivity and skepticism. The best news sites tend to be those with links to established newspaper, magazine, or television news organizations. Some, but not all, of these sites charge a subscription fee.

Financial newswires are an important component of many Web sites, including those run by newspapers, television networks, brokerage firms, and Internet-only information providers. News from the biggest wire services, including Associated Press, Reuters, and Dow Jones Newswires, are all widely available on the Web, though in most cases only a slimmed-down version of each of these organizations' financial wires is available online. Like brokerage firms, the news wires reserve their most timely and authoritative information for their clients who pay the highest prices. They aren't willing to provide premium services that cost hundreds of dollars a month to a low-price Internet site.

Some of the best business news sites include: CBS MarketWatch (**www.cbs.marketwatch.com**), MSNBC (**www.msnbc.com**), and CNNfn (**www.cnnfn.com**)—all free, and linked to broadcast networks; *The Wall Street Journal Interactive Edition* (**wsj.com**) and *The New York Times* (**www.nytimes.com**)—a subscription site and a free site, respectively, both tied to major newspapers; and TheStreet.com (**www.thestreet.com**)—an independent site. Many of the major portal sites offer news from financial newswires, and some wires run their own sites. Among them are Reuters Moneynet (**www.moneynet. com**), which offers some Reuters news for free, and SmartMoney.com (**www.smartmoney.com**), which offers a selection of business news stories from Dow Jones for free. Quote.com (**www.quote.com**), which offers some Reuters, Dow Jones, and AP news for free, requires users to register. It provides more in-depth news to paying subscribers.

NARROWING YOUR SEARCH
AND GETTING TECHNICAL

Stock Screening

Trying to decide which companies to research and follow in the news can be daunting. Thousands of companies are publicly traded, and it can be difficult to find the ones whose stocks mesh with your investing goals. For example, some investors, especially those of retirement age, may want stocks that tend to have relatively stable share prices and pay out lots of dividend income to cover living expenses. These investors may want to scan the market for utility stocks, which tend to have these characteristics. Once they find all the utilities, these investors may wish to identify those that historically have had the biggest dividends. From there, they can do more rigorous research into just a handful of companies that seem to best meet their needs and identify the individual stocks they may want to purchase.

As we saw with mutual funds (see Chapter 4), the Web has given investors easy access to tools that can identify investments tending to have certain characteristics. With mutual funds, an investor may use one of these screening tools to find funds that invest in certain industry groups and have had a certain level of annual performance in the past. With stocks, investors can look for companies involved in certain businesses that have grown their earnings at a desired rate in the past. Stock screening devices work the same way that mutual fund screening tools work. The user fills out an online form to identify the characteristics he or she finds important, and the site chugs through a database to find stocks that meet all of these requirements.

Intuit's Quicken.com (**www.quicken.com**) offers some of the best screening tools, some geared to beginners and others to advanced investors. The most elementary stock searches are based on popular investment strategies, like choosing just small stocks or undervalued stocks—shares of companies whose stock price is low relative to other companies in the same business and with the same earnings power. The more sophisticated screens allow investors to examine up to 33 variables, including specific industry groups, minimum and maximum requirements for things like price-to-earnings and price-to-book ratios and growth rates over various time periods.

Once you have come up with a list of stocks using Quicken's screening tool, you can move on to a similar tool that the site calls a stock evaluator. It lets you compare 12 data measures for up to 30 companies, and provides the results in a polished chart format. This is a good, quick way to comparison shop for stocks, letting you compare things like dividends and revenue-per-employee figures, which divide a company's total receipts by the number of people on its payroll. In theory, the higher the number, the more productive its workers are.

Some sites charge a subscription fee for access to their stock screening tools. Morningstar (**www.morningstar.com**), for instance, charges $9.95 a month or $99 a year for a subscription that includes the use of its best screening tools. Subscribers to Wall Street City (**www.wallstreetcity.com**), a Web site run by Telescan of Houston, are charged $9.95 a month for a subscription that gets them access to one screening tool. The site offers a more advanced screener for $34.95 a month, which attempts to identify "What's Working Now"— a rundown on the types of companies whose share prices are rallying at the moment. It can help identify other companies that may be good short-term investments.

At the more costly end, Zacks Investment Research (**www.zacks. com**) offers its Research Wizard product for $600 a year. The service, originally marketed only to institutional investors, provides research and tracking tools, in addition to a high-powered screening tool that includes 300 potential variables.

J. P. Morgan runs a free Web site that allows you to screen for non-U.S. companies that trade on major U.S. markets in the form of American depositary receipts, or ADRs. These securities, which are sometimes called American depositary shares, or ADSs, are sponsored by U.S. firms and represent a specific number of foreign company shares. The sponsor holds the actual shares in the company's home market, and issues ADRs that can be traded in the United States. The J. P. Morgan site (**www.adr.com**) allows investors to look for specific types of companies in particular countries. A search for beverage companies located in Mexico, for instance, came up with Coca-Cola FEMSA and Fomento Economico Mexicano, both traded as ADRs on the New York Stock Exchange.

Charting

A company's financial standing and business prospects are the most important factors that investors should consider when choosing a stock in which to invest. In Wall Street's parlance, examining these types of issues is called fundamental research. But many investors, including those on Wall Street, also rely on so-called technical research, particularly when it comes to predicting the movement of stocks over a relatively short period: days or weeks, rather than months or years. Technical research largely ignores things like earnings expectations, and concentrates instead on trading patterns of stocks, both in terms of price and volume. The number one tool of the technical analyst is the stock chart.

Charting the performance of stocks is an investing tool that goes back decades, and, of course, it started out as a time-consuming process that was done by hand. One of the most common technical tools, the moving average, required an incredibly cumbersome process of plotting and calculating stock prices. The moving average is the average price that a stock has traded at over a recent period—say, fifty days. Stocks have a tendency to stay above or below their moving average: Technical analysts usually view a move through a moving average as a significant event, one that could foreshadow continued gains (when a stock rises above the moving average) or continued losses (when a stock falls below its moving average). Because of all of the arithmetic involved in charting by hand, even simple things like moving averages were special.

Computer automation made charting far easier, of course, but until recently, charts still were accessible only to a few people. Subscriptions to chartbooks were available to individual investors, but even in the early 1990s, any degree of interactivity in charting required a special connection to a charting service—via modem, FM radio signal, or satellite—and could cost hundreds of dollars a month.

As with so many other investing tools and resources, it took the Internet to bring charting to ordinary investors. Quote.com was the first commercial Web site to offer charts, introducing a limited charting feature in late 1994 that allowed investors to look at historical data over varied time periods. Quote.com brought on additional charting features over the next several years, allowing investors to do things like compare the performance of two stocks side by side. Today it offers a robust charting package that allows investors to explore analysis like a stock's relative strength and its money flows—two indicators designed to help predict stock movement—for free.

Charting tools are available for free on scores of Web sites today. Many offer charts produced by a few big charting services, including Big Charts (**www.bigcharts.com**) and Stockpoint (**www.stockpoint. com**). Those companies operate their own Web sites as well. Only the most sophisticated charting functions, and those involving so-called real-time stock prices, are kept behind subscription walls. (Real-time stock quotes represent prices of trades that occurred no more than 90 seconds earlier. Most quotes available on the Net are delayed by 15 or 20 minutes.) For instance, Quote.com charges $100 a month for its high-level real-time charting package.

STOCK QUOTES AND PORTFOLIOS

Once you have identified the right investments and made your purchases, you can use the Internet to keep track of their performance in the market. Stock quotes can be retrieved from a wide range of Web sites, including Internet portals, news sites, financial research sites, and online brokerage sites. Some corporations even provide up-to-date stock quotes for their shares right on their corporate home page. Investors waiting for stocks to reach certain levels can—and do—check quotes repeatedly during the market day, no longer forced to wait for daily price updates in the newspaper or for a conversation with their stockbroker.

For most investors, the delayed stock quotes offered on most sites are sufficient. When you are investing for the long term, a 20-minute delay in the delivery of a price quote is of no consequence. Delays are built in by the major stock exchanges and by the Nasdaq Stock Market as they seek to hold on to the value of real-time information for the traditional players who have access to that data. Indeed, up-to-the-minute information is important for traders who need to move into and out of stocks based on very small price movements. But it has also helped to foster the traditional two-tiered structure to investment

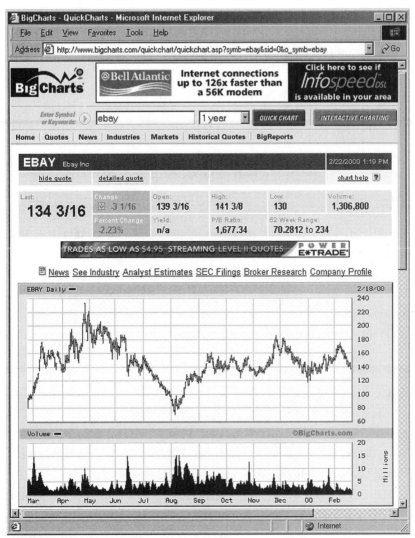

Used by permission of www.BigCharts.com.

information on Wall Street: Professional investors have the first crack at information and individual investors are beholden to the professionals.

But the Internet—and financial television networks—have helped to pry stock-quote information loose. The exchanges now allow CNBC to run real-time quotes along the bottom of viewers' television screens, instead of the delayed quotes they were forced to use at first, and the exchanges have adopted a fee structure that has allowed Web sites to more easily offer real-time quotes. Traditionally, services that provided stock quotes had to pay a fee based on every computer screen on which their data were provided. On the Net, where millions of people can in theory use every Web site, that model just didn't work. So, the exchanges established a payment scheme that charges Web site operators a small fee for every real-time quote they deliver to users. As a result, many sites now offer real-time quotes, but users are forced to provide information through a registration process, and most sites limit the number of quotes users can see each day.

Although not an issue for buy-and-hold investors, who are saving for retirement or the like, there are plenty of individual investors who trade actively and aim to snare small, short-term gains in stock prices. For them, real-time quotes are a must, and often they feel they need more than many sites offer. Online brokerage firms—typically the low-commission houses such as Datek Online (**www.datek.com**) and E*Trade (**www.etrade.com**)—have tried to attract clients by offering unlimited access to real-time quotes. Many other online brokerage firms offer users 100 real-time quotes when they open an account, and sometimes reward them with additional quotes based on the number of trades that they make. Non-brokerage sites, such as Market Guide (**www.marketguide.com**), Thomson Investors Network (**www.thomsoninvest.net**), and TheStreet.com (**www.thestreet. com**), allow readers 50 or 100 quotes each day.

Historical stock quotes—the price that a stock traded at in the past, say three months or three years ago—are somewhat more difficult to come by. Free charting services can give you a good idea of what the price was, but most don't give specific prices. Those that do, such as BigCharts (**www.bigcharts.com**) and some of the other sites that use Big Charts, serve up historical quotes only one at a time, not in batches that cover a number of days. (One exception is Yahoo! Finance, which allows users to retrieve batches of quotes for free.) Paid services usually allow you to retrieve whole sets of stock prices, which some people use with spreadsheet software that allows them to do their own home-brewed analysis. For instance, America Online provides historical quotes on its dial-up online service, which has a variety of monthly price plans. Wall Street City (**www.wallstreetcity.com**), meanwhile, allows access to its historical-quote database for free.

Online portfolio services are a good way to keep track of all of your investments at once, and the good ones allow you to enter the price that you paid for your stocks so that you can always keep track of your investment gains or losses—for individual stocks as well as your entire portfolio. Portal sites, financial news and research sites, and brokerage firm sites all offer online portfolios. The ones kept behind subscription walls are the best, but even the free ones offered by sites such as Yahoo! Finance (**finance.yahoo.com**) are useful—and a far cry from the pencil, paper, and calculator method that many people were forced to use not so long ago.

Most portfolios allow you to track U.S. stock prices and the net asset value of your mutual funds. (Net asset values, often referred to as NAVs, are akin to a stock's share price. They are calculated once a day, by dividing the total value of all the fund's holdings by the number of shares it has sold, and are updated on most Web sites several hours after the close of stock-market trading.) The best portfolios also allow investors to track the value of non-U.S. stocks, bonds, and stock options. (Stock options are securities that give investors the right to purchase a stock at a particular price, during a particular time period.) Other advanced services will send you a daily rundown of your portfolio value by electronic mail. Quote.com, for instance, offers portfolio updates via e-mail, as well as news alerts when a wire service runs a story about a company you follow.

SEVEN

Message Boards

I t's hard to believe that someone known only as Tonto could be taken seriously by investors. But he is, and for good reason. Tonto and others like him who participate in stock-chat message boards often have useful nuggets of information to share about companies and their stocks—and some insightful (or at least entertaining) opinions about investments. Their postings on online message boards—also sometimes known as electronic bulletin boards or investment forums—have become a valuable resource for investors, another online tool for people trying to decide whether, and what, to buy and sell.

Tonto is really Tod Pauly, part-time investor and full-time owner of a manufacturing business in Manitowoc, Wisconsin. But on Silicon Investor (**www.siliconinvestor.com**), a popular online forum where he's known only by his alias, Mr. Pauly has a reputation for using the boards to hammer away at companies he believes aren't quite on the level. "I post a lot about companies that I think have problems . . . and other people on those boards don't like that very much," he said. Indeed, he's repeatedly been accused of being a short seller, someone who bets that the price of a stock will fall (an allegation he denied). Tonto has achieved quasi-celebrity status in the world of online message boards, but he is just one of thousands of people who make postings each day.

Online forums have exploded in popularity—each day investors swap tens of thousands of messages, debating everything from stock picks to their thoughts on politics. You'll find plenty of people willing to show you the ropes of online investing, and you'll meet other investors who are interested in stocks that you like. But, like all destinations on the Net, you have to be careful. The boards are also favorite hangouts for stock promoters and con artists. Emotions tend to run high, and it can be easy to get swept in by hype. Meanwhile, as scraps of information are passed around, it can be difficult to determine what is fact and what isn't.

Still, one of the biggest draws of message boards is the belief that the users there regularly uncover valuable information. And to be sure, sometimes they do. A Motley Fool (**www.fool.com**) message board dedicated to computer disk drive maker Iomega, for instance, once carried dispatches from an investor whose grandparents lived near an Iomega plant. The user posted updates on the number of cars his grandparents saw in the plant's employee parking lot during off-hours. Readers concluded that Iomega workers were being kept for long shifts and that business must be booming. They bought the stock before it raced in the market.

Nuggets of exclusive information like that are tough to come by on the boards. Facts posted on the boards are often just recycled news that participants retell (not always accurately) from CNBC or financial news wires and Web sites. Other times, message-board postings amount to little more than speculation and amateur analysis. Reading these can be fun, but they offer little of substance. They're empty calories.

Online bulletin boards work with the same basic premise of traditional cork bulletin boards. Using your Web browser, you wander up to read the messages other users have posted, and, if you wish, write your own. For the most part, your postings are public. Anything you write can be read by everyone else, potentially forever—something to keep in mind when choosing your words. Separate message boards are created for separate topics, usually for a particular company, but sometimes on a broader category, like an industry or technology stocks as a whole. Groups of boards are maintained on Web sites or online services.

Message boards owe their heritage to another part of the Internet that predates the World Wide Web: newsgroups (also called Usenet). Newsgroups still exist, and are the home of active investment discussion, but they are often more difficult to navigate. Investment discussion Web sites, for instance, do a better job of presenting and organizing different subjects than can newsgroups, which are organized using cryptic codes such as "alt.misc.stocks." Web sites, such as Deja (**www.deja.com**), help to make sense of newsgroups, but many investors still find message boards easier to use. Investing, meanwhile, is just one of the thousands of topics that are discussed in newsgroups and on message boards.

There are two general types of message board forums: those that are proprietary and those that are open to all. The message boards on America Online's dial-up service, for instance, are proprietary—you can't access them unless you're an AOL subscriber. But anyone with Internet access, including AOL subscribers, can reach the message boards on Yahoo! (**finance.yahoo.com**) and other Web sites. (There is a separate set of boards on America Online's Web site that is open to all, but those boards are less comprehensive than the boards on the dial-up service).

Message boards are sometimes referred to as chat rooms, though in reality a chat room is something different. Online chats are conversations carried out in real-time: Each posting immediately appears on each participant's computer screen. While stock-market chat rooms often remain open around the clock, the conversation is most intense during market hours. During off-hours, the chatter may dry up. Unlike message boards, chats sometimes require special software to participate. One of the most popular types of online chat is called Internet Relay Chat, or IRC. (You can find out more about IRC, and download software, at

a Web site run by mIRC Co. [**www.mirc.com**], a software
company.) Other live chats can be found on America Online's dial-up service.

Live stock chats are mostly used by day traders, investors who aim to make rapid investments in and out
of the market. As a result, the discussion in chat
rooms often deals little with companies' prospects and
business plans, and focuses instead on rumors and technical analysis. Technical analysis attempts to divine
the likely direction of stocks based on patterns in
their share prices or trading volume.

You don't need any special software to use the boards that are on
the Web, and most of the message-board sites are free (one notable exception is Silicon Investor: You can read its messages for free, but must
be a paying subscriber to use many features). Most sites require you to
go through a registration process, where you'll be asked for your name
and other information, before you're allowed to post any messages on
the boards. But while there are hundreds of Web sites that offer message boards, there are only a handful of established sites that receive a
significant volume of messages each day. Many people are most interested in the busiest sites because that is where they will have the best
odds of coming across useful postings.

Participants in online stock discussions often use aliases, motivated
partly by privacy concerns but also because it's just more fun that way
("FutureZillionaire1" sounds more interesting than John Smith). Still,
as in the offline world, you should be skeptical of people you don't
know and can't identify. Likewise, understand that when people think
they're anonymous, they often don't speak with the same care that
they would use under other circumstances (you may find yourself
doing this if you post messages).

GETTING STARTED

First, you need to find a discussion forum you like. (The most popular sites are profiled later in this chapter.) Most users pick one or two sites and stick with them. Keeping up with message boards can be time-consuming (not to mention addictive). It's not uncommon for hundreds of messages to be posted in a single day about a particular company.

To figure out which message-board sites suit you, start by reading some messages to try to get a feel for the site as a whole. If you already own stocks, boards dedicated to those companies would be a good place to start. (On most sites, you navigate to specific message boards by entering a company's stock, or ticker, symbol into a search box—MSFT for Microsoft, for instance.) Boards tend to have their own unique identities. Some are rowdy, where squabbles (or "flames," in Net lingo) are common. Others may be more laid-back and reflective. Read through a few messages and you'll quickly realize which type of board you're looking at.

THE BIGGEST MESSAGE BOARD SITES

Yahoo! Finance   (finance.yahoo.com)
Silicon Investor   (www.siliconinvestor.com)
Motley Fool   (www.fool.com)
Raging Bull   (www.ragingbull.com)

Once you select a Web site, spend some time reading the recent postings on the specific boards that you are interested in before posting messages yourself. This is known on the boards as "lurking." Many people find they never wish to go beyond this stage: They are content to read what others have to say, and stay out of the discussion themselves.

Sites differ on how much information they require during registration. Some will force you to supply a valid e-mail address that they'll verify so that they can get in touch with you if they need to. Others are wide open, not even requiring your real name. On most sites you'll be asked to pick an alias, a nickname you'll be known by on the message boards. Some users use their real names; others prefer to give that information out only to those who they want to have it. Pick this name wisely because you probably won't be able to change it later. Also, keep in mind that even if you don't use your real name, it's still fairly easy for the message-board operator to track you down if need be. More on that later.

When you do decide to start posting messages, choose your words carefully. What you're writing is very much "on the record," and you should assume that it will be available for all to read on the Internet, perhaps for years to come. Most sites keep an archive of postings that users will be able to search long after you've forgotten about what you have written.

A good first rule, of course, is that you should have something to say before you post a message. Posts like "right on" and "I agree" get tiresome when you have to wade through them to find messages with substance. This is particularly annoying on boards that receive hundreds of posts each day. Keeping up with the daily glut of messages can be impossible with so many superfluous comments.

People often make "off-topic" posts on message boards, and usually they put the letters OT in the subject line, so that users browsing a list of messages know they can skip that particular post if they're just trying to keep up with the board's main focus. Still, jumping in the middle of a heated debate with a comment about a movie you just saw probably isn't going to make the other participants very happy, even if you include an OT notation.

Most systems have some sort of "private message" feature that allows you to send a note to a particular user without it going on the board for all to see. Use private messages to carry on private conversations (and to settle disagreements).

But remember that stock-chat message boards are a lot more than just financial debate. People tend to develop online identities, which they become very sensitive about. Fights (or flames) break out constantly—the subtle nuances of "normal" conversation are easily lost when you go online, and what you think is a joke could be taken as an insult by someone else.

If you're critical of a stock, you'll likely run into harsh opposition from many of the message-board regulars who don't like to see someone bashing one of their investments. Be specific in your criticism, and offer examples to back up your claims. You'll find users far more receptive to your comments if you spend a little time proving your case.

UNDERSTANDING WHAT YOU READ

There's no question that message boards can be a great resource. But they can be dangerous places, and investors have lost fortunes by trading on information they read on the boards. Securities regulators say they are troubled by the fact that so many investors seem to believe the message boards are full of hot "sure-thing" stock tips.

Message boards shouldn't be viewed as any different from a crowded room full of strangers. Trading on advice there is akin to trading on stock tips you receive from a stranger's conversation you overhear at a party. Still, people do it all the time. In fairness, message-board users have at times come up with quality "scoops" about companies—catching wind of a merger before it happens, or learning that the company has secured a patent on a new technology. But often the information on the boards is pure speculation.

It's important to understand that just about everyone who posts messages has a motive, and it may be different from yours. When money is at stake—as it is with any investment—there's really no such thing as a completely objective discussion. People don't want to hear bad news about companies they invest in, and even the best-intentioned debates often end up in mudslinging. Likewise, it's important to remember that short sellers—those who bet that the price of a stock will decline—can profit by stirring up panic on a message board. People also can profit by stirring up excitement on the boards about stocks they own.

All these things point to the importance of not relying on information you read on the boards. "You should assume everything you read online is false until you can confirm it somewhere else," said John Stark, chief of the SEC's Office of Internet Enforcement. "People know not to believe everything they read, but think that somehow the Internet makes things more legitimate, and it certainly does not."

In one high-profile case, a person used a Yahoo! message board to refer readers to a phony Web site, designed to look like a news page from Bloomberg Business News's Web site (**www.bloomberg.com**), that announced computer-networking company PairGain Technologies was being acquired. PairGain's stock raced on the news before falling back. It turned out the anonymous poster was none other than a disgruntled PairGain employee. He later pleaded guilty to fraud charges.

Shortly after that case, Yahoo! briefly added a warning to all of its message boards, telling users not only that they shouldn't believe everything they see, but also that the service is "for entertainment only." That was a considerable departure from the way message-board operators have typically chosen to position their services: as a research tool. (Yahoo! later removed the "entertainment only" line, amid complaints from users.)

"One of the things I've had to learn and remember is that people have a motive to post on the boards," said Linda Kaplan, a psychotherapist who lives in New York and regularly participates in online forums. "People want other people to buy their stock so the stock will go up. You've got to remember that a lot of what's said on the boards is coming out of that motive."

Good advice, but easy to forget. Message-board participants tend to develop strong bonds, and quickly establish trust. Almost every board has a handful of people who are generally regarded as leaders, and are trusted to explain company news. But remember that stock promoters and others who want to manipulate prices also know this well, and certainly use it to their advantage. There is no way to know that people really are who they say they are.

Here are some things to watch out for, and ignore, on the boards:

Blatant hyping.   Believe it or not, do a search for "headed to the moon" or "this thing is going to explode" on message-board sites, and you'll find scores of messages from people cheerleading their favorite stocks. But that hyping can be dangerous, and contagious. When members of a message board get in the habit of explaining away bad news with statements like "I think things will get better soon," it's time for a reality check. Remember that a stock's performance has nothing to do with how much you—or anyone else—want the price to go up.

Claims of inside information. It's not uncommon to find users claiming to know the inner workings of companies—when press releases are coming out, the status of development of new products, whether the company will meet earnings expectations. Some users even claim to know when particularly large purchases are about to be made in a stock. Such a purchase, if large enough, could push a stock's price higher. But, as with all claims of this sort, you should question the likelihood of anonymous message-board posters having such potentially lucrative inside information (and you should also wonder why, if they do have inside information, they're so eager to share it with so many strangers).

Stock promoters. Message boards have become favorite hangouts for stock promoters, individuals who are paid to hype a company's stock. Such people are often paid in stock rather than cash, meaning they make more money if they're able to get the stock price to rise. You should beware of message-board users who seem to repeat the company line a little too closely and know such things as when the next press release is expected. They may be on the company's payroll, in which case you should be skeptical of anything they have to say.

Stock promoters are required by law to disclose whether or not they're being paid, exactly how much, and the nature of the compensation—even when they make postings on a message board. Still, the SEC has brought many cases against promoters who disguised the fact that they were paid, and it continues to track down offenders. (For more information about stock promoters, see Chapter 8.)

Bashers. Just as stock promoters and other hypesters profit by pumping a stock, bashers, or those critical of a company, can profit by getting a stock's price to fall. Message-board participants who are positive on a stock are always quick to suggest that anyone who bashes the stock must be a short seller—someone betting the stock's price will fall. Most of the time, that's just plain wrong. But the SEC says it is becoming more and more concerned that some people on the boards who appear to be critical observers are actually slamming a company so that they can profit from a short sale. It's irresponsible to dismiss anyone with a negative comment as a short seller, but it would also be a mistake to think that anyone bashing a stock is just trying to save you from a bad investment. Do your own research.

Call in your certs!   This is a strange one, but stranger still is how often you see this phrase pop up in message boards. "Certs" here refers to stock certificates, and the notion of "calling them in" means asking your broker to send you the actual paper certificates, rather than allowing the stock to be held for you in your brokerage account. The idea here is to prevent short selling in a stock. Short sellers make money by betting a stock's price will fall. Essentially, they borrow shares of stock in a company from a broker, paying a small fee for the service, and immediately sell those shares on the open market. Then, they hope, the company's stock falls in price, so that when it comes time for them to buy back shares to repay the ones they borrowed from their broker, they can buy them for significantly less than they sold the original shares for. The difference is their profit.

The reason message-board users try to organize a "call in your certs" campaign is that when the actual physical shares of a stock are in a client's possession, they can't be loaned to short sellers. Brokers who loan stock to short sellers are actually loaning out the shares that other customers keep in their accounts—the same way a bank lends money that it is holding in other customer's savings accounts. In theory, if a group of investors could buy up the available stock in a company, and then get hold of the actual stock certificates, they could absolutely guarantee that there was no short selling because they would own every piece of stock, and there wouldn't be any available for brokers to lend to short sellers.

The flaws in such a plan are, hopefully, obvious. It's not uncommon for companies to have many millions of shares available for trading, and it would be virtually impossible for a group of investors on a message board to manage to control all those shares.

Oh, those market makers... "The market makers don't want to let this baby run!" Market makers, or MMs, are the most evil people on the planet next to short sellers, according to message-board users. These are the professional traders who are responsible for organizing the buying and selling of stocks that trade on the Nasdaq Stock Market. They do this by posting a "bid" price at which they are willing to buy a stock, and an "ask" price at which they are willing to sell a stock. Nasdaq requires market makers to buy and sell at the bid and ask prices they post, and that helps to ensure that investors can buy and sell a stock if they need to. In the language of Wall Street, market makers are required to maintain an orderly market in the stocks they trade. One way market makers earn money is from the difference—or spread—between their bid and ask prices: If they are willing to buy for $10 and sell for $10.25, the 25-cent difference is their profit.

Many message-board users—you'll find this most often on penny-stock boards—believe that market makers conspire to keep the prices of some stocks down. Some go so far as to suggest that market makers themselves short stocks and then conspire to keep the price low so they can reap profits. Market makers do indeed short stocks. For instance, if an investor puts in an order to buy a stock and the market maker doesn't own any shares and can't find any other willing sellers, he or she will use a short sale to fill the buyer's order.

But the notion that market makers are involved in a plot to manipulate stocks in order to wring profits from their short-sale positions is a bit far-fetched—even for an industry that did face regulators' allegations of price fixing in the 1990s (market makers were accused of conspiring to bolster their profits by secretly agreeing to keep their spreads wide, and they ended up paying a huge settlement to resolve the matter). The idea that market makers would hold back the price of a stock that was in high demand is illogical. When faced with strong demand and lots of "buy" orders, surely the market marker could make much more money by buying shares, then selling them at higher and higher prices, than by trying to hold back a popular stock on which the market maker happens to be short. Indeed, market makers tend to avoid holding big positions in stocks, and they certainly don't try to get in the way of a moving market: At least when it comes to a stock that is listed on a major market, one market maker doesn't have enough money to stand in the way of all other investors in the market. There is a saying on Wall Street: "You can't fight the tape."

Price predictions. Message boards are full of predictions (many of them ridiculous) about where a stock's price will be in the near future. No one, including Wall Street analysts who do this for a living, can say with certainty where a stock is headed. Price predictions can quickly give way to hype—if a dozen people on a message board seem certain a $5 stock is headed to $25, you may start to believe it. But wanting a stock to go up doesn't make it happen.

THE SAGA OF MOUNTAIN ENERGY

It's safe to say that without the Internet—and, in particular, stock-chat message boards—few investors ever would have heard of a tiny Houston oil company named Mountain Energy. The company never did any advertising and was hardly a household name. Yet investors from coast to coast rushed to invest in Mountain Energy, thinking its oil and gas operations were going to be the key to their riches.

They couldn't have been more wrong.

The story began in the spring of 1998, when message-board users were first getting wind of a company called International Casino Cruises. International was shedding its gambling operations and going into the oil business through an acquisition of Mountain Energy. According to a press release at the time, Mountain Energy had just acquired assets that contained some $200 million worth of oil and gas, and investors couldn't wait to get a piece of the company.

Message-board users were quick to rally around the stock, predicting that the company's shares—trading around $1 at the time—would soon approach $5 a share, or more. It was called a sure thing, and investors were already talking about how they would spend the windfall that their Mountain Energy investments would bring.

But even in the beginning, there were signs of trouble. It seemed difficult to get information out of the company. Press releases were vague. And because the company didn't report to the SEC, there was no audited financial information available. Some investors began to get suspicious.

Still, the masses kept the faith. Through tens of thousands of messages on Silicon Investor and Raging Bull, users cheered on Mountain Energy. They pored over the company's press releases, dissecting every sentence and wondering aloud what great new announcements were just around the corner.

A small group of message-board users remained firmly against Mountain Energy, much to the frustration of the majority of board users who believed the company could do no wrong. The group, called "bashers" by those who disliked their anti–Mountain Energy postings, quickly turned the board into a war zone. The naysayers hammered away at the company's biggest cheerleaders, posting question after question about the company's history, finances, and business practices. Still, most of their posts were ignored, as the larger group of message-board participants dismissed the bashers as short sellers.

In July 1998, there was news, but this time the boards weren't quite so excited. The Securities and Exchange Commission had suspended trading in Mountain Energy's stock, citing concerns about the accuracy of the company's press releases. Mountain Energy immediately put out its own release, assuring investors that it was cooperating with the SEC and expected to have the inquiry behind it soon. But the company never recovered. When the trading halt was lifted after ten days, the stock plummeted. Frantic message-board users struggled to get information about the company's status, but most came up empty.

A month later, Mountain Energy put out its last press release, announcing that due to a lack of money, all employees had been let go and the company was going out of business. There never was any word about those $200 million oil and gas deposits.

Mountain Energy's complicated past should have been an immediate red flag for investors, but the crowd of cheerleaders seemed to have little interest in tracing the company's history—even though most of the information about Mountain Energy's former lives was available to investors on the message boards. Part of the reason, no doubt, is that such trails can be hard to follow, especially since Mountain Energy (and its previous incarnations) drew more than 23,000 messages on Silicon Investor alone. A sprinkling of facts can be hard to find and digest when surrounded by thousands of hype-filled message board postings.

Mountain Energy's roots can be traced back to a company called Summary Corporation, which in 1995 was developing software to capture and organize scanned images. In September 1996, Summary Corporation changed its name to LumaNet, and reinvented itself as an Internet technology company focusing on e-commerce.

But not even a year later, in June 1997, the company was on the move again, this time evolving into Riviera International Casinos, which aimed to operate a gambling ship in Palm Beach County, Florida. The company claimed its ship would generate $2 million in revenue each month, and would open for business in August. But there were delays, and by December of that year, plans had abruptly changed again. The company was changing its name to International Casino Cruises and selling its Riviera ship, but remaining in the floating gambling business.

That lasted about two months. In February 1998, the business plan appeared to shift yet again as International Casino Cruises announced it was forming a new subsidiary called Convenience Concepts that would acquire convenience stores in Texas and Florida. Three months later, on May 21, 1998, the company underwent its biggest metamorphosis yet: The software company turned Internet firm turned riverboat operator turned convenience-store owner was being reborn as Mountain Energy.

WISHFUL THINKING

The Mountain Energy example is an extreme. Investors often get burned by relying on information they read on the boards, and it seldom involves any sort of behavior the SEC would be interested in.

Every time information posted on a message board proves to be wrong, it doesn't mean someone was trying to manipulate the stock. Often rumors grow out of control on message boards simply because the participants *want* them to be true, and want to feel as though they've uncovered something not widely known in the investment community.

For a good example of just how easy it is for all that message-board talk to have it dead wrong, consider an exchange that occurred over several months on a Silicon Investor message board dedicated to Open Market, a Massachusetts software maker.

As is the case on many boards dedicated to technology stocks, hopes that the company would be taken over were long a topic on the Open Market bulletin board. Still, shares of the company, which makes software for electronic commerce, weren't rising, and frustrated message-board participants were struggling to find any piece of news that could goose the stock price.

One day it seemed they had finally found it. A posting flashed on the board: "Buyout confirmed." No details were offered in the post, but message-board users quickly begin to post their theories. One had it that Cisco Systems Inc. would buy the company. Another said it was Compaq Computer Corp. Both agreed the purchase price was $25 a share, well above the price that Open Market's stock was trading at. That same day, there was another bullish item: Influential brokerage firm Goldman Sachs had prepared a report saying that Open Market's stock would hit $90 in a year.

All of this "news" sent Open Market's stock soaring. At the end of that day, the stock had jumped 15% to $14.75. Days later it climbed again, to just below $17. But within a week of the initial flurry of rumors, the gains were gone. There was no takeover, and no one could find a copy of the Goldman Sachs research. The brokerage firm later confirmed that it hadn't issued any investment reports on Open Market for nine months. The source of the rumors never emerged.

The saga continued. Open Market's shares fell into a holding pattern again for more than a month. Then, suddenly, the takeover talk was back. Fueled by news from the company that it would change its bylaws to make it less vulnerable to a hostile takeover, several investors on the board concluded that some rival must be preparing a bid. "Writing is on the wall! BUYOUT!" gushed one message-board writer. "A buyout will be announced after the close today." But the next day dawned, and Open Market was still independent.

Days later, message-board participants seized on news that Open Market's chief financial officer, Regina Sommer, had resigned. They came up with theories, this time bearish, that Ms. Sommer's departure was a harbinger of trouble. "I think that they are going to make a very bad announcement after the close. Like the CEO is leaving or something like that," wrote one user. The company's stock fell 6% that day, but no additional bombshells emerged in the news.

It wasn't long before optimism returned. A user who identified herself only as "Batgirl" claimed to have some inside information: Open Market would soon be partnering with a new company. It seemed the board's participants had finally come up with a scoop, because just days later Open Market did indeed announce an agreement to resell software made by OpenSite Technologies, a Research Triangle Park, North Carolina, maker of software for online-auction companies. But like so much on the message boards, the user hadn't offered up any inside information. Batgirl later admitted that she was simply repeating what she had read in a news story.

THE BIG FOUR

There are many places to go on the Net to chat up your favorite stock, but four sites attract the most attention. Here is a rundown of what to expect from the leaders:

Yahoo! Finance
(finance.yahoo.com)

Yahoo! doesn't release any statistics about traffic on its boards, but it's safe to say it's one of the most popular stock-chat destinations on the Net. Drop in on a board dedicated to a stock that is in the news, and you'll probably find an avalanche of postings analyzing the latest developments on the company. (One day after AOL released a better-than-expected quarterly earnings report, users posted more than 3,400 messages to its Yahoo! board.)

But Yahoo! has been criticized for its lax approach to monitoring its message boards. It's not uncommon to find irrelevant, or off-topic, postings in its message forums. Sprinkled among those 3,400 messages on the AOL boards, for instance, were user-posted advertisements for pornography sites, and messages touting unrelated microcap stocks. The service doesn't require much in the way of identification before it lets users set up accounts, and doesn't verify the information that users provide during registration.

Yahoo! has taken steps to rein in its boards. Even before it posted the warning in the wake of the PairGain hoax, it banned some of the most problematic boards: those that discuss stocks quoted on the loosely regulated OTC Bulletin Board service.

Still, the sheer volume of messages on Yahoo! can prove useful for someone digging for research on a company, and Yahoo!'s boards are closely integrated with the rest of the Yahoo! Finance site, which includes links to company profiles, news, and SEC documents.

Yahoo!'s boards are fairly easy to use. From the main Yahoo! Finance screen, enter the ticker symbol of the stock you're interested in. You'll be taken to a screen that shows some brief statistics on the stock, including current price and volume of shares traded. You can click on the stock's ticker symbol, on the far left, to be taken to a screen that has some more detailed information, like past performance. You access the stock's message board through the "More Info" box. If Yahoo! has a message board for the stock—and it does for practically every non-OTC public company—you'll see a link to "Msgs." Click on it.

The first screen you'll see inside the message board is a list of the 40 most recent messages, with the newest on top. You can scroll down through the list of messages and read the different subject lines. You can also click on the "Previous 40" and "Next 40" buttons to cycle through the list of messages. Note the dates of the messages, displayed on the right side. Scroll through the subject descriptions for a few days' worth of messages to get a sense of what the discussion has been about. When you see a message you'd like to read, click on its subject.

Silicon Investor
(www.siliconinvestor.com)

Started by brothers Brad and Jeff Dryer in 1995, Silicon Investor is one of the oldest of the popular stock-chat Web sites—and the only one that charges a fee for access.

New users continue to pony up $60 a year to participate in the service, which claims 200,000 active members. Silicon Investor is the only service of the big four that lets its users create discussion topics on any subject they choose, which explains why it's not uncommon

to stumble into a heated debate over, say, the president's job performance.

In 1998, the Dryer brothers sold Silicon Investor to Go2Net, a Seattle company with a variety of Internet properties, for stock then valued at $33 million. Since then, the service has been integrated with Go2Net's StockSite, a competitor to Yahoo! Finance that provides financial data and news.

Silicon Investor regulars often turn up their noses at competing message boards, claiming their own pay-to-post service draws a more intelligent clientele than its competitors. (Some users have gone so far as to circulate nicknames for Silicon Investor's rivals that can't be printed here.)

But the site's users still sling mud with the best of them, and the service has had no shortage of renegade posters who pepper the message boards with worthless stock tips.

And just as with its rivals, some of Silicon Investors' more active message boards—and most troublesome to patrol—are those dedicated to penny stocks. For instance, a forum to discuss Digitcom, a small Los Angeles telecommunications company, drew more than 43,000 messages in a little more than a year. An IBM message board, meanwhile, received only 5,100 posts over a three-year period.

To get started, just plug in a ticker symbol or company name in the main search box. Because Silicon Investor lets its users create message boards, you may find several different boards that discuss the stock you're looking for. (Type in MSFT, for Microsoft, and you'll find more than 20 boards.)

Pick the board you want from the list by clicking on its title.

You'll see the first message on the board, which usually tells you a bit about the discussion, and the list of the most recently posted messages (newest on the top). To read a message, click on its subject.

You can cycle through messages by using the "previous" and "next" buttons, or by entering a message number in the "Reply #" box and pressing enter.

There are lots of other nifty features on Silicon Investor, but you have to pay the $60 registration fee before you can use them. There's a "hot topics" list that helps you quickly see which message boards are getting the most attention for the day, and registered users can also use bookmarks to keep quick track of their favorite message boards—and other users.

Raging Bull
(www.ragingbull.com)

A relative newcomer to online chatter, Raging Bull initially carved a space for itself by targeting users who were unhappy with the rowdiness of other online forums. Indeed, many of its users are refugees

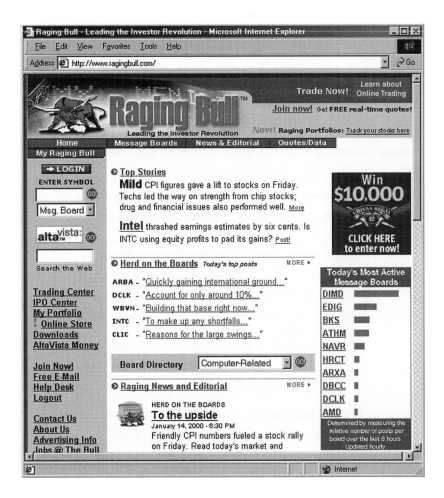

from other services, some drawn by Raging Bull's "ignore" feature—a button that lets users muzzle rowdy posters (or just those they disagree with). Enter the screen name of the bothersome individual, and his or her posts will be filtered out when you view the boards. The poster's comments, of course, are visible to all users who haven't selected "ignore."

Raging Bull was started in September 1997 by three college students, and didn't gain much notoriety until a $2 million investment in late 1998 from venture-capital firm CMGI Inc. Since that investment, the three have dropped out of school and moved the business from their basement to CMGI's headquarters in Andover, Massachusetts. They also used the money to beef up technology—the service was painstakingly slow when it began—and hire a public relations staff.

The service offers a hodgepodge of original content, including daily market commentary, and was the first discussion forum to offer its users free real-time stock quotes.

Raging Bull started off as a bare-bones messaging system and long lacked some key features provided by its competitors, like links to company news and financial statements—and even the ability to do a full-text search of the message boards. Still, that hasn't stopped investors from signing up for the free service. Raging Bull said it has about 150,000 members, and is adding new members at the rate of about 1,500 a day.

A lot of chatter on Raging Bull is dedicated to risky microcap stocks. Since all users are anonymous, and it's relatively easy for one person to set up multiple accounts, you've got to be careful. The chorus of criticism that your favorite stock is enduring may actually be the work of just one person with many screen names.

The Motley Fool
(www.fool.com)

Brothers Tom and David Gardner set up shop as a "content provider" on America Online in 1994. Their Motley Fool message boards—the name comes from a line in a Shakespeare play—quickly became one of the most popular destinations on the online service.

TMF: Intel Corporation (INTC) - Microsoft Internet Explorer					_ □ ×
File Edit View Favorites Tools Help					

Address http://boards.fool.com/messages.asp?id=1140069000000000   Go

Home	Messages	Quotes/Data	My Portfolio	New Fool?	Register	FoolMart
Folders	Best of	Favorites / Replies	Register			Help

Fool.com
Message Boards

[Search]   [Quick Find]

Stocks I / Intel Corporation (INTC) Quote , News , Chart

Post New   💜 (◀SKIP) 7 Days ▼ (SKIP▶)   Prev • Next

UnThreaded · Threaded	Author	Recs	Date	Number
Re: Econdropout, Put up or....	EconDropout	--	1/16/00 6:03 PM	11543
Re: Econdropout, Put up or....	EconDropout	--	1/16/00 6:20 PM	11544
Re: Econdropout, Put up or....	EconDropout	--	1/16/00 6:36 PM	11545
Re: Equal time	viditor	1	1/16/00 7:11 PM	11546
Re: Econdropout, Put up or....	viditor	--	1/16/00 7:52 PM	11547
Re: Intel's valuation...	rongrong99	--	1/16/00 8:16 PM	11548
Re: Intel's valuation...	Redhed5909	--	1/16/00 10:06 PM	11549
Re: Another View	smclark206	--	1/16/00 10:36 PM	11550
Re: YES !!!!!!!!!!!!!!!!!!!!!!!!!!!!!!	kirk123	--	1/17/00 12:40 AM	11551
Re: Econdropout, Put up or....	LouieLouieLouie	--	1/17/00 2:19 AM	11552
Re: intel.com	Scott64	--	1/17/00 2:21 AM	11553
Re: Question	tenamaxtli	--	1/17/00 8:50 AM	11554
Re: Econdropout, Put up or....	elgatogordo	--	1/17/00 9:30 AM	11555
What's this! "The Crusoe Processor"	TMFSpirit	--	1/17/00 10:03 AM	11556
Re: What's this! "The Crusoe Processor"	TMFSpirit	--	1/17/00 10:11 AM	11557
Re: To All Longs	rvbradish	--	1/17/00 10:16 AM	11558
Re: Econdropout, Put up or....	rvbradish	--	1/17/00 10:29 AM	11559
Re: Econdropout, Put up or....	rvbradish	--	1/17/00 10:35 AM	11560

Done   Internet

The Gardners' early goal was to give the little guy the tools necessary to make his own investment decisions, without relying on the Wall Street elite. But in recent years the Fool itself has grown into something of a Wall Street institution, boasting more than 1.5 million visitors to its Web site each month. And the Gardners have essentially joined the elite. They regularly appear on financial television programs and have written several books on do-it-yourself investing.

The Motley Fool says it takes an aggressive position on monitoring the chatter on its message boards. Its staff of community "strollers" patrols the boards, looking for off-topic or abusive posts. And, like Yahoo!, the service doesn't allow discussion of speculative microcap stocks.

Membership in Motley Fool is free, and required to use some of the more interesting features of the site. Navigating is straightforward; you search for boards by ticker symbol (remember, microcap stocks aren't represented) and flip through messages using "previous" and "next" buttons.

Any of the major message board Web sites can be useful, another way to keep track of the companies whose stocks you own—or are considering. But it is important to remember that the boards are simply a starting point for information: Check in regularly to see what is being said—the same way you may chat about investments (or any common interest) with the fellow you always seem to run into at the health club or convenience store. But don't buy or sell based only on what you hear from the boards. If a posting refers to news about a company, find a relevant article from a news source you trust, or call the company. If a posting says a stock is poised to surge, dig up some investment research from professional analysts to see if they agree. If a posting pitches an investment guaranteed to double—ignore it.

EIGHT

Scams and Deceptions

There's no question that the Net has empowered a new generation of investors, giving them access to information and tools that were once available only to the privileged Wall Street few. But cyberspace has also become a nightmare for the unwary. Con artists are using computers to breathe new life into old scams with frightening success.

Online fraud comes in all shapes and sizes; it's a safe bet that, as you read these words, someone, somewhere is devising a new way to try to separate you from your money. The growing popularity of online investing and the ease with which the Internet allows scam artists to reach millions of people has turned cyber-fraud into something of a cottage industry. Millions of dollars are being made at the expense of unsuspecting investors, often through sophisticated scams that have lasted months and even years.

Regulators have prosecuted a handful of high-profile cases, but the vastness of the Internet—and its anonymity—makes it difficult to police. Instead, regulators try to make investors aware of the dangers they face when they venture online in search of investment information. Unfortunately, far too often those warnings fall on deaf ears.

Some scams are easy to spot: guarantees of outrageous returns on an investment with little or no risk, for instance. But others are the work of seasoned pros who understand how to make people excited about an investment—and, in many cases, convince them to abandon common sense. Even the most cautious investors can get duped.

At its heart, online fraud—just like a more traditional scam—is about getting you to put your money somewhere you shouldn't. Most fraud involves "once in a lifetime" investments: an opportunity to get in on the ground floor of the next Microsoft or an offer to buy into some sort of lucrative (and sometimes bizarre) new business venture. Almost all involve companies or ventures you've probably never heard of—and likely never would have if it weren't for the Internet.

Consider what happened to Kristin Morris. While surfing the Net one day, she came across what appeared to be an incredible offer: a ground-floor investment opportunity in a technology company that was billing itself as "the next Microsoft." The company, Interactive Products and Services, had big plans for a line of wireless handheld devices that would let users access the Internet without costly computers. According to its Web page, IPS was selling shares in minimum chunks worth $250, but its president was predicting that agreements with major computer companies would boost its shares to $500 apiece in just five years.

Ms. Morris, who worked for a computer firm and felt she had a good grasp of technology, talked the deal over with her husband, and the Berryville, Virginia, couple decided to invest $1,000 in the offering. "We knew of course we could lose this money if IPS didn't succeed, but I never dreamed it was an elaborate scam and my money would be stolen," she said.

In fact, IPS had no products or pending contracts with big firms, and its only employee was its founder, Matthew Bowin. In the end, Ms. Morris would learn that she was one of several investors duped in the scam. Mr. Bowin was convicted of defrauding investors of $190,000 and sentenced in December 1998 to ten years in a California state prison.

Ms. Morris's experience points up the troubling paradox of the Internet: Scam artists have evolved right along with technology, devising creative new ways to dupe unsuspecting investors in greater numbers and faster than ever before. Meanwhile, regulators and others responsible for patrolling the Net are largely playing catch-up, struggling to establish and build enough resources to put them on an even footing with technology-savvy online scammers.

Here are a few examples of scam artists' greatest hits, updated for the Information Age:

The pump and dump. It's a scheme as old as the stock market itself: Pump up the price of a stock through vigorous cheerleading that often involves outrageous claims, and then sell, or dump, shares once the price climbs. Sometimes individuals concoct elaborate pump-and-dump scams so that they can unload their personal holdings in a stock. But often the company itself is involved, dumping millions of shares of "insider" stock while investors are left holding the bag.

Paid promoters. Someone has to do all that pumping. Small or struggling companies sometimes hire stock promoters to drum up buying in their stock (and boost its price). Promoters use a variety of techniques for hyping stocks—some operate Web sites with online tip sheets where they list their "stock picks" or "stock profiles," often disguising the fact that the companies themselves have paid hefty fees to be featured. It's not illegal to promote stocks for pay, but it is against the law for promoters to hide or disguise the fact that they're being paid in exchange for their cheerleading. Promoters often go out of their way to pass themselves off as independent financial professionals, or even investors, just like you. Few actually refer to themselves as "stock promoters," instead portraying what they do as simply public relations or even stock analysis.

Spam. A favorite tool of stock promoters, spam—yes, the name comes from where you think it does—is the junk mail that floods your electronic mailbox. Con artists often use spam to tout worthless investment opportunities. And regulators say that while investors would likely discard such solicitations if they arrived by U.S. mail, anonymous e-mail messages often come off as hot inside information, and far too often investors are drawn in.

SPOTTING A SCAM

You don't have to look very hard on the Net to find these scams; they often find you. The trick is in recognizing them for what they are.

Many con artists understand the Internet far better than do casual investors—or even some securities regulators.

Spam, of course, comes directly to your e-mailbox, but other scams can be far more difficult to identify. Online message boards, for instance, have become fertile ground for stock scams, largely because of their inherent anonymity. The forums are like large digital bulletin boards. Users carry on public debates—by reading and replying to messages posted by other users—about companies and investments. There's no way to know if that message-board post about a hot stock tip is from someone who truly has inside information—which is about as likely as Bill Gates giving you the inside goods on Microsoft—or from someone trying to pump up the price of the stock, possibly as part of a paid stock-promotion campaign. Similarly, a slick-looking Web site, seemingly produced by a credible research firm, often turns out to be nothing more than a vehicle for promoting stocks owned by the site's operator or a company that hired the site.

Moreover, while you often can't trust good news on the Net, you can't trust bad news either. Hiding behind the cloak of anonymity afforded by most online stock discussions, investors will sometimes provide false negative information about a company in which they hold a short position—essentially, a bet that the shares' price will decline. Large, well-known companies are usually immune to such pressures, but small, already volatile issues can sometimes swing wildly on the basis of a few negative reports.

Regulators say duping investors is becoming easier and easier, largely because online investing has boomed, while general investor literacy has lagged behind. Philip Rutledge, deputy chief counsel of the Pennsylvania Securities Commission, said that regulators were caught off guard by online investing's popularity, and weren't ready with warning messages to match the hype. "People can now make investment decisions in an instant, with just the click of a mouse. They surf the Net, collecting all these hot tips, which we all know are basically worthless," said Mr. Rutledge, pausing, then adding, "Or at least we should know better."

But do we really know better? Despite a chorus of warnings from securities regulators, investors continue to flock to the Net for investment advice. And more often than not, when it comes to free advice on the Internet, you get what you pay for.

Part of the problem is that investment philosophies have changed. Old "slow and steady" investment strategies are being thrown out the window in exchange for what many regulators say is an attempt at a new kind of get-rich-quick scheme: using an online trading account to harvest fast money from the stock market. Mr. Rutledge believes the online brokerages themselves bear much of the responsibility. "A lot of people who have never invested a dime before are now being lured in by heavy advertising from brokers," he said. "Many of these people just don't understand what they're doing. They were lucky to have a CD. Now they are thinking that the Net may be the key to riches."

Of course, investors who trade online don't get rich overnight. (The odds of doing so are about as good as those of winning the lottery.) People who believe they can get rich quick are particularly susceptible to stock scams, and in their hands, an online trading account can be dangerous. "I think people read about the fraud, but they somehow believe it won't get them. People always want to believe that they're going to strike it rich and be more savvy than the next guy," said Mr. Rutledge.

Regulators Take Notice

The first case involving Internet manipulation that was brought by the Securities and Exchange Commission remains one of the agency's most prominent. Throughout 1995 and 1996, a McLean, Virginia, company called Systems of Excellence (often referred to by its memorable stock symbol, SEXI) produced a flood of press releases. The news announcements championed the company's line of high-tech video teleconferencing products, and reported that there was strong demand for its devices. The company went so far as to say it had snagged large clients like Johns Hopkins University.

Systems of Excellence became an online favorite, vigorously cheered in online message boards and widely regarded as a runaway success. The company even appeared to have the ear of Wall Street insiders: A company called SGA Goldstar promoted Systems of Excellence as a stock pick in its online "Whisper Stocks" newsletter. According to press releases—and filings made directly to the SEC—things seemed to be going well for the company.

But on October 8, 1996, investors who had been cheering the stock got a jolt: The SEC suspended trading in the company's stock and launched an investigation into some of the company's claims. Investors scrambled to make sense of what was happening. Emotions ran high in online message boards, and many investors refused to acknowledge there was anything amiss at their beloved Systems of Excellence. Some message-board users criticized the SEC for being on a "witch hunt." Others described the suspension as "routine."

But it seems there was trouble at the company. One month after suspending trading, the SEC filed a $10 million lawsuit alleging "massive" securities fraud against the company, its chairman, Charles O. Huttoe, and several of his relatives and business associates. The SEC also filed suit against Theodore R. Melcher Jr., the author of the "Whisper Stocks" Web site that touted the company.

Systems of Excellence was never the business it led investors to believe it was. The SEC said Mr. Huttoe spent more time building his own wealth at the expense of investors than he did developing the company's vision. Calling it a classic "pump and dump," the SEC said Mr. Huttoe secretly distributed nearly 42 million shares of Systems of Excellence to his family and friends, who later sold those shares in the frenzy created by all the glowing press releases and online hype. The releases were largely lies—the deals with big clients didn't exist, and the company's books had been cooked by an auditor who later faced his own SEC fraud charges. It turned out there was also trouble with SGA Goldstar and its inside scoop on the company: It had been paid to write positively about Systems of Excellence in SGA Goldstar's online newsletter.

Even as the SEC investigation marched forward—and damaging evidence against the company was reported in the press—Systems of Excellence tried to remain in business. The company pledged to clean up its act, and begged investors to give it a second chance. Amazingly, some message-board users continued to support the company, predicting an imminent turnaround. But the stock price never rose much higher than a few pennies a share.

In the end, the SEC fined Mr. Huttoe $12.5 million, and both he and Mr. Melcher were sentenced to federal prison. But by then it was too late for investors: Mr. Huttoe had spent most of his ill-gotten gains, and those who had been swindled did not get back any of their money. On March 7, 1997, Systems of Excellence filed for bankruptcy protection.

The case was a wake-up call for securities regulators, and prompted them to step up their patrols of the Internet. The SEC formed a new Office of Internet Enforcement to serve as its watchdog in cyberspace (that office now receives hundreds of reports each day about potential fraudulent online activity). In October 1998, the SEC brought its first wide-ranging crackdown on online stock fraud. The agency accused 44 companies and individuals of illegally touting the stocks of small companies over the Internet. In total, the stock promoters took in $6.3 million and nearly two million shares of free or cheap insider stock and options in exchange for hyping companies.

Sometimes the reach of such scams can be staggering. In one case, the SEC received more than 500 complaints about Francis A. Tribble and his public-relations company, Sloane Fitzgerald Inc. of New York. The SEC said Sloane sent more than six million electronic mail messages to investors, built bogus Web sites, and distributed an online newsletter over a ten-month period to promote two tiny companies—all without disclosing the companies had paid them in cash and stock.

Sometimes the schemes are just plain bizarre: In April 1999, the SEC won an emergency restraining order to halt what it deemed a bogus bond offering in a venture called New Utopia. According to an extensive promotional Web site, New Utopia was to be a new country, perched on giant concrete platforms in the Caribbean, about 115 miles west of the Cayman Islands. The SEC said New Utopia's leader, Howard Turney—who was to be supreme leader of New Utopia, and preferred to be called Prince Lazarus—used the Web site to solicit investment in a $350 million bond offering. (Mr. Turney has maintained the SEC is on a witch hunt, and said he will continue with his plans to build New Utopia.)

The SEC has also gone after companies seeking to develop everything from coconut plantations to a rocket that would visit a near-Earth asteroid. Why are investors falling for these scams? "You've got one of the greatest bull markets in history smack up against one of the greatest information revolutions in history, and things are getting dangerous," said John Stark, director of the SEC's Office of Internet Enforcement. "People aren't investing, they're gambling."

The OTC Bulletin Board Service

Most online fraud involves tiny companies quoted on the OTC Bulletin Board, a service of the National Association of Securities Dealers, which also operates the Nasdaq Stock Market. The OTC-BB, as it's often called, is really nothing like the Nasdaq market. In fact, it isn't a stock market or exchange at all, but rather an electronic quotation system that disseminates price quotes from brokers looking to buy and sell stocks quoted there. Its securities are mostly—though not all—tiny companies with limited assets and often few or no sales. They are often thinly traded, and have very low "floats"—shares not held by insiders or the company itself and available for public trading. As a result, the OTC-BB stocks are often quite volatile. Drastic price swings are not uncommon, and regulators have referred to it as the Wild West of the stock market. What's more, there are virtually no minimum eligibility requirements placed on the stocks quoted on the OTC-BB (unlike the national exchanges, which require companies to be of a certain size and financial stability before being listed). Because of all this, these "microcaps"—so named because they have a tiny market capitalization, or market value—are considered highly speculative investments.

OTC Bulletin Board companies have only recently been required to file regular financial statements with the SEC (just as companies on major exchanges are required to do). But stock in companies that choose not to file can still be traded. In response to the new regulations, and subsequent de-listings, a publication called the Pink Sheets that has been around for decades has taken its no-minimum-requirements quotation service online.

"Before the Internet, the Bulletin Board wasn't a problem, because you had never heard of these companies and had no way of getting information on them. All that has changed now," said Mr. Stark, the SEC's top Internet cop.

Con artists love microcap stocks. Their relatively unregulated nature makes them fertile ground for stock scams. It can be nearly impossible to get basic information on these types of companies, including such basic details as address and telephone number. Stock promoters capitalize on this, carefully constructing hype for companies with little regard for their actual performance, past or present.

One April Fool's Day, a group of message-board regulars set out to prove a point: No matter how ridiculous investment hype sounds, someone, somewhere will want to buy into it.

The five created an artificial company called FBN Associates. They built a Web site for the company, drafted press releases, and set up an e-mailbox to handle investor inquiries. FBN, according to its Web site, was based in Sedona, Arizona, and had an impressive list of products including devices that could flawlessly fix Year 2000 problems in all sorts of machines, from computers to toasters. One of its products, the EZSounder 2000, was a modified Timex watch that could detect the millennium bugs just by being worn near faulty computers.

Investors flocked to the idea. "My broker can't find the stock symbol. Help! How can I buy this?" wrote one participant on an online message board.

Janice Shell, an art historian in Milan, Italy, who served as "investor relations manager" for the gag company, said she received a flood of e-mail inquiries from people looking for an investment prospectus. There were certainly clues on the Web site that FBN—which stood for "fly by night"—wasn't on the level: The company claimed its products had been endorsed by the pope, and flaunted various multi-million-dollar contracts with various unnamed companies. The site also listed job openings, touting employee perks at FBN's headquarters, including an Olympic-sized pool and full gymnasium.

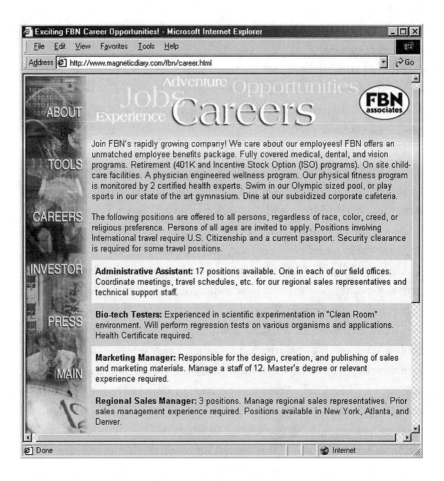

Ms. Shell and others who created FBN continued to participate in message boards after the hoax. Since then, she has become something of a vigilante, spending much of her time online trying to expose scams in tiny companies. "FBN was nothing compared to what some people believe about some of these companies they invest in," she said. "It's just crazy."

MANY WAYS TO BE DECEIVED

Spam

Chris Johnson, an insurance salesman in Gallatin, Tennessee, received an e-mail message on America Online that he thought sounded too good to ignore: Maxnet, a company he had never heard of, was being called "the next Yahoo!" and unnamed analysts were predicting that the company's stock, which was trading around $3 a share at the time, could hit $50 a share.

Mr. Johnson immediately went to the Web to do some research. He found a slick Web site at www.maxnet.com and descriptions of some products he thought looked promising. He also found an impressive client list that included Liz Claiborne, Norfolk Southern, and Miami Children's Hospital.

He called his broker and bought 7,500 shares for $3.75 a share. "It looked like a great investment," he said. "And for a few days, it was."

But the company Mr. Johnson found on the Internet wasn't the one he bought stock in, and he wasn't alone. Thousands of America Online users received that unsolicited e-mail message—called spam in the on-line world—promoting Maxnet Inc. The Maxnet those investors actually bought stock in was a recently formed company based in Freehold, New Jersey, that was still developing its only product: a Web site directory service.

The company that many investors believed they were buying into— and the company that owns the Web site Mr. Johnson found—was actually Maxnet Systems, a privately held network engineering company based in Dania, Florida, that often refers to itself simply as "Maxnet" and has nothing to do with the New Jersey Maxnet or the spam. Maxnet Systems received scores of e-mail messages and phone calls from irate investors who were confused by the spam.

It's not clear how many people invested in Maxnet Inc. based on the e-mail tip, but the stock responded: In the three-day period that many investors say they received the e-mail, and subsequently bought the stock, trading volume surged to well over one million shares a day, and the stock rocketed from around $1.50 a share to as high as $4.50 a share on the OTC Bulletin Board. But as is often the case when stocks are lifted by such anonymous e-mail tips, Maxnet's stock dropped below $1 a share just one week after the spam.

Maxnet Inc. denied having anything to do with the spam. Maxnet Systems, the Florida company, has sued Maxnet Inc., claiming infringement of its trademark, and Maxnet Inc. has since changed its name to MaxPlanet Corporation.

But that is of little comfort to Mr. Johnson, the insurance salesman who bought 7,500 shares at $3.75 each. He watched his investment steadily dwindle in value in the days after the e-mail announcement. When it became clear to him that the stock wasn't going anywhere near the $50 a share the spam had suggested, or even near the price he bought it at, he sold all of his shares for 59 cents each.

"For about four or five days I just couldn't sleep. My wife kept asking me what was wrong. I hadn't told her that I had bought the stock. It was hard telling her I took a $23,000 loss," he said.

Mr. Johnson said Maxnet was the first stock he ever bought based on an e-mail tip, and said it will certainly be the last. "I got had here. And I think somebody knew exactly what they were doing." Mr. Johnson was not alone; investors from coast to coast were duped by the spam, including a Massachusetts college student, a homemaker in Dayton, Ohio, a retired teacher in Santa Rosa, California, and a retired police officer in Pewaukee, Wisconsin. Many said they were otherwise cautious investors who just couldn't resist an opportunity to tap into the frenzy surrounding Internet stocks—in other words, they were the perfect targets for con artists.

Tracking down the people behind a spam is difficult, and often impossible. You may not realize it, but it's easy to fake a return address on an e-mail message. That can make it tricky to communicate with the person sending the unwanted mail, since chances are the person listed on the "from" line has nothing to do with the spam. Talented spammers take this a step further, actually hijacking computer systems owned by others to distribute their dirty work. For example, a spammer in California may be able to find a security loophole in the computer servers of a company in Utah. Without that company even realizing what was happening, the spammer could send thousands of pieces of mail through those servers to e-mail users around the country, all the while covering his own tracks because the messages would be traced to the Utah company.

It may seem strange that spammers are able to send you e-mail in the first place. Where did they get your e-mail address?

If you're a typical Internet user, your e-mail address isn't all that private. Spammers use sophisticated software programs to "harvest" e-mail addresses from the Net. Such programs prowl cyberspace, scouring messages posted in discussion forums and passed in chat rooms that may contain an address. Sometimes just submitting your e-mail address to a Web site, even one you trust, can be a risk. Sites are prohibited from selling your personal information—like e-mail addresses—if you tell them not to, and legitimate sites usually provide an easy way to notify them if you want your information kept private. But it can be difficult to keep track of every site you've given personal information to, and if those sites do indeed pass along your data, it's impossible to know what the companies who received it have in turn done with it.

Your best bet, regulators say, is to know that at some point in your online life, you're going to get junk mail, so be ready. Spams touting stocks almost always sound urgent—part of the goal of the sender, no doubt, is to spur a quick run-up in the stock's price. In the Maxnet spam, the sender wanted investors to believe they had to act fast, which prevented many of them from actually calling the company (and, presumably, learning the message was bogus). A lack of verifiable contact information should be an immediate red flag. If you can't ascertain the source of the mail, it's impossible to judge the credibility of its content.

Spammers often focus on "hot" issues like technology—"something that can turn a dime into a dollar overnight," said Mr. Stark, the SEC Internet regulator. He said investors often get so caught up in the excitement of the stock market—and those often-soaring Internet stocks—that they often abandon common sense.

Take the case of 21st Century Frontier Group, a tiny company that trades on the OTC Bulletin Board. Thousands of e-mail users received a spam touting the company's stock. According to the spam, insiders at 21st Century had leaked word that the company had developed software to fix the so-called Y2K problem that threatened to cripple computers in the year 2000. What's more, the anonymous tipster said this new technology was at the center of a bidding war between two large software makers. The spam included a street address for 21st Century in "Silicon Valley, California."

But 21st Century Frontier Group wasn't a high-tech Silicon Valley firm, nor did the company appear to have any solutions for the Y2K problem. The company was actually based in Elmer, New Jersey, and, according to press releases issued in the months before the spam, was trying to establish a recycling business and angling to buy a motorcycle dealership in Arizona.

There was little public information available on the company at the time, and the few press releases that were available indicated the company was struggling to secure funding for its operations. And unlike the anonymous stock analysts quoted in the Maxnet spam, the author of the 21st Century e-mail wrote that his information came from a somewhat more dubious source: his eavesdropping "at a local pub."

But all that didn't stop investors from rushing in. Just before users began receiving the messages, shares of the company were quoted at less than 10 cents on the OTC Bulletin Board amid little trading volume. But after the spam, the price climbed dramatically, reaching as high as 64 cents a share, while volume spiked to as many as 1 million shares a day. And just like the Maxnet case, the shares dropped just a few weeks later.

As is often the case with spam, it's difficult to determine the source of the e-mail promoting 21st Century. The sender used a fake return address, but also went a step further, using bogus credit card numbers to set up multiple e-mail accounts with an Internet service provider.

Phone numbers listed for 21st Century at the time of the spam had been disconnected, but a few days after the spam, 21st Century put out a press release denying rumors it was working on a Y2K fix. The company has since gone out of business.

Pay-for-Promotion Web Sites

A now-famous cartoon in *The New Yorker* put it best: Two dogs are sitting in front of a computer screen, and one says to the other, "On the Internet, nobody knows you're a dog."

That pearl of wisdom may help explain the success of online stock promoters, who often pass themselves off as financial professionals—or sometimes casual fellow investors—without revealing they've been paid to hype a company's stock. Stock promotion has quickly become big business on the Internet—and one of the SEC's most vexing problems. New sites constantly spring up offering "hot stock tips" and "news" about undiscovered companies. Some promoters go so far as to publish official-looking research reports, which almost always include "strong buy" recommendations and astronomical price targets. What's often unclear is that the content on these sites is simply paid advertising.

Stock promoters have always existed in one form or another. Not that long ago, sophisticated "boiler room" operations flourished, where promoters using banks of phones would cold-call investors, touting often worthless stocks. Such operations were expensive to operate, and somewhat limited in their reach.

But the global nature of the Internet has turned stock promotion into a lucrative business. Where investors once might have just hung up on a stranger pitching such investments, they now pay close attention, lured in by slick Web sites and the illusion that they're dealing with someone in the know. Moreover, using the Internet, promoters can reach thousands of investors far more quickly than even the biggest boiler room could using one-investor-at-a-time phone calls. Promoters are making millions of dollars touting companies, often at the expense of unsuspecting investors who buy into what turns out to be nothing more than empty hype.

Though some promoters' methods are crude at best—issuing research reports peppered with spelling and grammatical errors, for instance—investors continue to buy on the recommendations. Some investors say they regularly watch for promoters' "stock tips" not because they believe in the promoter's stock-picking prowess, but rather because they know others will fall for the hype and bid the stock price higher.

Many investors are surprised to learn that touting stocks in exchange for pay is, in fact, legal. But the laws that govern stock promoters are clear: Promoters are free to tout stocks, but they must disclose if they were paid and the terms of that compensation, including the amount and whether they were paid in cash or stock. Stock promoters are also subject to antifraud regulations, of course. The SEC has gone after promoters who have made ludicrous claims about their clients.

Promoters often go out of their way to avoid looking like stock promoters. Sometimes they construct Web sites that profile stock tips as if
they were little investment gems the Web site operator had stumbled
upon. Other promoters use financial message boards, taking advantage
of the anonymity they offer, to blend in with other investors and talk
up stocks. Other message-board participants are unaware, and often
assume that others posting on the investment boards are amateur investors like themselves.

Many promoters maintain that what they do is no different than
what larger, more established public relations firms do: tell the story
of "undiscovered" companies. But many of the companies that turn
to stock promoters are small, with unproven histories. With few exceptions, companies that use stock promoters usually aren't listed on
a major stock exchange, but rather are quoted on the OTC Bulletin
Board. Many of the SEC's online fraud cases have involved stock
promoters.

Many stock promoters claim they only represent companies that
they truly believe have great potential, but it's reasonable to assume
that anyone receiving large payments in exchange for touting a stock
probably isn't an unbiased source. What's more, it's important to
remember that stock promoters—unlike brokers or other financial
professionals—aren't bound by "suitability" requirements. A broker,
for instance, could be found in violation of suitability rules if he ad-
vised someone of modest means to make a big investment in a particularly speculative stock.

A financial professional, such as a stock analyst, who issues a "strong
buy" recommendation on a stock that goes south would face scrutiny
and ridicule. But stock promoters operate with relative impunity. Many
operate their Web sites anonymously—a red flag for investors digging
for online information.

One site, Stock Genie, has advertised heavily on financial sites like
Silicon Investor. Stock Genie's site features monthly "stock profiles"
including glowing reports on small, unknown companies.

Stock Genie is sometimes paid by the companies listed on its Web
site, but investors have to look closely to discover that relationship.

The details of the compensation are laid out in lengthy disclaimers that run at the end of Stock Genie's reports on companies. Stock Genie is often compensated in shares of a company's stock that can be sold at any time. Stock Genie discloses no information about itself, such as a mailing address, telephone number, or even the names of the people running the site.

When promoters like Stock Genie receive stock as compensation, it's in their best interests to see the stock prices of companies they feature race higher. Some promoters even receive extra bonuses for getting a company's stock to a certain price. As a result, promoters try to convince investors to buy shares and hang on to them—ironic, since the usual way a promoter makes money is to dump his shares into the market.

Popular tactics include predicting news will be released soon, since positive news releases often boost a stock's price. When prices of recommended stocks decline, promoters will often attribute the slump to manipulation from market makers—the professional traders that oversee trading in particular stocks. Other times they'll claim it's because an overall sector is slumping, though stocks quoted on the OTC Bulletin Board rarely move in step with their much larger counterparts on major exchanges, like the New York Stock Exchange.

By definition, promoters are positive on a company's prospects. They're paid to be. As with everything on the Web, always verify the information you get from promoters with another source. And remember that it's fair to ask why a company is paying someone to hype its stock.

When Cashco Management wanted to attract investors to its stock, it turned to Global Penny Stocks, an online investment newsletter. Cashco had a strange product mix: The company sold software to fix the Y2K computer bug, and wood-based kitty litter.

In exchange for a payment of $3,950, Global Penny Stocks' publisher, George Schlieben, issued a "special research report" on Cashco and gave it a "buy" rating. He predicted the company's stock—trading at around 44 cents a share on the OTC Bulletin Board when Mr. Schlieben issued the report—would hit $2 to $2.50 a share in the next year, and $4 in two years. A few days after the report, the stock climbed to 51 cents a share, before beginning a steady decline, later trading for just a few pennies.

In small print above the research reports, Mr. Schlieben indicated he had received a fee, but didn't say how much. Mr. Schlieben also didn't disclose that all of the information in his research report—including the price targets for the stock—came directly from the company.

In October 1998, the SEC filed a civil complaint against Mr. Schlieben for failing to disclose the details of his compensation. In its complaint, the SEC said Mr. Schlieben's favorable research reports were "nothing more than paid advertisements." In November 1999, Mr. Schlieben settled the case with the SEC. Without admitting or denying guilt, he agreed not to violate the SEC's disclosure rules.

The fee that Mr. Schlieben charged Cashco for preparing the research report was relatively low by stock-promotion standards. The Future Superstock—another online investment newsletter targeted in an SEC sweep of stock promoters—received hundreds of thousands of dollars for some of its stock picks.

The SEC alleged that Jeff Bruss, editor of the Future Superstock Web site, had also engaged in another practice common to stock promoters: selling into a stock rally that he helped create. At the time, the SEC said Mr. Bruss had recommended to the newsletter's subscribers the purchase of about 25 microcap stocks that were predicted to double or triple within months. In most cases, the SEC said, the prices of the recommended stocks did in fact increase for a short period of time after being promoted in Future Superstock, but then dropped substantially. The SEC said that in many cases, Mr. Bruss sold stock in companies just after recommending that others purchase those same stocks.

The SEC claimed that Mr. Bruss never disclosed he had been paid, in cash and stock, from nearly every company he promoted on the Web site. What's more, the agency said Mr. Bruss presented the company profiles as "independent research and analysis," when in fact they were just advertisements.

Mr. Bruss denied any wrongdoing in the case.

Many stock promoters operate Web sites that they bill as "investment newsletters." These sites usually feature a collection of stock tips, called everything from "stock tips" to "featured company profiles."

The first thing you should do any time you come to a Web site that appears to offer stock picks or investment advice is check to see if the site is being paid for its opinion. Stock promoters are required to disclose this information, and most do, though it's not always easy to find. Look for a section labeled "disclaimer" or "disclosure." Sometimes the disclaimer is attached at the bottom of the individual stock picks.

Some disclaimers can be long and rambling, and it can be difficult to determine whether the site has been paid. Most of the notices include general legal disclaimers warning you that the site is not any sort of registered financial adviser, and that despite what you may think "stock pick" or "strong buy recommendation" means, the site is not suggesting you buy any particular security (only registered professionals can offer investment advice).

Some sites say only that "XYZ newsletter may from time to time receive compensation from the companies it covers," but the SEC has said such disclosures are inadequate because they don't clearly spell out whether the information on the site is a paid advertisement.

Be sure to note the nature of the compensation the site is receiving. Again, if the promoter is being paid in stock, he's going to have to sell that stock at some point to make a profit—no doubt after he's suggested everyone else buy.

Also be aware of other conflicts of interest the dis-

(continues)

claimer may reveal. Some promoters, for instance, may not be on a company's payroll, but may still have personal holdings in a stock they're recommending. Those promoters are likely trying to drum up excitement in a stock so that the price will rise, and they in turn can sell their shares into that rally.

Be suspicious of claims about a promoter's stock-picking prowess. Many investment newsletters list tables that show the performance of past stock picks. Often promoters use tricky language, like listing the price the stock was at when they recommended it, and then listing the high the stock reached since that recommendation. No mention is made of the stock's performance *since* it reached that high; in many cases stocks do race after being hyped by a promoter, only to collapse later.

And finally, research the promoter. Run the name of the site—and the stock promoter—through the SEC's Web site (www.sec.gov), and check with the securities regulator for the state the site operates from. If you can't find any information on who runs the site, consider going elsewhere.

Paid Touts on Message Boards

While Web-based investment newsletters remain tools of the trade for stock promoters, many have ventured onto Internet message boards, where each day scores of investors gather to swap stock tips. Stock promoters wage carefully constructed—and often anonymous—hype campaigns on the boards, whispering about great things to come, and generally whipping investors into a frenzy. Because users of message boards are allowed to post using aliases, promoters are able to hide their identities and "blend in" with other investors.

Disclosure rules still apply in message boards, of course. The SEC has said promoters who participate in the boards should tack a notice onto every post that details whether they're being paid by the companies they're chatting up. But it's rare to find such notices on boards—though that certainly doesn't mean stock promoters are staying away.

Daryn Fleming was a regular participant on the popular Silicon Investor online message boards (**www.siliconinvestor.com**). He often urged others to buy stock in certain companies, cheering their management teams and business plans. "Rumors abound about . . . oh, I won't say what. I will say BUY BUY BUY," he wrote about one company.

But what wasn't always clear from his message-board posts was that Mr. Fleming's firm, Wall Street West, was paid to promote the companies he mentioned.

Wall Street West described itself as a "stock research firm and holding company." In exchange for payments of cash or stock, Wall Street West promoted companies as stock picks on its Web site, and in several instances wrote glowing research reports that included "buy" recommendations on the stocks. It also sent out e-mail and press releases promoting the companies.

Mr. Fleming has maintained that he hasn't violated any SEC regulations. Over time he added disclosures to his Web site detailing his compensation arrangements with the companies he promotes there. But even when he was beginning to add the detailed disclosures to his site, Mr. Fleming continued to tout stocks on Silicon Investor, often without revealing his name or his connection to Wall Street West.

Other Deceptions

The SEC has also seen an increase in online affinity fraud—scams that target specific groups, like a particular religion or race. Sophisticated e-mail tools make it easy for spammers to assemble targeted mailing lists, and the SEC said specific groups are sometimes more susceptible to fraud because of the personal nature of such invitations.

Foreign investment scams are also flourishing on the Net. Because there are no borders in cyberspace, scammers from countries near and far are flooding the United States with investment opportunities. A common scam, said the SEC, is an offer to invest in some sort of bank note in a foreign land, almost always at an astronomic rate of return. But not only is it much harder for regulators to identify foreign con artists, prosecuting them—and getting investors' money back—is often nearly impossible.

WARNING: HERE ARE SOME TIPS THAT MAY HELP YOU IDENTIFY A WEB SITE HOAX.

- Beware of Web sites that have only numbers for their addresses, rather than the typical ".com" you're used to. These are called IP addresses, and are sometimes used by Web site operators who want to hide their identities. An IP address is a unique string of numbers that identifies every computer on the Net. People use IP addresses because in order to get a ".com" address, they must register and provide a name and address. But an IP address doesn't require such registration, and can make it more difficult to know who you're dealing with. (Note, however, that such addresses have been used by law enforcement to track down scammers. Always make a note of any IP addresses you come across.)

- Also, be aware that it's relatively easy to move content from one Web site into another. Some unscrupulous site operators build pages that appear to be their own, but actually draw in data from a more reputable financial site. Some scammers copy graphics onto their sites to create elaborate hoaxes—making a page look like a news page from Bloomberg.com, for instance, as in the PairGain

case discussed earlier. Taking a graphic from a
Web site is as easy as saving a file on your PC.
- Check a Web site's registration. Go to an Internet
registration site, such as **www.networksolutions.
com,** and type in the address you're curious about.
You'll get a screen telling you who the site is
registered to, including an address and telephone
number. You should note that site registration
information is frequently out of date or inaccu-
rate, and there's no process to verify that the
information a registrant gives is valid. Still,
this can be a good starting point if you're
having trouble figuring out who is behind a
Web site.

PROTECTING YOURSELF

"I've said it once, and I'll say it again: Never, ever make an investment decision based on something you read online," warns Mr. Stark, the SEC's top Internet cop.

Good advice, but too often ignored. Of course, Mr. Stark isn't suggesting you disconnect your computer from the Net. People make informed investment decisions every day based on things they read online. Rather, he's pointing out that the Internet is a wide-open playground for con artists, and it's far too easy to get burned. Investors must do their own research before they buy or sell a stock based on what they read on the Net.

Regulatory agencies like the SEC have intensified their efforts to clean up the Net, but they acknowledge fraud has grown much faster than their resources to fight it. It is ultimately up to investors to protect themselves.

Here are some tips for avoiding online investment scams:

Be skeptical.   Almost everyone with an investment opinion also has some sort of financial stake in that recommendation, either directly or indirectly. They may want you to believe they're just trying to help you out, but rest assured they're more interested in their own pockets than yours.

Never rely on just one source of information.   Most investors who get into trouble online do so because they quickly buy a stock based on one hot tip, or on a dispatch put out by a stock promoter. Always verify information you read online with other sources. If you read something about a company, call the company directly. Many companies have investor relations departments and are happy to answer questions. And avoid anonymous sources; they're unaccountable for their information, making them far less likely to be reliable.

What's in it for the promoter?   Remember, stock promoters are paid to get you excited about stocks, and promoters are required to disclose the details of those payments. Many bury such information in fine print on their Web sites (a practice that should give you pause in itself). If you're not sure if a promoter has been paid, ask. If a promoter has been paid in stock, try to find out if they've sold any shares (if the stock is such a good investment, why are they selling?). Many promoters make extravagant claims about their stock-picking ability, but remember there's no way to verify those claims—everyone is a great stock picker with 20/20 hindsight.

Ignore anonymous stock tips.   Contrary to what some folks will have you believe, hot stock information doesn't come in the form of unsolicited e-mail or anonymous message-board postings. Senders of such messages are almost certainly trying to manipulate the price of a stock for their own personal gain. Trying to "front-run" such schemes—thinking you can buy in on the stock at the beginning of a rally and sell before the stock pulls back—is a dangerous practice, since it's impossible to guess when those behind the scheme will begin dumping their holdings.

Search Edgar.   Securities laws require many companies to file annual reports with the SEC, which are stored in the Edgar database.

All companies traded on a major stock market like Nasdaq or the New York Stock Exchange must file such reports, as must those companies with more than 500 investors and $10 million in net assets. But many "microcap" companies don't meet those guidelines, and so aren't required to file annual reports or audited financial information. The absence of such reports should be a red flag in itself—why won't the company go on the record with its financials and business plan? Many tiny companies string investors along for months, or even years, claiming they're working on their SEC filings (and, subsequently, working to get listed on a major stock market). Still, even some tiny companies must make certain filings with the SEC, and such filings will at least reveal the names and addresses of the company's owners (something that can be unusually hard to find when it comes to such companies). If you can't find a company in Edgar, call the SEC at (202) 942-8090 to find out if the company has filed any documents with the agency.

Check with other regulators.   Whether there's information on file with the SEC or not, it's always a good idea to check in with other securities regulators. They can see if there have been any complaints about the company, or about promoters touting the company. A complete list of addresses and phone numbers for state regulators is available on the SEC's Web site at **www.sec.gov/consumer/state.htm.** Some contact information is also available in Chapter 9.

Understand the OTC Bulletin Board.   The fact that most companies quoted on the OTC Bulletin Board are there because they can't actually qualify for a listing on a major market should give you pause. It would be unfair to accuse a company of being a fraud just because it's quoted on the OTC-BB. But it can be said that companies quoted there are often riskier investments than those listed on national exchanges. Many of the investor-protection regulations that govern stocks traded on the major exchanges and Nasdaq don't apply to the microcaps. OTC-BB stocks are also often thinly traded, meaning it could be much harder to sell the stock when that time comes (many of the stocks don't even trade every day). You should also note that clients of stock promoters are often OTC companies.

Beware of foreign investments. Some fraudulent companies set up shop in foreign lands, believing that makes them less likely to be caught by securities regulators. And in many cases, they're right. It's very difficult for the SEC or other regulators to track down fraud outside the U.S. If you send money outside the country, and something goes wrong, you'll likely be on your own.

WEB SITES

U.S. Securities and Exchange Commission
(www.sec.gov)

It can be difficult to find what you're looking for on the SEC's Web site, but there's still a wealth of cautionary information here for investors. The Enforcement Division's part of the site (found directly at **www.sec.gov/enforce.htm**) contains the latest news on SEC crackdowns. It's a good idea to check out a Web site or a stock promoter here before believing anything he or she says. You can use the enforcement page to search all SEC information. Plug in the name of the company you're thinking of investing in, or the name of the person offering you stock advice, to look for signs of trouble. It's not foolproof, but it is foolish not to give it a try.

The North American Securities Administrators Association
(www.nasaa.org)

NASAA is an organization made up of state securities regulators. The Web site features an in-depth "Investor Education" area that provides detailed information on many popular frauds, including Internet stock schemes. It also provides tips on spotting hard-to-identify scams, as those on the Net often are. Much of the information is based on actual questions from investors.

NINE

Recourse

I t happened: You lost money on your investment. It wasn't supposed to be like this. You were careful, you did your research.
That ninth-grader down the street is using his computer to trade
his way into what seems like five figures, and somehow you—
you!—managed to lose money. Now what?

People lose money every day in the stock market. Sometimes (well,
actually, most of the time) it's their own fault, and the only thing to do
is learn from the mistake and move on. But sometimes, someone else
helped them out of their money. Maybe a con artist duped them.
Maybe an unscrupulous stock broker pressured them into a poor investment, or maybe an online broker simply didn't process a sell order
until it was too late.

The first thing to do when you lose money on an investment is to
figure out exactly what happened. In the case of fraud, it can be somewhat easy to figure out—though you may be embarrassed to admit
that you were taken in. It sometimes takes years to sort out the details
of a well-planned scam, and it's unlikely you'll see your money anytime
soon. Still, acting quickly is the key. Internet con artists can disappear
in no time, and the sooner you alert regulators, the better.

In other cases, particularly while dealing with an online broker,
losses can be much more difficult to sort out. No online broker is
going to compensate you for making a poor trade. Remember, you're

paying such a low commission because you've opted for the do-it-yourself route. Still, online brokers are responsible for the promises they make to you, particularly about how they'll handle the orders you give them. Regulators say investors are sometimes too quick to chalk a loss up to their own inexperience with online trading, when in reality a glitch in the trading system may have played a role.

You don't necessarily need a lawyer to handle all of this. Regulators offer lots of guidance to individuals seeking to report a scam, and the securities industry runs an arbitration process to settle claims against brokers that you can use without an attorney. All of that said, though, you still may want to consider hiring a lawyer to file a lawsuit against a scam artist or to represent you in arbitration (your broker surely will have an attorney). Two lawyers' groups run referral services to help find legal representation, and both run Web sites: the American Bar Association (**www.abanet.org/referral/home.html**) and the Public Investor Arbitration Bar Association (**www.piaba.org**), an organization for lawyers who represent investors in securities-related cases.

SCAMMED

The Securities and Exchange Commission receives a flood of e-mail *every day* tipping off the agency to suspected scams. Internet con games have become big business, and are becoming more and more sophisticated all the time. (For more on online fraud, see Chapter 8.)

In some cases, fraud is a very subjective thing. If a company says it's going to be the next Microsoft but turns out to be the next big flop, did it scam you? If you buy a stock based on the cheerleading of a stock promoter who has been paid to promote a company and the investment drops in value, can you go after him? Questions like this are answered in court.

Most online fraud involves small, relatively unknown companies. Such companies tend to be good vehicles for scams for several reasons: They usually have small "floats"—the pool of shares available for public trading—and millions of shares of "insider" stock that can be unloaded on the public. Those small floats make it easy for scam artists to orchestrate dramatic price swings in a stock that can quickly leave you with losing stock trades. What's more, tiny companies are relatively easy to set up with minimal documentation, making it easier for them to disappear (and harder to track down).

Securities regulators on both the state and federal levels have stepped up their surveillance of online fraud, and several states have set up special task forces to focus on the Internet. Still, regulators have limited resources, and the Internet has given online con artists a wide reach. Despite all of these efforts, online fraud remains rampant, and you need to keep up your guard and be prepared to work aggressively to seek recourse if you believe that you have been duped. The SEC only prosecutes a limited number of fraud cases each year, and investors only receive some of their money back in a handful of those cases. And beware: When a company goes bankrupt, there may not be anyone left to sue for your money.

Securities regulators like the SEC are the key to shutting down the fraud. Getting them involved early is absolutely essential.

The first step, even before you're sure that you were scammed, is to do some research and assemble all the evidence you have. "Save everything, period," said Denise Voigt Crawford, a regulator for the state of Texas. "Once the paper trail is gone, we don't have anything to go on." That includes things like company press releases, advertisements, or any other documents upon which you based your decision to invest. If you had any direct correspondence with the company through e-mail, print out those letters. If it was traditional mail, save it. If a stock promoter's hype was one of the reasons you bought the company, you should print out that material, too.

Regulators say it's important to create a detailed timeline of the events that happened while you owned the stock. You should include:

- When did you first hear about this company? How? Was it a Web page? A stock promoter? A friend? Be as detailed as possible. The events that led you to purchase the security in question will be among the most important facts in proving that you were deceived. You should find copies of your trading records from your broker, detailing exactly when you bought the stock, and at what price.

- Why did you buy this stock? Was there something specific about the company's business plan or background that interested you?
- What happened at the company while you owned the stock? What promises did the company make through press releases, and did those promises come true? If not, did the company offer a reasonable explanation? Be sure to document particular spikes or drops in the price of the stock. Did there appear to be any particular reasons for these changes? Did they correspond to particular company news announcements?
- When did the investment first begin to lose value? What did you do? If you had any conversations with the company, document them thoroughly, including the date and time of the conversation and the names of the people with whom you spoke.

No one is going to reimburse you for a poor investment decision. And failing to do your homework on a stock is no defense. But there is no shortage of people on the Internet who are looking to pump stock prices—and to pressure you into buying up worthless stock—so that they can profit.

Once you decide you've been the victim of one of these scams, and you have assembled a detailed record of the events, it's important to contact securities regulators right away. The SEC has an Office of Internet Enforcement dedicated to investigating fraud on the Internet. That office can be reached by e-mail at **enforcement@sec.gov**. (For tips on what to include in your complaint to the SEC, visit **www.sec. gov/enforce/comctr.htm**.)

You'll also want to contact your state securities-regulation representative. There may be special laws in your state that could make it easier to prosecute someone for the scam. Also, because states receive far fewer complaints than the SEC does, you may get a faster response to your problem. You'll find a complete list of state securities regulators at the end of this chapter.

Finally, if a broker was involved in the incident, you'll want to notify the National Association of Securities Dealers, a regulatory group in

Washington that all brokers must register with. The NASD (known as a self-regulatory organization because it is funded by the brokerage industry, but also regulates brokerage firms) can help you figure out whether the broker has been in trouble before. You also have the option of initiating an arbitration claim against the broker to try to get your money back (arbitration is described in detail in the next section).

Again, timing is key. Sending an e-mail to the SEC before you yourself have even figured out what is going on probably won't expedite your case. But at the same time, waiting several months to unravel every detail only gives the scammer time to cover his or her tracks. Alert regulators as soon as possible, and send them every piece of information you have. Be sure to keep each regulator informed about developments in the case.

COMPLAINTS AGAINST BROKERS

The booming popularity of online trading has also led to a spike in the number of reported problems. The Securities and Exchange Commission says the number of complaints involving online brokers has risen dramatically.

Most complaints involve technical trading issues—the broker's computer system didn't process a sell order as you instructed it to, or maybe it purchased 1,000 shares of General Motors stock when you only wanted 100. In many cases, brokers will correct these types of mistakes when they are brought to their attention. Regulators say you should write to the firm's compliance officer as soon as you realize the mistake, clearly stating the problem and clearly asking to have your account credited accordingly. Always put your complaints in writing, they say, even if you have already talked by telephone to someone at the firm.

But other disputes aren't settled that easily, and regulators say they expect the number of arbitration proceedings against online brokers to mount as the number of online brokerage accounts grows—sometimes at a faster pace than the technology behind them.

"We are taking a very hard look at what brokers are promising to their customers, and we're going to hold them to it and make sure they deliver," said Philip Rutledge, deputy chief counsel for the Pennsylvania Securities Commission. He said he has been alarmed by the number of investors he has talked to who don't understand the potential technical limitations of online brokers, particularly on heavy trading days.

"Many of the cases we handle are those where the customer is promised certain things, like good execution times, and the firm doesn't deliver. They don't tell you that for $14.95 you're going to get a terrible execution," said Phil Aidikoff, a Beverly Hills, California, attorney who has represented brokerage customers in arbitration cases. "Many times, these are seasoned investors who know how the markets work, and they have an absolute right to expect that their orders will be handled as they've instructed. But too often, that doesn't happen."

As in cases where you've been scammed, the first step is figuring out who is at fault. That can be a difficult process with an online trade. If you received confirmation for a trade that the brokerage later says never went through, your case should be relatively simple. But what about system outages? Exactly how long do brokers have to process your order?

The stock markets, like the Nasdaq Stock Market or the New York Stock Exchange, do, at times, suffer outages that affect trading. But such outages aren't nearly as common as with online brokers, or as frustrating. It's one thing if no one can execute a trade because of a glitch that affects the entire stock market, but another if it's only *your* broker whose systems are down. Technical problems hit entire markets perhaps once or twice a year, typically, but hardly a week goes by that doesn't include at least a brief outage at one of the major online brokerage firms.

Online brokers will typically provide you with an alternate trading method, like an automated telephone trading system, to use when they are having troubles on the Web. Firms like Schwab often let customers walk into a local brokerage branch to execute trades. These routes may allow you to trade during an online outage, but regulators say you should ask for the same discounted online commissions for telephone or face-to-face trades when it's the broker's fault that you can't trade on the Web.

Because brokerages allow these alternate trading methods in cases of system failures, an outage in itself probably isn't enough to base a claim of loss on, attorneys say. This issue is particularly thorny, though—several state regulators have formed task forces to analyze online brokerages and their growing system problems. Some have suggested that brokers with a pattern of system failures should be reined in by the SEC until they can beef up their technology to support demand.

Outages come in different forms: Not all of them mean the broker's Web site is entirely inaccessible. In some cases, investors are able to continue to trade, but they can't reach their account information. In other cases, they find that getting responses from brokerage sites—like trade confirmations—are excruciatingly slow. This can be particularly dangerous, because it can lead to confusion about whether an order was completed or not.

The problems aren't unique to smaller firms. Online giant Charles Schwab and online pioneer E*Trade, two of the biggest Internet brokers, have experienced their share of computer problems. "Investors don't know what they're getting into when they sign up with online brokers, and they definitely don't know what to do when they run into a problem," said Denise Voigt Crawford, the Texas securities commissioner.

Common Disputes

Aside from system outages, slow trade executions are perhaps the most common complaints that are lodged against online brokerage firms. An investor identifies a stock he or she wants to buy, sees a price that seems reasonable, and places an order—only to find out later that the online brokerage firm was too slow. By the time the trade was made (or executed, in the language of Wall Street), and a confirmation was returned, the stock's price had moved sharply. The bargain price was missed and the order was filled at a level the investor would never have considered paying. Conversely, an order to sell stock may have been completed at a price far lower than the investor would care to accept. Although these are mostly problems for investors who buy and sell stocks for just short-term gains (anywhere from a day or two to several weeks), these types of foul-ups can leave even long-term investors smarting.

Investors also complain about "double orders," which happen when an investor clicks a button on a Web site to submit an order, and then clicks again a short time later after it appears the order hasn't been filled. In some cases, the order really had been filled on the first click, even though the confirmation hadn't reached the investor yet. Clicking again sends the order through a second time.

Another problem is the establishment of an unwanted short position in a stock. Sometimes an online brokerage customer will issue a buy order for a stock and neglect to check for confirmation that the trade went through as instructed. Later, if the buy order did fail, and the customer puts in a sell order for that stock, the online brokerage may think the customer is trying to short the stock.

Investors sometimes complain that they were confused by stock quotes they received from their online broker, said Mr. Rutledge, the Pennsylvania regulator. Sometimes, it's not clear whether quotes are delayed, or real-time. (Online brokerage firms tend to distribute real-time quotes sparingly, because they are charged a small fee by the stock markets for each real-time quote they use. Delayed quotes are free to firms.) Although delayed quotes are only 15 or 20 minutes old—which may not seem like a big deal—on a fast-moving Internet stock, that can seem like a lifetime.

Mr. Rutledge said he also believes that many customers don't know the difference between market and limit orders, and while online brokers may not be at fault for that, he believes they can do more to make sure customers know what type of order they're placing. A market order is an order to buy a stock at the best price the brokerage is able to secure in the market at the time the order is executed. That price could end up being far greater than the price quoted at the time the customer taps his order into his computer. Some stocks move sharply in very short periods of time, especially if they are the subject of a news development. Because of this, regulators suggest customers place limit orders, which specify the maximum price at which they're willing to buy the stock. If the broker can't complete the transaction for that price, the order isn't filled.

Arbitration

You may not realize this, but when you open an account with an on-line broker you typically sign away your right to take the broker to court over a dispute. That's because brokerage contracts—with both online and off-line firms—regularly include a clause that requires all disputes must be settled through arbitration. "People don't realize that when they sign that brokerage agreement that they're not going to have the same legal rights as they do when they go down to the local car dealership and get a car that turns out not to be as it was repre-sented," said Michael Richards, a Memphis attorney.

Arbitration has long been a contentious issue. Lawyers for investors claim that the process, which is often run by the industry itself, is stacked in favor of securities firms. But the firms insist the system is fair, quicker than going to court to settle disputes, and argue that it's less expensive for both sides. The National Association of Securities Deal-ers said most cases are resolved in 10 to 12 months, compared with court cases that can span years.

But it can be intimidating for an investor unfamiliar with the way ar-bitration works. "People think they walk in and Judge Judy will give them justice. But it's a very complex process, and the brokerage side is very, very good at it," said Phil Aidikoff, the securities lawyer.

More often than not—about 63% of the time—investors do walk away from arbitration with some money. Lawyers for investors say that num-ber is low, and shows a bias for firms. But securities firms say it proves that hearing panels are more sympathetic to investors who have lost money. They say investors are often upset that they made a bad trade, and want the firms to bail them out. "There are many people who go into the market, and you have to believe they're fully cognizant of the risks, but when they lose a lot of money they figure they can cut their losses by initiating a claim," said John Peloso, a securities attorney with Morgan, Lewis & Bockius in New York and a former arbitrator. "But many times, these cases are very unclear, and there is fault on both sides."

Arbitration is usually far less costly than a typical court case. You're not required to hire an attorney to represent you. But almost everyone does, because you can bet that the firm you've filed the claim against will have at least one attorney working on the case. What's more, there are "forum fees" that must be paid to the arbitrators for their time. Often these fees are paid by the losing side, but sometimes they're split equally among both parties.

Your rights in an arbitration proceeding may not be as broad as they would be in court. For instance, there may be limits placed on the amount of money you may seek as damages, and you may not be allowed to pursue punitive damages (claims for money over and above the amount you lost, which are awarded at times in court cases that involve particularly egregious behavior). Also, your rights to investigate your case (known as "discovery" in legal parlance) may be narrower than you would have in a lawsuit. All of these things are seen as trade-offs for the quicker turnaround and lower cost of arbitration.

Arbitration begins when an investor files a claim against a broker. Claims are most often filed with the National Association of Securities Dealers (**www.nasdr.com**), which regulates brokers, but they can also go to other arbitration groups—sometimes called forums—that hear cases, including the major stock exchanges and the American Arbitration Association (**www.adr.org**), a nonprofit group. Your brokerage account agreement probably includes a list of the arbitration forums from which you can chose.

In the claim, the investor will need to document exactly how he believes he was wronged by the firm, whether it was through a technical glitch or high-pressure sales tactics from a broker (not usually an issue in claims against online firms). For small cases—where less than $10,000 is at issue—there probably won't be an arbitration hearing at all. Instead, an arbitrator will request written statements from both sides, and will make a ruling based on the documents. When your claim is for more than $10,000, you'll get a hearing. A hearing is similar to small claims court, but more informal. Hearings are held at NASD offices around the country, or in hotel meeting rooms. One arbitrator will be assigned to your case, unless your claim is for more than $25,000, in which case three will be assigned.

Most people who serve as arbitrators do so on a part-time basis. They must pass qualification guidelines with the NASD or another arbitration forum, and performance is regularly reviewed. Many arbitrators are attorneys, or retired securities professionals who want to remain active in the industry. Some have argued that the presence of current or former securities professionals constitutes something of a conflict of interest, because such people, they argue, are more likely to be sympathetic to firms. But each side gets a chance to exclude arbitrators who they believe shouldn't hear the case. When a hearing is scheduled, the NASD gives each side a list of candidates eligible to hear the case. Both sides rank the arbitrators, and the NASD selects the arbitrator based on those rankings.

During the proceedings, the arbitrator will question both sides about the claim. Generally, you or your lawyer won't get a chance to pose questions directly to the other side, but the arbitrator will try to ask the firm about the issues you've raised. The arbitrator may ask both sides to produce documentation. Lawyers say it's important to remember that firms—particularly large firms—are very good at the arbitration process because they've done it a lot more than you have. Coming to the hearing prepared with documents is essential, they say, as is remaining calm and focused on your case.

ASKING FOR HELP

Some regulators say they're seeing an increase in the number of brokerage customers going after online brokers over a curious claim: failing to protect them from themselves. The cheap commissions and do-it-yourself nature of online trading have made it too easy for novice investors to get in over their heads, these people have argued. They say firms are far more interested in attracting new customers than they are in educating them on how to be responsible investors.

And that very well may be true, but don't expect an arbitration panel to reward you for your lack of investment savvy.

"There comes a point in time where we have to accept the fact that people have to have some responsibility for getting themselves into trouble," said Bill Singer, an attorney with Singer Frumento in New York. "When you walk into a casino and put your life savings on the craps table, you don't get it back just because you claim that the casino shouldn't have let you place the bet."

Still, carelessness is one thing, and being duped is another. If you were tricked by a shady company that lied about itself or by an online broker that failed to keep its end of the bargain, you do have options. Just because you made your trades alone, without the help of a broker, it doesn't necessarily mean you're responsible for everything that goes wrong. When in doubt, contact regulators.

"There is nothing wrong with holding someone responsible if they've wronged you. People who trade online tend to be far more self-reliant than others," said Ms. Crawford, the Texas regulator. "But that doesn't mean they should sit idly by when there's a problem."

Here is how to contact the Securities and Exchange Commission and state securities regulators. Web pages or e-mail addresses are included where available:

SEC

Washington Headquarters
202-942-7040
E-mail: **help@sec.gov**

Northeast Regional Office
New York
212-748-8000
E-mail: **newyork@sec.gov**

Boston District Office
617-424-5900
E-mail: **boston@sec.gov**

Philadelphia District Office
215-597-3100
E-mail: **philadelphia@sec.gov**

Southeast Regional Office
Miami, Fla.
305-536-4700
E-mail: **miami@sec.gov**

Atlanta District Office
404-842-7600
E-mail: **atlanta@sec.gov**

Midwest Regional Office
Chicago
312-353-7390
E-mail: **chicago@sec.gov**

Central Regional Office
Denver, Colo.
303-844-1000
E-mail: **denver@sec.gov**

Fort Worth District Office
817-978-3821
E-mail: **dfw@sec.gov**

Salt Lake District Office
801-524-5796
E-mail: **saltlake@sec.gov**

Pacific Regional Office
Los Angeles
323-965-3998
E-mail: **losangeles@sec.gov**

San Francisco District Office
415-705-2500
E-mail: **sanfrancisco@sec.gov**

ARBITRATION FORUMS

National Association of Securities Dealers
Washington, D.C.
202-728-8958
(**www.nasdr.com**)

American Arbitration Association
New York
800-778-7879
(**www.adr.org**)

Boston Stock Exchange
617-235-2000
(**www.bostonstock.com**)

Chicago Board Options Exchange
312-786-7705
(**www.cboe.com**)

Chicago Stock Exchange
312-663-2222
(**www.chicagostockex.com**)

Cincinnati Stock Exchange
312-786-8803
(**www.cincinnatistock.com**)

New York Stock Exchange
212-656-2772
(**www.nyse.com**)

Pacific Stock Exchange
San Francisco
415-393-4000
(**www.pacificex.com**)

STATE SECURITIES REGULATORS

Alabama
Securities Commission
334-242-2984 or 800-222-1253
E-mail: **alsecom@dsmd.state.al.us**

Alaska
Department of Community and
  Economic Development
907-465-2521
(**www.dced.state.ak.us/bsc/bsc.htm**)

Arizona
Corporation Commission
602-542-4242
(**www.cc.state.az.us**)

Arkansas
Securities Department
501-324-9260
E-mail: **arsec@ccon.net**

California
Department of Corporations
213-736-3481
(**www.corp.ca.gov**)

Colorado
Division of Securities
303-894-2320
(**www.dora.state.co.us/securities**)

Connecticut
Department of Banking
860-240-8230
(**www.state.ct.us/dob**)

Delaware
Division of Securities
Department of Justice
302-577-8424

District of Columbia
Department of Insurance and Securities
  Regulation
202-727-8000

Florida
Office of Comptroller
Department of Banking and Finance
850-410-9286
(**www.dbf.state.fl.us/**)

Georgia
Office of the Secretary of State
404-656-3920
(**www.sos.state.ga.us**)

Hawaii
Department of Commerce and
  Consumer Affairs
808-586-2744
(**www.state.hi.us/dcca/**)

Idaho
Department of Finance
208-332-8004
(**www.state.id.us/finance/dof.htm**)

Illinois
Office of the Secretary of State
217-782-2256 or 800-628-7937
(**www.sos.state.il.us/depts/**
  securities/sec_home.html)

Indiana
Office of the Secretary of State
317-232-6681
(**www.ai.org/sos/security/**)

Iowa
Securities Division
515-281-4441
(**www.state.ia.us/ins/security**)

Kansas
Office of the Securities Commissioner
785-296-3307 or 316-337-6280
(**www.ink.org/public/ksecom**)

Kentucky
Department of Financial Institutions
502-573-3390 or 800-223-2579
(**www.dfi.state.ky.us/security/**
  security.html)

Louisiana
Securities Commission
504-846-6970

Maine
Department of Professional and Financial
  Regulation
207-624-8551
(**www.state.me.us/pfr/sec/sechome2.**
  htm)

Maryland
Office of the Attorney General
410-576-6360
(**www.oag.state.md.us**)

Massachusetts
Secretary of the Commonwealth
617-727-3548
(**www.magnet.state.ma.us/sec/sct/**
  sctidx.htm)

Michigan
Department of Consumer and Industry
  Services
517-373-1820
(**www.cis.state.mi.us**)

Minnesota
Department of Commerce
651-296-4026
(**www.commerce.state.mn.us**)

Mississippi
Secretary of State's Office
800-804-6364
(www.sos.state.ms.us)

Missouri
Office of the Secretary of State
573-751-4136
(mosl.sos.state.mo.us/sos-sec/
sossec.html)

Montana
Office of the State Auditor
406-444-2040, 800-332-6148
(www.state.mt.us/sao/secbib.htm)

Nebraska
Department of Banking and Finance
402-471-3445
(www.ndbf.org)

Nevada
Secretary of State
702-486-2440 or 775-688-1855
(sos.state.nv.us)

New Hampshire
Bureau of Securities Regulation
603-271-1463

New Jersey
Department of Law and Public Safety
973-504-3600
(www.state.nj.us/lps/law/home.htm)

New Mexico
Regulation and Licensing Department
505-827-7140
(www.rld.state.nm.us)

New York
Department of Law
Bureau of Investor Protection and
Securities
212-416-8200
(www.oag.state.ny.us/investors/
investors.html)

North Carolina
Department of the Secretary of State
919-733-3924
(www.secretary.state.nc.us/sec)

North Dakota
Securities Commissioner
701-328-2910
(www.state.nd.us/securities/)

Ohio
Division of Securities
614-644-7381
(www.securities.state.oh.us)

Oklahoma
Division of Securities
405-280-7700
(www.securities.state.ok.us/)

Oregon
Department of Consumer and Business
Services
503-378-4387
(www.cbs.state.or.us/external/dfcs)

Pennsylvania
Securities Commission
717-787-8061 or 215-560-2088 or
412-565-5083
(www.psc.state.ps.us)

Puerto Rico
Commissioner of Financial Institutions
787-723-3131

Rhode Island
Department of Business Regulation
401-222-3048
(www.state.ri.us/manual/data/
queries/stdept_.idc?id=19)

South Carolina
Office of the Attorney General
803-734-4731
(www.scattorneygeneral.org)

South Dakota
Division of Securities
605-773-4823
(**www.state.sd.us/dcr/securities**)

Tennessee
Department of Commerce and Insurance
615-741-2947
(**www.state.tn.us/commerce/securdiv.**
  html)

Texas
State Securities Board
512-305-8300
(**www.ssb.state.tx.us**)

Utah
Division of Securities
801-530-6600
(**www.commerce.state.ut.us**)

Vermont
Department of Banking, Insurance,
  Securities and Health Care Administration
802-828-3420
(**www.state.vt.us/bis**)

Virginia
State Corporation Commission
804-371-9051
(**www.state.va.us/scc/division/srf**)

Washington
Department of Financial Institutions
360-902-8760
(**www.wa.gov/dfi/securities**)

West Virginia
State Auditor's Office
304-558-2257
(**www.wvauditor.com**)

Wisconsin
Department of Financial Institutions
608-261-9555
(**www.wdfi.org**)

Wyoming
Secretary of State
307-777-7370
(**soswy.state.wy.us**)

TEN

Banking and Other Personal Finances

C ompared to online stock trading, electronic banking seems downright dull. After all, using your computer to pay your bills or apply for a credit card can't compete in the thrills department with making a tidy bundle on some hot little stock. Yet online banking can be a valuable tool to organize and manage your finances. The ability to transfer money between accounts with just a few clicks can help you maximize the return on your cash assets. Online bill paying can save hours of stuffing and licking envelopes—not to mention trips to the post office for stamps—while the growing field of online bill presentment promises to streamline the process even further. And the Net's transparency makes it easier than ever to shop for and compare loans, insurance, and other financial services.

In 1998, slightly fewer than 4 million households in the U.S. regularly used their modem-equipped PCs to perform such banking transactions as viewing their balances, transferring funds between accounts, and paying bills, according to Forrester Research. That was only a small fraction of the approximately 40 million people who logged on to the Internet in a typical week. But that situation is rapidly changing. The number of online-banking users is expected to grow dramatically, with 17 million people using some type of Web-based banking service by 2002, according to Forrester.

Many large commercial banks have offered some type of PC-based service since the mid-1980s. The earliest systems, introduced by such industry behemoths as Citibank and Bank of America, were based on proprietary software customers had to install on their PCs to connect via the financial institution's private data network. These in-house systems left much to be desired: The banks' network reliability and the software's ease of use were major obstacles. Moreover, banks seemed convinced that PC-equipped yuppies would pay hefty fees for online banking and bill paying, at first charging as much as $10-$15 per month. Eventually, many banks shuttered their early home-banking systems after spending tens of millions of dollars and attracting only a few thousand users.

Second-generation home banking systems centered on personal financial management software such Intuit's Quicken or Microsoft's Money. These programs were—and are—a vast improvement, providing many planning and budgeting capabilities. In their early versions, though, they required users to enter all of their handwritten checks, ATM, and credit card transactions manually—time-consuming tasks that discouraged all but the most financially obsessed. Eventually, both Intuit and Microsoft introduced upgrades, allowing users to download and upload transactions with a participating bank or broker. Banks still charge fees for this service, although the price has fallen at many banks to $5 to $6 per month for the bill-payment function.

Some big commercial banks, particularly those with geographic ties to Silicon Valley, such as Bank of America (**www.bofa.com**) and Wells Fargo (**www.wellsfargo.com**), quickly recognized the Web as the perfect way to reach tech-savvy customers. But many other banks initially perceived the Internet as a hacker heaven that posed myriad privacy and security concerns. The introduction of stronger encryption systems—security software that scrambles data so it cannot be viewed or altered by interlopers—in both Netscape's and Microsoft's Internet browsers have helped assuage bankers' fears. Now, most large and midsize banks—even such relative laggards as Citibank (**www.citibank. com**) and Chase Manhattan Bank (**www.chase.com**)—have set up interactive Web sites. Most of these sites still have the same features of older home-banking systems: You can view account data, move money around, and pay bills. In addition, some bank Web sites allow consumers to apply for loans online. Smaller, so-called community banks with fewer than 10 branches have been slower to jump on to the Web banking bandwagon due to the up-front development costs, but analysts say it's only a matter of time before these institutions offer online services as well.

Meanwhile, a growing number of "virtual" financial institutions have also arrived on the scene. Some—such as Security First Network Bank (**www.sfnb.com**), Wingspan Bank (**www.wingspanbank.com**), Net.B@nk (**www.netbank.com**), eBank (**www.ebank.com**), and Telebanc (**www.telebanc.com**)—are full-fledged banks. They offer traditional bank products without any brick-and-mortar branches; customers can access their accounts through the Internet, but must use other banks' ATMs to get cash. But many other Web sites offer increasingly bank-like services. For instance, Charles Schwab (**www. schwab.com**) and Fidelity Investments (**www.fidelity.com**) offer products such as CDs, check writing, ATM/debit cards, and even electronic bill paying. The advantage to investors is potential one-stop shopping for a full array of financial services. E*Trade took that trend a step further in 1999, when it agreed to acquire Telebanc, which does all its business online or by phone.

The next frontier for online banking is likely to be electronic bill presentment, or electronic bill delivery. Electronic bill presentment addresses the main drawback to paying your bills via PC: It's still too much of a chore. Current bill paying systems require you to set up all the payee information (biller's name, address, phone number, and account number) before a transaction can be sent out. Also, not all billers are currently equipped to receive electronic payments, forcing banks and their payment-processing partners to print out paper checks and mail them, which adds to the cost of the service.

In electronic billing systems, though, cable TV companies, utilities, credit card firms, and other businesses issue electronic bills instead of paper ones. These e-bills are then consolidated by a payment processor, such as Checkfree Corp. (currently the biggest processor of PC-initiated payments) or Transpoint (a joint effort of Microsoft and credit card processor First Data Corporation, with Citibank as minority investor). You can then "pick up" your bill at your bank's Web site. After reviewing the bill, you can simply click to make your electronic payment. No muss, no fuss—and no mountain of paper bills to organize and store.

The key to acceptance may be whether banks are willing to reduce their fees for online transactions. Already, many online customers grumble—with good reason—that the additional fees tacked onto online accounts don't reflect the bank's diminished need for physical branches and human tellers. Perhaps consumers' best hope may be that competition from nontraditional players in the billing-and-payment game—brokerage firms, maybe even Web portals like Yahoo! (**www.yahoo.com**) and Quicken.com (**www.quicken.com**)—will compel banks to pass on more of their savings.

HOW TO CHOOSE AN ONLINE BANKING SERVICE

Here are some questions to ask yourself before you establish an online banking relationship:

- Are you an ATM fanatic? Most people have learned to accept the $1–$2 fee they get charged for using the automated teller machine of a bank other than their own. But if you use a cash machine 2–3 times a week, it can add up to $150–$200 a year. That's a major problem for online brokers and virtual banks that mostly rely on other institutions' ATM networks. So if you're a frequent cash-withdrawer, you're probably better off keeping your checking account at a big bank.

- Do you still want to speak to a person? As online banking and investing increasingly becomes a unified service, the complexity for consumers is only going to go up. Before opening an account with an online bank or broker, make sure you are comfortable with the customer service options available to you. While an e-mail inquiry may suffice in some instances, if your mortgage payment disappears into the ether, you're going to wish you had the ability to access an intelligent life form.

- How much money do you have? Online brokers like Fidelity and Schwab offer a soup-to-nuts menu of financial products, including money-market checking accounts linked to brokerage accounts (known as "cash management accounts," in broker parlance), as well as traditional saving instruments like certificates of deposit. Unfortunately, the account maintenance fees they charge relative to banks are high. The good news is that many online brokers will waive account maintenance charges and other fees if you maintain a certain level of assets with them, usually at least $20,000. But if you're just starting your first job out of college, you may find a better fee deal if you go to a bank.

CREDIT CARDS

These days it seems as if no corner of the Web is safe from credit card ads. Clickable credit card banners are as ubiquitous as snail-mail credit card solicitations—or America Online disks, for that matter. The reason is simple: Issuers realize that the Web is the next great frontier for attracting new customers.

By 2003, nearly one out of every six credit cards will be obtained online, estimates Forrester Research. Given that U.S. consumers hold credit card lines worth $5.2 billion, and that the figure is expected to balloon to $21.5 billion by 2003, online credit looks to be a big piece of a huge pie, and most issuers are smart enough to want a part of it. A 1999 survey conducted by bankrate.com (**www.bankrate.com**), a news site affiliated with Bank Rate Monitor that follows the credit card industry, found about 300 online card offers from 59 different cyberspace issuers.

As is usually the case, all of that competition is a boon for consumers. For one thing, the Web makes getting cards and comparing rates and other features much easier. But there are still some issues that should command consumers' attention.

The biggest changes the Internet is bringing are speed and convenience. No longer does applying for credit take several weeks through the mail or require a long phone call and a conversation with a telemarketer. Now a host of issuers let consumers apply right over the Internet, and a number of them will tell you right away whether you qualify. These include some of the biggest names in the business. For example, First USA's e-card series (**www.firstusa.com**) allows customers to obtain instant credit approval, check balances, and make payments online. Providian Financial Corp. (**www.providian.com**) offers similar services, including instant approval, on its Web-based Aria family of cards. So does NextCard (**www.nextcard.com**), a Web-based card issuer. First USA takes extending credit a step further, offering consumers instant credit on the Web: If you qualify, you may immediately receive a card number, expiration date, and line of credit to start charging within minutes. Who needs plastic?

Other big players in the industry are moving toward offering instant credit as well. Meanwhile, they and smaller issuers are offering consumers the chance to apply for cards online, although once the information is submitted, it usually takes the standard few weeks to determine if a potential customer is creditworthy and deliver a card.

Thanks to all that competition, issuers are continually piling on benefits and services. Many Internet-oriented issuers—along with a host of traditional credit card companies—offer full fraud protection on Internet transactions, meaning that consumers are not responsible for even the first $50 if they are the victims of any sort of fraud.

Also, several card issuers are offering special deals patterned after bonuses offered by traditional card issuers but tailored for Web users. First USA, for example, offers users of its Internet-issued e-card 5% cash back on purchases from a host of Internet merchants, including retailer Amazon.com (**www.amazon.com**), wine seller Wine.com (**www.wine.com**), and movie store Reel.com (**www.reel.com**). Both NextCard and Providian offer consumers the chance to earn points based on their spending, which can be redeemed for goods and services such as airline tickets, car rentals, restaurant meals, and products from a wide array of online and off-line merchants.

In 1999, American Express launched its "Blue" smart card, featuring an embedded chip for online shoppers worried about giving out their credit card numbers on the Web. In most ways Blue works just like a regular credit card, but the chip also allows consumers to shop online by swiping their card rather than entering the card number or other personal information. It works like this: For $25, consumers can buy a card reader from American Express. Then, instead of sending sensitive information over the Web, they can just run their cards through the reader and enter a personal identification number, or PIN, to make online charges. With identifying information from the chip and the PIN, American Express will automatically fill out those pesky online forms needed to complete most transactions.

The companies are also competing on personalization features. First USA allows consumers applying for the card it co-markets with portal site Yahoo! to choose between a black card that features the Yahoo! logo and a swirl design, and one that carries the logo over a silver metallic background. NextCard takes the personalization a step further and allows consumers to design the look of their card by choosing from a set of hundreds of images, or submitting their own digital picture to be used on the face of the card.

And, as is true for off-line issuers, there is stiff competition on the interest rate front. In fact, rates for Internet cards are among the lowest around, with some issuers offering introductory interest rates as low as 2.9% for the first few months and 9.9% thereafter.

Of course, there are a few catches. For many of the best introductory rates, users must transfer balances from other credit cards. And, just as with the traditional credit card offers, the lowest longer-term rates are reserved for consumers with the best credit ratings. Moreover, depending on the company, only a minority of applicants may actually get credit cards: NextCard, which targets consumers with strong credit histories, offers cards to about 20% of those who apply, with the best offers going to those most likely to rack up finance charges by not paying off their entire balances. On the other hand, Providian—which built its name offering credit cards to people with less than sterling credit histories—says it is granting Aria cards to as many as 55% of the people who apply for them because of the broad array of cards it offers with different interest rates, credit limits, and other features.

Luckily for confused consumers, a number of Web sites offer tools for comparing various card offers. For instance, CardWeb (**www. cardweb.com**) allows users to comparison shop by such criteria as rates, annual fees, and credit history requirements. Bankrate.com, meanwhile, provides tables of credit cards that consumers can compare based on features such as the best rates, special cards for frequent fliers, low introductory rates, and the best deals on certain categories of cards, such as gold and platinum cards. Both sites also offer lots of news about credit cards that consumers can use to learn about the latest offers from issuers and about scams and bad deals that they should avoid.

Once you apply for a card online, be careful to make sure that the card you're offered is in fact the one you want. While you may apply for a card offering one set of terms, the one the company offers you might be quite different—once it analyzes the data you submit and checks your credit history. If you don't carry balances on your cards, for example, you won't qualify for the super-low rates NextCard offers as an introductory special. NextCard, however, is alone among the big three online issuers in showing consumers the cards they qualify for and asking which they want.

At First USA, once you've submitted your personal data and been approved, your card is on its way. The only way to cancel a card is to call the company, and that can be difficult to do before the card has arrived and a record of it is in their system. Since First USA's e-card doesn't carry an annual fee, there's little harm, except for the inconvenience factor, in getting and then canceling the card. At Providian, though, there is a bit more to be concerned about: Many of its cards carry steep processing or annual fees or have automatic credit-insurance coverage charges. The company says customers who don't like the terms of the card they're issued can simply not pay the initial bill, and the card will never be activated. That gives consumers some protection, but it still pays to read the terms and conditions on a card carefully before using it.

Brian O'Connor, managing editor of bankrate.com, noted that his organization receives many complaints from users who apply for credit cards online and then find out they haven't gotten the terms they expected. "They apply for one rate, and they're surprised when the bill comes and it's for another."

In addition to reading fine print, you should make sure you are dealing with a reputable company and that they are using a secure Web server, since you'll be providing a lot of personal information. "You want to make sure of who you're dealing with," observed Robert McKinley, president of CardWeb.com. "If you're not sure or you have some question about it, then you need to back off. If there is a name of a bank but no physical way to contact anyone, no phone number or address, then that is a red flag." Some scamsters have created bogus sites that purport to accept card applications—but in reality are fronts for obtaining sensitive personal data.

MORTGAGES

With interest rates on home mortgages across the country falling, Andre Lukas decided it was time to refinance the loan on his San Diego home. Mr. Lukas, 58, had refinanced before, but as an active stock and options trader, he didn't feel like leaving his computer to visit a bank or mortgage broker. Nor did his wife, a senior programmer at a hospital, want to interrupt her schedule.

So Mr. Lukas started inquiring about rates on home loans from his PC. He got a quote from E-loan Inc. (**www.eloan.com**), an online mortgage broker based in Dublin, California, for a 30-year fixed-rate mortgage at 6.75% interest plus 0.75 point. He determined the rate was competitive after checking the rates in his Sunday newspaper. Not only did E-loan offer a good rate, but it agreed to cut Mr. Lukas's appraisal fee by $75 after he found someone who would do it for less. To seal the deal, E-loan sent a notary public to his house to sign the closing papers.

"It wasn't the first time I refinanced," Mr. Lukas said, "but it sure was the first time I refinanced without leaving my house."

Though a small part of electronic commerce, online mortgage shopping is growing rapidly. Countrywide Credit Industries (**www.**

countrywide.com), of Calabasas, California, the biggest independent mortgage lender, said that only $648 million of the $25 billion in mortgage loans it originated in 1998 were funded over the Internet. But that number represented better than a six-fold increase over a year earlier. By 2003, market researchers estimate that as many as 10% of mortgage loans could be originated on the Internet.

But there are still some obstacles to getting a good deal on a mortgage online. Getting useful information from an online source usually requires disclosing more personal and financial information than most people are comfortable with. Picking a mortgage banker or broker online can be difficult—there are literally hundreds of Web sites from lenders known and unknown, and understanding their myriad offers can take some doing. And while E-loan gave Mr. Lukas a break on his appraisal fee and many online mortgage companies may be willing to waive certain costs to get your business, getting a mortgage online is not necessarily cheaper than going to a local banker or broker.

There's no denying that the information available on the Internet has made shopping for a mortgage more convenient, even if it doesn't always reduce costs or the amount of paperwork involved. And the days of a nearly paperless mortgage may be close. A handful of lenders have emerged who conduct virtually the entire mortgage application and approval process online, and they require many fewer financial documents to approve a loan.

Because a home mortgage is the largest financial obligation you may ever undertake, it's wise to ensure your financial affairs are in order before you start hunting.

You can order a copy of your credit report, the same one a mortgage lender is going to scrutinize, from the Web sites of the major credit bureaus: Equifax (**www.equifax.com**), Trans Union (**www.tuc.com**), or Experian (**www.experian.com**). Reports cost $8. If you're married, consider getting your spouse's credit report, too. You should contest any errors that appear on the reports in writing with the bureaus—agencies that claim to clean up your credit history are unable to do anything more than write letters on your behalf to the bureaus.

Assuming your credit history report is accurate, you can use the data to estimate your credit "grade" before a lender assesses it. The better your credit history, the higher your grade and the better mortgage rates you'll be able to get. Credit is scored by analyzing the frequency of delinquent credit cards bills, taxes, and so forth, and expressing all that in a single number.

The Web site of HSH Associates (**www.hsh.com**), based in Butler, New Jersey, is one of the best places on the Internet for anyone thinking about getting or refinancing a mortgage. It contains an interactive calculator that will estimate your credit score by asking the same questions a lender would. Questions range from how many times you've been late paying your credit card bills, to whether you've ever filed for bankruptcy. Understand that this score is only approximate, and lenders may reach different conclusions using the same information.

It's also a good idea to figure out just how high a mortgage loan you can afford. Most mortgage-related Web sites contain a calculator that will help you figure this out. Mortgage lenders generally suggest that no more than 36% of your monthly income should go to pay your mortgage, and many sites offer calculators to help you figure out how much debt you can reasonably expect to carry.

Before you start hunting for quotes on mortgages, you can brush up on the going rates and types of loans available by checking the sites of HSH or bankrate.com. These outfits have been tracking the mortgage industry for years; they offer not only daily national average rates, but also break down rates down by state, metropolitan area, and lender. The sites also contain useful information to help you decide whether you should opt for a fixed- or adjustable-rate mortgage.

Besides figuring out the length and type of mortgage you want, you should decide whether you are willing to pay points. Points are essentially a transaction charge that lenders tack on to mortgage loans. For example, if you take out a loan of $100,000 and pay 1.50 points, that means you'll really be taking out a loan of $101,500. The advantage of paying points is that in exchange you'll probably get a lower rate of interest on your loan, which lowers your monthly payments. Plus, the points are tax deductible. On other hand, if you're stretching your finances to buy a house and don't want to put up any more money up front than you absolutely have to, it's probably better to forgo the points and pay a slightly higher rate of interest over the years. Bankrate.com's site contains a calculator that helps figure out the costs of the different options.

Be aware, too, that some lenders quote mortgage rates as an annual percentage rate, or APR. The APR is not the same as an interest rate, though it is a useful number because it is derived by combining the interest rate, points, and other applicable fees over the life of the loan. If you plan to keep your house only a couple of years, a loan with a higher interest rate but lower APR could be better.

Another thing you should decide before shopping online is whether you want to be prequalified, preapproved, or approved for a mortgage. To be qualified simply means that your cash, assets, and debt meet the lender's guidelines for the type of loan you want. Preapproved means that the lender has actually done a credit and employment check on you. Final approval means the preceding conditions have been met, the property you want has been appraised, and the lender has signed off to grant you your loan.

There is no shortage of places to hunt for a mortgage online. The trick is settling on the kind of site you want. Most of the best-known lenders, such as Countrywide, Bank One (**www.bankone.com**), and the big commercial banks, will offer you a quote online, but do not feature the rates of other lenders.

A more informative kind of site is run by LendingTree (**www. lendingtree.com**). LendingTree collects information electronically— not a full loan application, the site contends, but enough information to send to up to four lenders, who may then offer you a loan. The site has relationships with more than ninety lenders. This can be an efficient way to quickly collect and compare terms offered by several lenders. The downside is that you may not get a response from the lender that you are interested in dealing with.

Other sites include Microsoft's HomeAdvisor (**www.homeadvisor. com**) and Intuit's Quicken (**www.quickenloans.quicken.com**). Seconds after you fill out an electronic application form, you are presented

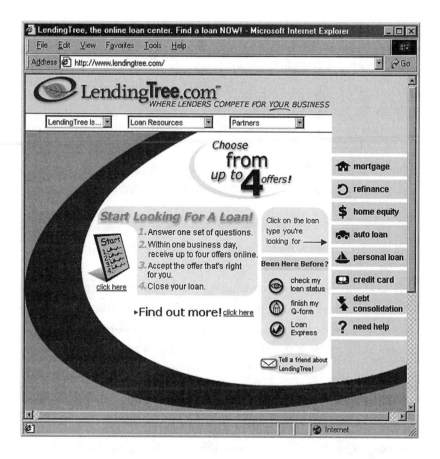

with several offers tailored to your specifications. You might not like answering probing questions about your personal finances on the Internet, but these sites are secure and they say they do not share information with anyone else. There is no charge for window shopping—charges only start when you apply for a loan.

Another way to get a mortgage online is to bid for it. Priceline.com (**www.priceline.com**), the company that auctions airline tickets by matching online bidders with willing airlines, has taken this process to the mortgage business as well. Bid on a mortgage and Priceline.com will forward the offer to four lenders, who will reply within six business hours (8 A.M. to 8 P.M. Eastern time, Monday through Friday). If the bid is not accepted, you can make another offer. But know too that if your bid is accepted, interest rates are not guaranteed until the mortgage is obtained. A lender who accepts your Priceline.com bid might levy a $200 "good faith" deposit to your credit card. The fee is credited to your closing costs if you decide to take the mortgage, but you'll owe the money even if you don't take the loan.

RealEstate.com (**www.realestate.com**) of Atlanta also offers an online mortgage auction service, and says it will pay $250 if your bid is accepted and you later find a "better overall loan package."

Finally, there are sites that aim to conduct the entire process online until closing. Many of these sites are run by small mortgage companies that are eager to compete with the big names on the Internet. They tend to require many fewer financial documents than other mortgage lenders.

RockLoans (**www.rockloans.com**), a unit of Intuit, is one such site. The company says it will approve mortgage loans, whether or not customers have a specific property in mind, and does not require that customers mail in their W-2s, tax returns, or other forms mortgage lenders typically require. All RockLoans requires is a single pay stub showing you've been employed for thirty days, and all the pages of one monthly bank statement. The company says its fees may be lower because in 30% of its loans, only a "drive-by appraisal" of the property is necessary. iQualify.com (**www.iqualify.com**), a unit of Finet Holdings Corporation, of Walnut Creek, California, also requires no tax forms for mortgage applications, which it says are processed "in minutes" with multiple lenders. The risk in all this, of course, is that should things go wrong, you've little recourse but to dial a "call center." That's not the same as dealing with a person you've met at an office.

While these two sites come closest to selling mortgages directly online, it will be necessary to leave your desk and meet a real person to sign the deal at closing. Until electronic signatures are safe and accepted, mortgage executives say, some paperwork will be necessary to complete an "online mortgage."

At E-loan, for example, you start by filling out an electronic version of the standard mortgage application form. Then E-loan returns your forms via regular mail, which you sign and mail back. After your application is officially submitted, it is analyzed and sent to different lenders. After one of those lenders offers a loan, E-loan will identify the lender and notify you. While your loan is pending, you can check its status online until the transaction is ready to be completed.

But getting to the finish line can be tricky. E-loan is based in California, and 83% of its business is done in that state. Should you apply, the company will request you choose a city in which to sign the final papers. E-loan says it will makes every effort to close the deal in your choice of location, but makes no guarantee that will happen. Conceivably you could be traveling some to get that loan, or you might have to pay an extra fee for the company to send someone for the signing.

You should be careful when dealing with a Web site from a banker or broker you've never heard of. If the Web site is run by a mortgage bank, then it must be licensed by the banking department or real estate division in each state in which it does business. But not all states regulate mortgage brokers, the category that applies to most Internet mortgage sites. If you have any doubts about the authenticity of an online mortgage broker, the best you can do is find where the site is based and contact the area's Better Business Bureau.

Closing costs—the fees for appraisals, lawyers, searches for outstanding claims on the property, etc.—can add anywhere from 3% to 6% to the final cost of buying a house, according to the Mortgage Bankers Association of America. Minimizing these fees is a key to reducing the costs of getting a mortgage. For example, on Quickenmortgage.com, applying for $100,000 30-year fixed-rate mortgage for a home in New Jersey resulted in eight quotes, with rates ranging from 7.25% plus 0.75 points from Countrywide, to 8.625% and zero points from Chase Manhattan Bank. Fees ranged from $2,914 for a loan from Cendant Mortgage to $3,479 for the Countrywide offer—a $565 difference on the same loan.

Because these fees vary from state to state and lender to lender, they can make comparing offers online difficult. A site run by a mortgage banker may offer lower fees than a broker's because brokers tack on a commission for finding loans. But with cutthroat competition on the Internet, this guideline doesn't always apply.

The best way to keep fees low is to ask what they will be at the start. Some sites are more forthcoming with this information than others. For example, Keystroke.com (**www.keystroke.com**) of Seattle offers a line-by-line breakdown, while Quickenmortgage.com just mentions a lump sum estimate. Others just mention the initial mortgage application fee, with no hint of what's to come later.

Don't hesitate to ask about closing costs; federal law requires that mortgage companies give a "good faith" estimate of fees within three days after taking your application. If you haven't received it by then, call the lender—most online mortgage lenders offer a toll-free number. An online lender located in a faraway state might have trouble meeting the deadline because they might not have the same access to appraisers, surveyors, and other local services needed to complete a mortgage. Review the good faith document carefully to make sure it lists all fees to be paid to third parties by you. Remember that this list will be just an estimate; some fees will not be finalized until just before closing.

Going online for a mortgage doesn't always mean reduced closing costs. Occasionally online brokers tack on charges you wouldn't likely see from a traditional mortgage banker or broker. For example, Rockloans.com may charge customers a "document preparation fee" when the closing of a mortgage takes place far from one of their offices (most are in Michigan), and the company must hire a third party to sign the final papers.

But because the online mortgage business is young and growing, many companies are willing to cut some slack on fees to win your business. For example, Countrywide responded to a recent online application by e-mailing back the next day and volunteering to waive appraisal or credit report fees.

INSURANCE

The online insurance business has developed slowly; currently only a handful of Web sites offer information about insurance policies, and nowhere can you buy a policy entirely online. Still, a growing number of online brokers are making it easier to compare prices for insurance policies. That's important, because prices vary widely from company to company for similar policies.

The most useful online insurance sites are Insweb (**www.insweb. com**), Intuit's Quicken Insurance (**www.insuremarket.com**), and QuoteSmith (**www.quotesmith.com**). All offer quotes on auto, term life, individual health, homeowner's, and renter's insurance from a variety of insurers. More than 80% of Insweb's business is done in auto insurance.

These sites don't sell policies, but act as brokers and receive fees from insurers for providing leads. You fill out a form online about what you're looking for, and the sites forward the information to about 30 insurance companies. Window shopping is free, and the sites will save your data to invite you to check with them every few months for price updates.

Often a request for quotes results in an instant real-time price. But sometimes you are required to wait or even get on the phone and repeat the same information to get a quote. For example, a request for a quote for auto insurance for a California driver on Insweb.com resulted in nine companies offering quotes, ranging in price from $49.85 per month to $114.33. But only six companies could generate quotes instantly; the other three said they would e-mail information in a few days. Progressive Insurance (**www.progressive.com**) runs one of the best sites of any insurance company, offering instant online quotes on its own policies and those from up to three other companies. Don't expect big discounts for transacting business electronically. Insurance executives say many state regulators frown on the practice, because that would be unfair to people who do not have access to the Internet. The only way you can get any sort of discount online is if an insurer is willing to waive administrative fees to get your business; they aren't allowed to undercut the prices they file with state regulatory bodies.

Appendixes

GETTING ONLINE

If you plan to manage your investments online, your only technical requirements are a computer and Internet access. Here are the minimum requirements you'll want from your system—and a look at some high-end options:

HARDWARE

If you're looking to buy a desktop computer, your likeliest choices are either a Windows-based PC, by far the most common, or an Apple Macintosh. Both handle Internet browsing and trading transactions equally well, but some supplementary trading-related software is designed with Windows in mind, and there is a greater variety of options available for Windows. On the other hand, your decisions are simplified if you buy a Macintosh: The consumer-oriented iMac package gives you pretty much everything you'll need right out of the box, and many people still consider the Mac easier to use than a Windows machine.

The most important requirements for your hardware are memory and hard-disk capacity. The amount of memory (often referred to as RAM, for random-access memory) determines how many programs you can run simultaneously, and how well each performs. All you really need to know is that the 32 megabytes of memory that come standard on most new PCs are more than enough for you to trade online. In fact, if you have enough RAM to run a Web browser, you have enough to trade.

In terms of a hard drive, which provides permanent storage for information, around four to six gigabytes will suffice. Web browsing doesn't necessarily take up a lot of hard-disk space, and many new machines are shipped with bigger hard drives anyway. (Other storage capabilities—high-capacity cartridge-based Zip drives, for instance—are strictly optional.)

Perhaps the least important consideration for trading is your computer's processor. In a Windows machine, any Pentium II, Pentium III, or Celeron chip, or comparable chip made by one of Intel's competitors, will do just fine for purposes of online trading. In an iMac, don't even worry about the processor; whatever's under the hood will meet your needs.

Don't forget a good printer as well: You'll be glad you have hard copies of your trading records when tax time rolls around.

SOFTWARE

The only software you really need is a Web browser. The two most popular are Netscape Navigator and Microsoft Internet Explorer. There's little distinction between the two, and the odds are one or both came already installed on your computer.

Some online brokers also offer their own proprietary software. This can in some cases help speed up the trading process or add more features, but it is by no means necessary. Some traders find financial-management software such as Intuit's Quicken or Microsoft's Money useful for tracking their finances. There are plenty of useful personal finance and portfolio tools on Web sites, too.

CONNECTING TO THE INTERNET

Spending money on a powerful processor and a large hard drive will do little to improve your online experience without a sufficiently fast Internet connection. The speedier the connection, the faster you'll be able to navigate the Web, download information, and make trades.

There is a growing number of ways to connect to the Internet. Many companies use high-speed dedicated lines. For individuals, options include traditional dial-up modems, ISDN, cable connections, and DSL.

A modem uses the telephone lines to provide the link between your computer and the outside world. Modems can be connected either internally or externally—the former are generally cheaper, while the latter are easier to install. But it is the connection speed that makes the biggest difference. The faster the better: You don't want to sit around waiting for Web pages to download, and a transaction that takes longer to send to your broker increases the risk that you won't complete the trade at the specified price. While modems operating at 28.8 kilobits per second (Kbps) are still common, you'll be happier with 56Kbps. Most new computers come with a 56K modem already installed.

Next, you'll need to choose an Internet service provider, or ISP. Internet access is a very competitive sector of the online industry, and choices abound—thousands of providers offer free trials and software to potential subscribers. Your local phone company probably offers Internet access; so do major long-distance carriers like AT&T, MCI, and Sprint. National dial-up providers like Earthlink are also popular options, and there are probably smaller local and regional ISPs in your area as well. Expect to pay about $20 a month for unlimited Internet access.

In choosing a provider, make sure first of all that it offers a phone number that's a local call for you. Ask also about connection consistency and customer support. (You want to be able to reach a person 24 hours a day if something goes wrong.) You might also want to ask about the ratio of users to available modems; nothing is more frustrating when you're trying to connect than a busy signal. (A ratio of one modem per three customers is considered good.)

Online services like America Online and Compuserve offer a combination of their own content plus access to the wider Internet, and their software can make it easier to get online. Many members appreciate the security and ease of navigation such services provide.

If you're doing some serious trading—going online every day or several times a day—you might want to consider connection technologies with even greater speeds and improved consistency. The downside: They cost more and require special equipment.

Many telephone companies offer ISDN (Integrated Services Digital Network) service, which is more than twice as fast a regular dial-up connection. But high costs—$50 to $100 a month, plus the purchase or rental of special modems—have limited the use of ISDN in the U.S., and it is quickly being supplanted by other technologies.

For instance, cable companies are beginning to offer Internet access—often under the names At Home or Road Runner—over the same wires that they use to pipe television channels into homes. These connections can be far, far faster than modems or ISDN. They are also expensive: an installation charge of perhaps $150 (which the companies sometimes waive), the purchase or rental of a cable modem, and a monthly bill of $40 or so.

DSL, or Digital Subscriber Line service, is another new technology with a growing coterie of fans. DSL also requires more equipment and money: About $50 and up per month for service, plus about $150 to $300 for a DSL modem and a onetime installation fee of about $100. While it may not be quite as fast as a cable modem, it works over ordinary phone lines; you won't have to run any special cables. (One caveat: The technology is distance sensitive, so the distance between the user and the ISP's equipment affects its performance.)

While the markets for cable and DSL are growing, the services aren't yet available everywhere. Ultimately, your geography, needs, and bank account will determine what technology you should use.

GLOSSARY OF
MESSAGE-BOARD JARGON

Message-board users have a language all their own. Some of it is simply shorthand to cut down on the amount of typing they must do. Other things are technical terms, or merely colorful phrases, that they have adopted from Wall Street—or invented themselves. Here's a quick guide to understanding some of the lingo you'll find on the boards:

AFAIK: As far as I know.

Basher: A person who makes derogatory posts on message boards in an effort to drive down a stock's price. As in: "He's a well-known basher. I've seen some of his posts wreak havoc on the penny boards."

Break out: When a stock rises above its 52-week trading high, or out of an established range of prices. This is a term from traditional technical analysis.

BTW: By the way.

Certs: Stock certificates. Some investors like to take delivery of the actual paper certificates, though most leave them in their brokerage accounts.

CNP . . . : Continued in next post. "For 2001, we can expect to see a further slowdown in the company's . . . CNP . . ."

DD: Due diligence, or in-depth research and analysis of a company's fundamentals. "Thanks for posting the information on the new product line. Your DD is greatly appreciated."

Double-bagger, Triple-bagger: A stock that has doubled or tripled in price. "Keep an eye on that stock. If this Internet rally keeps up we could see a double-bagger."

EOM: End of message. Usually found at the end of a brief post that fits entirely into the subject heading of the message link. Used as a courtesy so that board participants won't waste their time clicking on a link that contains that same information as the subject heading. "I'll call the company and get back to you. <EOM>"

FWIW: For what it's worth.

Flames: Disagreements and personal attacks contained in posts that are irrelevant to the stock discussion taking place on the message board. "It's hard to find any good DD on this board, what with all the flames."

Float: The number of shares of stock in a company available for public trading. "Outstanding shares" includes the float, plus any shares held by the company itself.

<G>: Grin, often with sarcasm. "I guess the plummeting stock price could be viewed as a buying opportunity <GGGG>."

Gapping Up: When a stock jumps in price. A gapping stock will move perhaps a point or so in a single jump, rather than in small fractions of a point, as is typical. "Yahoo!'s really gapping up on earnings news."

Hypester: A person who makes enthusiastic posts on message boards in an effort to drive up a stock's price. The opposite of basher. "I wouldn't touch a stock that hypester is touting."

IMO: In my opinion. Some variations are IMHO (in my humble/honest opinion) and JMO (just my opinion). "Your earnings projections for 2001 are a little overinflated, IMO."

IR: Investor relations. "I'll call the company's IR and get back to you."

L2: Nasdaq Level II, a data service popular with professional traders because it allows them to see individual quotes from market makers. "Where are the market makers on this stock? Can somebody check L2?" (See **MMs.**)

LMAO: Laughing my, uh, rear off.

LOL: Laughing out loud.

Lurker: A person who spends a lot of time perusing Internet chat rooms and message boards without contributing to discussions. "I've been lurking at the board for a while and want to commend all contributors on the great DD."

MMs: Market makers. These are the professional Nasdaq traders who organize the buying and selling of a stock, posting "bids"—the prices at which they'll buy stock—and "asks"—the prices at which they'll sell stock. They are required to keep the market functioning smoothly. They are often criticized strongly on the message boards.

MOMO: A momentum stock—one that seems to be moving in a particular direction based more on investor's opinions than for reasons having to do with the company's underlying business. "Stocks that trade under $5 tend to be momos."

OT: Off-topic. The post includes subject matter unrelated to the stock discussion. Often used so that board participants in a hurry know they can skip the post. "***OT*** Anyone know the spread on the Jets–Miami game?"

Penny Boards: Message boards devoted to discussing stocks that trade under $5 a share. "The flames on that penny board turned me off the stock."

POS: Piece of, uh, stuff. "This stock is a real POS."

P&D: Pump and dump. When used as a noun, describes a stock that rises dramatically based solely on online hype. Investors get caught up in the hype and buy shares, in the process driving up the price. As the price rises, hypesters sell to lock in profits. The price then tends to drop dramatically, leaving novice investors holding the bag. "With all the hype I've seen on the boards, it sure sounds like a P&D."

PM/IM: Private message or instant message. A communication system that allows discussion participants within a site or online service to communicate one-on-one, akin to e-mail. "If you can't agree on the matter, please stop wasting public space and take it to PM."

Profile: A Web page that lists information about a particular message-board user. Most of the online forums allow their users to create these pages to share things like hometowns, interests, and favorite stocks. The word profile is also used on pay-for-promotion Web sites to describe the packages of information about companies that the sites have been paid to disseminate. These profiles are often little more than advertisements.

ROFL: Rolling on the floor laughing.

Shorts: Short sellers, people who bet the price of a stock will fall. Short sellers borrow stock in a company from a broker, and then immediately sell it. If all goes as they hope, the stock's price will eventually decline, allowing them to buy back the shares—and repay the broker's loan—and still clear a profit. "All the shorts are trying to keep this stock down."

TA: Transfer agent—a firm, often a commercial bank, appointed by a corporation to maintain records of stock and bond owners, and to cancel and issue stock certificates. "Can somebody call the TA and find out the float on this one?"

Thread: A particular message board or continuing topic in a discussion forum.

Thread lice: Off-topic posts on a message board, usually containing advertisements. "This would actually be a good place to discuss stocks if it weren't for all the thread lice."

Thx: Thanks.

Tip sheet: An online newsletter, often distributed through e-mail, that offers stock picks. Beware: Many of these sheets are little more than paid advertisements for the companies mentioned.

Weak hands: Nervous investors who tend to follow the herd and sell shares at the first sign of weakness. "The stock has stabilized now that all the weak hands have cleared out."

MAJOR ONLINE BROKERAGE FIRMS

AB Watley	(www.abwatley.com)	888-229-2853
Ameritrade	(www.ameritrade.com)	800-454-9272
Brown & Co.	(www.brownco.com)	800-225-6707
Datek Online	(www.datek.com)	888-463-2835
DLJdirect	(www.dljdirect.com)	800-825-5723
E*Trade	(www.etrade.com)	800-786-2575
Fidelity	(www.fidelity.com)	800-544-7272
Firstrade.com	(www.firstrade.com)	888-988-6168
Investrade	(www.investrade.com)	800-498-7120
JB Oxford	(www.jboxford.com)	800-799-8870
Morgan Stanley Dean Witter	(www.online.msdw.com)	800-584-6837
Mr. Stock	(www.mrstock.com)	800-467-7865
My Discount Broker	(www.mydiscountbroker.com)	888-882-5600
National Discount Brokers	(www.ndb.com)	800-888-3999
Quick & Reilly	(www.qronline.com)	800-837-7220
Charles Schwab	(www.schwab.com)	800-435-4000
Scottrade	(www.scottrade.com)	800-619-7283
Muriel Siebert	(www.siebertnet.com)	800-872-0711
SureTrade	(www.suretrade.com)	401-642-6900
TD Waterhouse Securities	(www.waterhouse.com)	800-555-3875
Web Street Securities	(www.webstreetsecurities.com)	800-932-8723
Wit Capital	(www.witcapital.com)	888-494-8227

URLS USED IN THE TEXT

BANKING

Bank of America (**www.bofa.com**)—This site allows you to check account balances, pay bills, and transfer funds between linked accounts.

bankrate.com (**www.bankrate.com**)—This news site (affiliated with the Bank Rate Monitor) follows the credit card industry as well as mortgage rates and checking account fees.

Chase Manhattan Bank (**www.chase.com**)—In addition to online banking, the site's customer service staff are reachable by e-mail around the clock.

Citibank (**www.citibank.com**)—This site lets you view account data and pay bills online.

eBank (**www.ebank.com**)—This bank focuses accounts and loans for small business entrepreneurs.

Net.B@nk (**www.netbank.com**)—The largest bank operating exclusively via the Internet, it offers a full range of financial services, from loans to checking accounts and credit cards.

Security First Network Bank (**www.sfnb.com**)—Aside from general financial services, Security First has alliances with firms in several industries, including tax preparers, insurers, and online retailers.

Telebanc (**www.telebanc.com**)—Open a savings account or an Internet checking account, get online account information, even transfer funds.

Wells Fargo & Co. (**www.wellsfargo.com**)—A bill-paying service is free with a minimum balance of $5,000.

Wingspan Bank.com (**www.wingspan.com**)—Offers banking, lending, and insurance products and services.

BONDS

BondAgent.com (**www.bondagent.com**)—Provides trading in about 10,000 municipal, corporate, Treasury, and zero coupon bonds. Offers free research, news, bond calculators, and a learning center.

BondsOnline (**www.bondsonline.com**)—Sponsored by Twenty-First Century Municipals Inc., this site offers free research, news, and ratings; the "bond professor" answers questions posted by investors.

Bondtrac (**www.bondtrac.com**)—Lists bond prices for professional bond traders, but also is useful for individual investors.

BMI Quotes (**www.bmiquotes.com**)—Provides free pricing on all manner of bellwether corporates, Treasurys, and mortgage-related products.

Bureau of the Public Debt (**www.publicdebt.treas.gov**)—Run by a unit of the Treasury Department, this site includes information on U.S. Savings Bonds and Treasury securities. Users can join auctions of Treasury securities for free.

Garban Information Systems (**www.garbaninfo.com**)—Offers extensive bond quotes in real-time, for a fee.

GovPX (**www.govpx.com**)—Offers free quotes on bellwether Treasury bonds, and some trading volume statistics.

Investing in Bonds.com (**www.investinginbonds.com**)—A nonbrokerage site run by the Bond Market Association that provides rudimentary information about bond investments.

Quote.com (**www.quote.com**)—Posts updated Treasury prices every 15 minutes, courtesy of Bear Stearns.

BROKERS

Alaron Trading (**www.alaron.com**)—Gives quotes and charts, daily research, news from Bridge, free reports, and trading booklets.

Ameritrade (**www.ameritrade.com**)—Provides retail discount-brokerage services and related financial services, including electronic trading, and market data and research services.

Charles Schwab (**www.schwab.com**)—Online arm of the brick-and-mortar discount brokerage firm.

Datek Online (**www.datek.com**)—Discount brokerage firm run by privately held Datek Online Holdings Corp.

DLJdirect (**www.dljdirect.com**)—Online brokerage arm of Donaldson, Lufkin and Jenrette Securities; helps make shares of IPOs more accessible to individual investors.

E*Trade (**www.etrade.com**)—An industry pioneer, and one of the largest online discount brokerage firms, E*Trade offers online trading, virtual community interaction, and 24-hour customer service.

Friedman Billings Ramsey (**www.fbr.com**)—U.S.–based broker-dealer that offers online trading, a primer on investor education, and another "in" for investors interested in IPOs.

Jack Carl Futures (**www.jackcarl.com**)—A division of ED&F Man International, Jack Carl offers free content, including news headlines, historical price charts, market commentary, and economic reports.

LFG Linnco Futures Group (**www.lfgllc.com**)—A futures brokerage firm.

Lind-Waldock (**www.lind-waldock.com**)—The largest discount futures brokerage; Lind-Waldock also provides free end-of-day charts on futures contracts, free delayed quotes, and content from TheStreet.com.

Morgan Stanley Dean Witter (**www.online.msdw.com**)—Trade stocks, options, bonds, and more than 5,000 mutual funds.

National Discount Brokers (**www.ndb.com**)—Online securities broker that also features NDB University, a primer with "lessons" on investing basics.

Quick & Reilly Online (**www.qronline.com**)—Discount brokerage firm offering trading in stocks, mutual funds, bonds, and options, as well as guidance from a Quick & Reilly Personal Broker.

SureTrade (**www.suretrade.com**)—A division of Quick & Reilly/ Fleet Securities Inc., SureTrade is one of the smaller online brokerages.

TD Waterhouse Securities Inc. (**www.waterhouse.com**)—Large U.S. discount brokerage firm, known for its competitive pricing.

Wit Capital Group Inc. (**www.witcapital.com**)—Online broker-dealer focusing on making initial public offerings and research accessible to do-it-yourself investors.

W. R. Hambrecht (**www.wrhambrecht.com**)—Offers advisory, research, and brokerage services. Highlights emerging companies and growth industries, and features OpenIPO, an electronic underwriting service to help distribute IPOs to individual investors.

ZAP Futures (**www.zapfutures.com**)—This division of Linnco Futures Group offers free delayed quotes, charts, research, and streaming commentary from trading pits at the Chicago Mercantile Exchange.

See a list of major online securities-brokerage firms on page 303.

CHARTING

BigCharts.com (**www.bigcharts.com**)—A free, user-friendly guide to interactive charting includes charts, quotes, reports, and indicators on stocks, mutual funds, and market indexes.

Stockpoint (**www.stockpoint.com**)—Provides personalized, information-driven financial content and tools for both individual and professional investors.

COMMODITIES & FUTURES

Commodity Futures Trading Commission (**www.cftc.gov**)—The government regulatory agency for futures trading.

Data Broadcast Corp. (**www.dbc.com**)—This fee-based quote service offers various subscription packages, under the brand name eSignal, that include a choice of delayed, real-time, or streaming quotes.

Freese-Notis Weather (**www.weather.net**)—In addition to weather forecasts, the site offers daily advice on commodities trading.

Futures Industry Institute (**www.fiafii.org**)—An information resource for the beginning trader.

Futures.Net (**www.futures.net**)—This site lists the most actively traded futures contracts.

Futures Online (**www.futuresmag.com**)—The online version of *Futures Magazine* provides comprehensive and continually updated information about the futures industry.

Futuresource.com (**www.futuresource.com**)—Offers free futures charts and quotes to registered members.

Ino.com (**www.ino.com**)—Offers charts, quotes, and other information for futures traders.

Linco Futures Group (**www.lfgllc.com**)—Gives its brokerage clients real-time quotes for a fee.

National Futures Association (**www.nfa.futures.org**)—Features disciplinary information on brokerage firms and their employees, including detailed records.

National Weather Service (**www.nws.noaa.gov**)—An independent weather forecasting site.

Options Industry Council (**www.optionscentral.com**)—This industry trade group provides access to educational material, and an online schedule of free U.S. seminars.

OptionSource (**www.optionsource.com**)—Run by Cincinnati options-research firm Schaeffer's Investment Research, the education tab of this site runs through an online tutorial on investing basics.

PC Trader (**www.pctrader.com**)—This unit of Jones Financial Network offers fee-based services for both the ordinary investor and day traders.

TradingCharts.com (**www.tfc-charts.w2d.com**)—Provides free commodities and futures information, as well as personalized chart menus for tracking specific futures.

Weather Channel (**www.weather.com**)—An independent site for weather forecasts.

World Link Futures (**www.worldlinkfutures.com**)—Offers educational articles for both the beginner and more advanced students; has many links to other information sources.

CREDIT CARDS

CardWeb (**www.cardweb.com**)—This site reviews credit cards based on criteria such as rates and frequent-flier miles.

First USA (**www.firstusa.com**)—This bank's e-card series allows users to make payments and check balances online, and provides instant credit—customers receive a credit number instantaneously over the Web if they qualify.

NextCard (**www.nextcard.com**)—A nontraditional Visa card available exclusively to Internet users; it can't be obtained via telephone or mail.

Providian Financial Corp. (**www.providian.com**)—Providian provides online bill payment and account balance access; the site also accepts applications for instant credit.

CREDIT REPORTS

Equifax (**www.equifax.com**)—International credit bureau Equifax provides consumer credit information in the U.S. and abroad.

Experian (**www.experian.com**)—Another international consumer-credit information custodian, Experian offers a range of business services available by subscription and by credit card purchase.

Trans Union (**www.tuc.com**)—Offers credit data and fraud-prevention information.

DAY TRADING

ActiveTrade (**www.activetrade.net**)

All-Tech Investment Group Inc. (**www.attain.com**)

Day Traders On-line (**www.daytraders.com**)

Digital Traders (**www.trading-places.net**)

Pristine Day Trader (**www.pristine.com**)

DIRECT STOCK OFFERINGS

Direct IPO (**www.directipo.com**)—A listing service for companies offering stock directly to the public.

Direct Stock Market (**www.dsm.com**)—This site, which requires investors to register, provides a listing of companies offering stock for sale directly to the public.

SCOR Report (**www.scor-report.com**)—The Web site for an industry newsletter that covers small-business finance, this site provides general and legal information about DPOs.

Virtual Wall Street (**www.virtualwallstreet.com**)—This site provides extensive information and resources on DPOs.

DIVIDEND REINVESTMENT PROGRAMS

DRIP Investor (**www.dripinvestor.com**)—This site, run by a company that produces a print newsletter on DRIP investing, includes selected columns and a message board.

Moneypaper (**www.moneypaper.com**)—This site provides comprehensive information, including tips for getting started and a list of companies that have no fees.

National Association of Investors Corp. (**www.naicstockservice. com**)—This site provides DRIP information for beginners.

Net Stock Direct (**www.netstockdirect.com**)—Provides a searchable database of 1,600 companies with direct stock investing plans.

EXCHANGES

American Stock Exchange (**www.amex.com**)

Chicago Board of Trade (**www.cbot.com**)

Chicago Board Options Exchange (**www.cboe.com**)

Chicago Mercantile Exchange (**www.cme.com**)

Kansas City Board of Trade (**www.kcbt.com**)

MidAmerica Commodity Exchange (**www.midam.com**)

Minneapolis Grain Exchange (**www.mgex.com**)

New York Board of Trade (**www.nybot.com**)

New York Mercantile Exchange (**www.nymex.com**)

Pacific Stock Exchange (**www.pacificex.com**)

Philadelphia Stock Exchange (**www.phlx.com**)

FINANCIAL NEWS SITES

Barron's Online (**www.barrons.com**)—News and analysis from *Barron*'s magazine as well as articles exclusive to the Web site.

CBS MarketWatch (**www.cbs.marketwatch.com**)—As with CNNfn and MSNBC web sites, the financial news is free and the site is linked to the broadcast network.

CNNfn (**www.cnnfn.com**)—News provided in conjunction with the broadcast network.

Institutional Investor magazine (**www.iimagazine.com**)—This magazine publishes annual reports on the best analysts in the business, based on their popularity among investors.

Kiplinger.com (**www.kiplinger.com**)—The online version of Kiplinger's personal-finance magazine covers many areas of investing, retirement money, and taxes.

MSNBC (**www.msnbc.com**)—Linked to the MSNBC broadcast network; selected news highlights from *The Wall Street Journal* and CNBC are in its business section, **cnbc.wsj.com.**

Quote.com (**www.quote.com**)—Offers some news from Reuters, Dow Jones, and the Associated Press for free, but requires users to register. Quote.com provides more in-depth news to paid subscribers.

Reuters Moneynet (**www.moneynet.com**)—Offers Reuters news for free.

SmartMoney.com (**www.smartmoney.com**)—The online edition of the personal finance magazine, a joint venture of Dow Jones and Hearst Corporation.

TheStreet.com (**www.thestreet.com**)—Online home of money manager and commentator James Cramer.

The Wall Street Journal Interactive Edition (**wsj.com**)—Subscription-based; offers 24-hours-a-day updated news, personalized news and alerts, and a number of research tools, including a searchable publications library of articles in more than 5,000 newspapers and magazines.

INITIAL PUBLIC OFFERINGS

Alert-IPO! (**www.ostman.com/alert-ipo**)—Subscription-based site that features daily reports on IPO activity, from filings and price moves, to weekly summaries on IPO action.

CatchIPO (**www.catchipo.com**)—Site offers free software to help individual investors obtain first-come, first-serve IPO shares via E*Trade.

FreeEDGAR (**www.freeedgar.com**)—Lets site visitors view and print IPO filings, and offers free, unlimited access to indexed SEC Edgar filings, free e-mail alerts of targeted company filings, and instant download of financial data directly into Microsoft Excel spreadsheets.

IPO Central (**www.ipocentral.com**)—Run by company-information specialists Hoover's Online, this site offers both free and subscription-based information on IPOs.

IPO Data Systems (**www.ipodata.com**)—In addition to the usual slew of IPO information on pricing and performance, IPO Data Systems offers fee-based services like custom reporting, data feeds, and tearsheets, or summaries of IPO filings.

IPO Intelligence Online (**www.ipo-fund.com**)—For a $50 fee, the site offers staff-written, detailed research reports on companies that have filed to go public.

IPO Maven (**www.ipomaven.com**)—Offers extensive data on deals in the pipeline, and the performance of IPOs.

IPO Monitor (**www.ipomonitor.com**)—This subscriber-based site provides statistics about recent IPOs and features the IPO Newsline, which presents the latest breaking news from companies that have recently begun trading publicly or are in the process of going public.

Multex Investor Network (**www.multexinvestor.com**)—Primarily a repository for free company research reports written by analysts, Multex Investor Network also features online discussion forums with analysts.

Primark (**www.primark.com**)—Its Disclosure unit gives subscribers access to company data, including filings, updates, and analysis of insider trading and thousands of recent research reports.

Quote.com (**www.quote.com**)—Offers extensive data on IPOs, including most actives, biggest gainers and losers, and recent filings and pricings.

INSURANCE

Insweb (**www.insweb.com**)—Site visitors fill out a customer profile and Insweb comparison shops for price quotes and policies. Get the pros and cons of different policies from participating companies, and then request coverage—or not.

Quicken Insurance (**www.insuremarket.com**)—Save insurance quote comparisons in a personal portfolio. There also are several tools on the site, including the Auto Risk Evaluator and the Family Needs Planner.

Quotesmith (**www.quotesmith.com**)—Instant insurance quotes from more than 300 participating companies. Offers quotes for dental insurance, annuities, and medical supplements.

Progressive Insurance (**www.progressive.com**)—Progressive offers instant online quotes for its own policies and those of up to three other companies.

INTERNET RETAILERS

Amazon.com (**www.amazon.com**)—The site sells books, music, video, toys and games, consumer electronics, and also offers online auctions.

Reel.com (**www.reel.com**)—The site features mainstream Hollywood movies, and a variety of cult classics and kids' favorites.

Wine.com (**www.wine.com**)—One of the first online wine sellers.

INVESTMENT RESEARCH

Briefing.com (**www.briefing.com**)—Frequently updated commentary, quotes, and interactive charting, as well as portfolio-building tools.

Edgar Online (**www.edgar-online.com**)—Provides access to the SEC's Edgar (Electronic Data Gathering and Retrieval) database without the one-day delay for a company's prospectus that the SEC site has, but for a fee.

Hoover's Online (**www.hoovers.com**)—The company profile provider's site includes detailed narratives on numerous businesses, biographies of their top executives, and a rundown on their competitors. Some information is free, some is fee-based.

Hulbert Financial Digest (**www.hulbertdigest.com**)—Dealing with both stocks and mutual funds, this newsletter provides ratings of more than 160 newsletters and 450 portfolios, with monthly updates.

Investor Communications Business (**www.icbinc.com**)—Through its alliance with several major newspapers, the site mails annual reports anywhere in the world for free.

Market Guide (**www.marketguide.com**)—A financial data publisher that provides fundamental and technical data on thousands of publicly traded firms.

Multex (**www.multexinvestor.com**)—Offers company reports, some of which are free, but mostly provided on a pay-per-view basis. Multex offers quicker access to reports from a different Web site (**www.multex. com**), but users must be approved by the firm that wrote the research.

Public Register's Annual Report Service (**www.prars.com**)—Order free annual reports on more than 3,600 public companies and get them delivered by mail.

Quicken.com (**www.quicken.com**)—Known primarily for the personal-finance software it's named after, the site serves up a strong selection of data and analysis, market commentary, mutual-fund analysis, and stock-picking tools.

Thomson Financial (**www.thomsoninvest.net**)—Provides summaries of analysts' reports and recommendations to many other sites, and maintains its own outposts on the Web. Thomson charges a fee for some of its information.

Wall Street City (**www.wallstreetcity.com**)—Run by Telescan Inc.; paid subscribers can access variably priced screening tools. Access to its historical quote database is free.

Zacks Investment Research (**www.zacks.com**)—Provides individual investors with research produced by more than 3,000 analysts at the top North American brokerage firms. Access to some information is fee-based.

MESSAGE BOARDS

deja.com (**deja.com**)—Offers a way to navigate some 45,000 newsgroup discussion forums on every imaginable subject.

mIRC (**mirc.com**)—mIRC users may download free Internet Relay Chat software, which allows people to converse in real-time via the Internet.

Motley Fool (**www.fool.com**)—Originally popular for its heavily trafficked financial message boards, the site gears its original content toward educating individual investors about investing basics.

Raging Bull (**www.ragingbull.com**)—This site's most distinguishing trait is its "ignore" feature—a button that lets users muzzle annoying posters.

Silicon Investor (**www.siliconinvestor.com**)—One of the oldest stock chat sites on the Net, and the only one that charges users a fee to participate. Also the only service that lets users create discussion topics on any subject.

Yahoo! Finance (**finance.yahoo.com**)—The front-runner for most popular stock-talk destination on the Net.

MORTGAGES

Bank One (**www.bankone.com**)—This lender offers online mortgage quotes.

Countrywide Credit Industries (**www.countrywide.com**)—The biggest off-line independent mortgage lender, CountryWide has more than 300 Internet-linked offices.

E-loan (**www.eloan.com**)—Borrowers can compare, apply for, and obtain home loans, and have 24-hour access to loan status information online.

HomeAdvisor (**www.homeadvisor.com**)—Customers can instantly compare different rates from a variety of known lenders.

HSH Associates (**www.hsh.com**)—HSH has an interactive calculator that will estimate credit scores for those seeking to refinance their mortgage.

Keystroke.com (**www.keystroke.com**)—Keystroke.com claims it has the highest closed-loan ratio on the Internet. It also provides a line-by-line breakdown of closing costs.

LendingTree (**www.lendingtree.com**)—This site takes information online and sends it to lenders, yielding a variety of quotes from which to choose.

Priceline (**www.priceline.com**)—Site visitors bid on mortgages, and Priceline matches them up with four possibilities.

Quicken (**www.quickenloans.quicken.com**)—Inquirers fill out an electronic application form and are matched with several offers.

iQualify.com (**www.iqualify.com**)—A unit of Finet Holdings, iQualify.com requires no tax forms for mortgage applications.

RealEstate.com (**www.realestate.com**)—Features an online mortgage service that will pay $250 if your bid is accepted and you later find a better deal elsewhere.

RockLoans (**www.rockloans.com**)—The online unit of mortgage bank Rock Financial Corp. conducts the entire mortgage process online with minimal paperwork, until closing.

MUTUAL FUND INFORMATION

Fidelity Monitor (**www.fidelitymonitor.com**)—A fee-based monthly newsletter focused on Fidelity's mutual funds.

FundAlarm (**www.fundalarm.com**)—This site advises investors on the best time to sell fund holdings.

IBC Financial Data (**www.ibcdata.com**)—Features data on money-market mutual funds, and ranks 2,400 funds.

Indexfunds (**www.indexfundsonline.com**)—A free information service for stock market index investors.

Internet Closed-End Fund Investor (**www.icefi.com**)—Combines free and subscriber-based services, provides online tutorials, and quarterly updated data on closed-end funds.

Invest-o-rama (**www.investorama.com**)—Besides fund screening, beginner investors likely will appreciate the many links to even more research on the Web.

Morningstar (**www.morningstar.com**)—Basic information about mutual funds and fee-based, subscriber-only access to the site's screening tools.

Mutual Fund Investor's Center (**www.mfea.com**)—Gives financial planning advice to novice investors.

Quote.com (**www.quote.com**)—A screening tool that sorts through more than 7,500 mutual funds.

SmartMoney.com (**www.smartmoney.com**)—Its "Fund Analyzer" compares and contrasts funds based on volatility, turnover, and returns for various time periods.

Standard & Poor's Personal Wealth (**www.personalwealth.com**)—Provides access to news and analysis, and recommends mutual funds.

MUTUAL FUND FAMILIES

Dreyfus (**www.dreyfus.com**)—Allows account holders to view their balance and see detailed fact sheets on all funds in the family.

Fidelity Investments (**www.fidelity.com**)—General information on investment planning, with emphasis on mutual funds and saving for college or retirement.

Janus Funds (**www.janus.com**)—Besides a monthly missive from the chief investment officer, the site provides daily performance figures, account histories, and Morningstar ratings.

Charles Schwab (**www.schwab.com**)—Its Mutual Fund OneSource, another so-called supermarket site, offers access to funds from hundreds of firms.

Scudder Funds (**www.scudder.com**)—Offers asset-allocation worksheets based on customers' investment horizon and risk tolerance.

T. Rowe Price Associates (**www.troweprice.com**)—This site includes shareholder reports, fund prospectuses, and information on funds' historical performances.

Vanguard Group (**www.vanguard.com**)—Provides online information about its broad range of funds and financial services.

ORGANIZATIONS AND REGULATORY BODIES

Nasdaq Stock Market (**www.nasdaq.com**)—Offers free stock quotes, IPO information, and portfolio-tracking and stock-screening tools.

The North American Securities Administrators Association (**www.nasaa.org**)—Devoted to investor protection and education, NASAA offers links to state securities regulators, and information on Internet stock schemes.

U.S. Securities and Exchange Commission (**www.sec.gov**)—Allows searching of the Edgar database of reports filed by companies traded on major stock markets.

See a list of additional regulatory Web sites in Chapter 9.

PERSONAL FINANCE/CALCULATORS

ADR.com (**www.adr.com**)—This site, operated by J. P. Morgan, offers information about American depositary receipts, global shares, and foreign shares.

Armchair Millionaire (**www.armchairmillionaire.com**)—Gives investors a commonsense approach to personal finance, using a friendly tone and simple language.

Financenter (**www.financenter.com**)—Broad information on all the ins and outs of home finance, from automobile advice to insurance caveats. Chock-full of calculators and worksheets.

Financial Engines (**www.financialengines.com**)—Site includes calculators and other tools to help you evaluate your investments and financial plans.

Gomez Advisors (**www.gomezadvisors.com**)—This market-research firm also posts detailed and updated information about brokers on its site.

InvestorGuide (**www.investorguide.com**)—Gives a broad overview of personal finance, and offers access to portfolio-building tools, research, quotes, and charting.

Media General Financial Services (**www.mgfs.com**)—Media General is a publisher that provides many other Web sites with financial data on more than 12,500 publicly traded firms on U.S. and Canadian exchanges.

Microsoft MoneyCentral (**moneycentral.msn.com**)—This area of the Microsoft Network includes an investing primer and a "Research Wizard," which pulls together information about companies or funds and presents its findings in a simple way.

Network Solutions (**www.networksolutions.com**)—Users can search for a domain name registration, download new Web site building tools, and learn more about the mechanics of Web site architecture.

SmartMoney.com (**www.smartmoney.com**)—Site includes a long list of calculators and other personal-finance tools.

Virtual University of Investing (**www.virtual-u.com**)—Offers some free educational information and introductory courses on investing and personal finance.

RECOURSE

American Arbitration Association (**www.adr.org**)—The AAA's Web site addresses mediation, arbitration, and all other methods of alternative dispute resolution.

American Bar Association (**www.abanet.org/referral/home.html**)—This section of the ABA Web site offers basic information on using lawyer referrals, and a state-by-state listing of local lawyer referral services.

National Association of Securities Dealers (**www.nasdr.com**)—The official site for the securities industry regulatory group includes descriptions of NASD responsibilities and procedures, as well as information on filing customer complaints, regulatory tips, and other forms of redress.

Public Investor Arbitration Bar Association (**www.piaba.org**)—The PIABA site consists mostly of information about the lawyers' investor protection organization and its members.

SEC Office of Internet Enforcement Complaint Center (**www.sec. gov/enforce/comctr.htm**)—This area of the Securities and Exchange Commission's site includes information on filing a complaint with the agency.

See a list of additional Web sites in Chapter 9.

STOCKS

See, Brokers, Charting, Day Trading, IPOs.

WEB PORTAL SITES

America Online (**www.aol.com**)

Excite (**www.excite.com**)

Lycos (**www.lycos.com**)

Netscape Netcenter (**www.netcenter.com**)

Yahoo! (**www.yahoo.com**), (**finance.yahoo.com**)

PERMISSIONS ACKNOWLEDGMENTS

Grateful acknowledgment is made to the following for permission to reprint screen shots from the following Web sites:

BondAgent.com: Reprinted by permission of BondAgent, LLC.

CBOT.com: Reprinted by permission of CBOT.com.

Charles Schwab: Reprinted by permission of Charles Schwab.

Datek.com: Reprinted by permission of Datek Online.

Etrade.com: Reprinted by permission of E*Trade Group, Inc.

Silicon Investor's Web Site: Reprinted by permission of Go2Net, Inc.

IPO Maven: Reprinted by permission of IPO Maven.

Lendingtree.com: Reprinted by permission of Lendingtree.com.

Magneticdiary.com: Screen shot from the "FBN Associates" part of the Magnetic Diary Studios Web site. Reprinted by permission of Magnetic Diary Studios, **www.magneticdiary.com**.

Morningstar.com: Reprinted by permission of Morningstar, Inc.

Fool.com: Copyright © 1996–1999 by The Motley Fool, Inc. Reprinted by permission of The Motley Fool, Inc.

Multex.com: Copyright © 2000 by Multex.com, Inc. All rights reserved. Reprinted by permission of Multex.com, Inc.

Netstock.com: Copyright © 2000 by Netstock Direct Corporation. Reprinted by permission of Netstock Direct Corporation.

Quicken.com: Copyright © 2000 Intuit, Inc. All rights reserved. Reprinted by permission of Intuit, Inc.

Ragingbull.com: Copyright © 1997–2000 by Raging Bull, Inc. All rights reserved. Reprinted by permission of Raging Bull, Inc.

Sage.com: Reprinted by permission of Sage.com.

SmartMoney.com: Reprinted by permission of SmartMoney.

TDWaterhouse.com: Reprinted courtesy of TD Waterhouse Investor Services, Inc.

INDEX

Net Stock Direct, 91, 311
Net.B@nk, 277, 304
Netscape, 9, 51, 276, 322
Network Solutions, 321
New Jersey Council on Compulsive
   Gambling, 32–33
New Utopia, 239–40
New York: attorney general's office of,
   25–26
New York Board of Trade, 159, 311
New York Mercantile Exchange, 154,
   157, 311
New York Stock Exchange, 17, 28, 31,
   41, 42–43, 154, 264, 271
The New York Times, 202
News: about bonds, 145; and day
   trading, 94, 95; and drawbacks to
   online trading, 25; about futures
   trading, 159, 163, 165–66, 169,
   170; and history and background of
   brokers, 67; and impact of Internet,
   3; about IPOs, 84; about mutual
   funds, 121; about options, 176; and
   scams, 249; and selecting online
   brokers, 63; sources of, 195; and
   tools for investing, 209; Web sites
   for, 201–2, 312–13. *See also*
   Newsletters; Newswires; Press releases; *specific source*
NewsAlert, 62
Newsgroups, 8, 212
Newsletters, 31, 91, 94, 95, 110,
   124–25, 238, 239, 251, 302. *See
   also specific newsletter*
Newswires, 202, 211. *See also specific
   newswire*
NextCard, 280, 281, 309
No-load mutual funds, 105–6, 114,
   120–21, 131, 193
The North American Securities Administrators Association (NASAA),
   93, 258, 320
Novice investors: and bond trading,
   144, 146; and complaints against
   brokers, 269; and futures trading,
   153, 158, 159, 160; investment
   goals of, 105; and mutual funds,
   106, 121, 123; and risk, 105; and
   self-directed investing, 184–87; and
   tools for investing, 184–87

O'Connor, Brian, 282–83
Office of Internet Enforcement (SEC),
   239, 258, 262, 322. *See also* Stark,
   John
Online investors: expectations of, 27
Online trading: advantages of, 15–18,
   95, 156; anonymity of, 95; draw-
   backs to, 24–33; early, 7, 13–14;
   number of accounts for, 14; popu-
   larity of, 236, 263
Open interest, 154–55
Open Market, 224–25
"Open outcry" system, 153
Opening accounts: *See also* Initial in-
   vestments
OpenSite Technologies, 225
Option Source, 309
Options Industry Council, 175, 309
Options trading, 28, 67, 136, 170–76,
   209
OptionsSource.com, 175, 176
Osinga, David, 32
OT (off-topic), 301
OTC Bulletin Board (OTC-BB),
   43–44, 63, 67, 226, 240–42, 243,
   245, 246, 248, 249–50, 257
The Outlook (newsletter), 39
Overvaluation, 39
Ownership, stock, 33, 36

P&D. *See* Pump and dump
Pacific Stock Exchange, 175, 271, 311
Pagers, 62
PairGain Technologies, 217, 226,
   254–55
Partes, 76
Passwords, 52–53, 54
Patterson, Marni, 192
Pauly, Tod (aka Tonto), 210
Pay-for-promotion Web sites, 246–52
PC Trader, 147, 162, 309
Peloso, John, 267
Penny boards, 301
Penny stocks, 43, 228
Pension plans, 4, 35, 183–84. *See also
   type of plan*
Personal digital assistants, 62
Personal finance: Web sites for, 320–21
Personal information, 54, 245, 255,
   283, 284

ABOUT THE AUTHORS

Dave Pettit is the deputy managing editor of *The Wall Street Journal Interactive Edition*. He launched the *Interactive Journal*'s "Heard on the Net" column, which examines online investing and strives to alert readers to misinformation and scams on the Net. He has written about business and financial markets for *The Wall Street Journal* and the Dow Jones News Service for ten years.

Rich Jaroslovsky is the managing editor of the *Interactive Journal*. A veteran reporter and editor, he has been national political editor of *The Wall Street Journal* and was responsible for The Wall Street Journal/NBC News poll. He teaches public policy at Duke University and is the first president of the Online News Association.

Jason Anders is a reporter for the *Interactive Journal*. He has written extensively about online message boards and investment fraud on the Internet. Lisa Bransten covers venture capital for *The Wall Street Journal*. She joined the *Interactive Journal* in 1997 to report on technology and Silicon Valley finance. Prior to that she covered capital markets and technology for *The Financial Times*.

Rebecca Buckman is a reporter for *The Wall Street Journal*. Previously, she worked at Dow Jones Newswires and as a metro and state house reporter at the *Indianapolis Star*. Terri Cullen is the Money & Investing editor of the *Interactive Journal*. She has written about financial planning and investing for ten years.

Aaron Elstein covers online investing for the *Interactive Journal*. Previously, he wrote about mergers and acquisitions for *American Banker* and covered state government for the *Illinois Times*. Andrew Fraser is the assistant Money & Investing editor for the *Interactive Journal*. Previously, he was an editor and reporter on the national business desk of the Associated Press.

Carrie Lee is a reporter for the *Interactive Journal,* focusing on on-line investing and personal finance. She is a regular contributor to CNBC and NBC television, and has worked as a financial reporter for five years. Brian Tracey is a news editor for the *Interactive Journal.* Formerly he was managing editor of *American Banker Online.* Nick Wingfield covers the Internet for *The Wall Street Journal.* He has been a reporter for the *Interactive Journal,* and a senior writer for CNET's News.com.

All of the authors would like to acknowledge the contributions of *Interactive Journal* staff members Cassell Bryan-Low, Sharon Cleary, and Elaine Rocchi, as well as the time and feedback given by other *Journal* editors and reporters.

ABOUT THE INTERACTIVE JOURNAL

The Wall Street Journal Interactive Edition—wsj.com—is the Web's most successful subscription-based site, with more than 375,000 paid subscribers. The site has dozens of features and more than 100,000 pages of information with continually updated news, research tools, e-mail alerts, portfolio tracking, personalization and archive/search capabilities. At the heart of the site, of course, is the unrivaled business and financial news coverage of *The Wall Street Journal,* including its international editions and the *Interactive Journal's* own reporting and editing staff. The *Interactive Journal* was launched in 1996.